CHAUCER AND THE SHAPE OF CREATION

CHAUCER AND THE

SHAPE OF CREATION

The Aesthetic Possibilities of Inorganic Structure

ROBERT M. JORDAN

Harvard University Press, Cambridge, Massachusetts, 1967

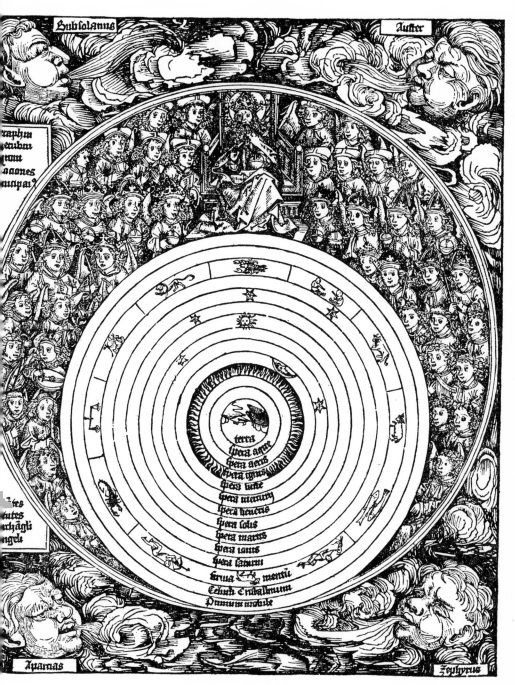

The Shape of Creation

FOR JEAN

For everi wight that hath an hous to founde
Ne renneth naught the werk for to bygynne
With rakel hond, but he wol bide a stounde,
And sende his hertes line out fro withinne
Aldirfirst his purpos for to wynne.

—*Troilus and Criseyde,* I, 1065

PREFACE

In the past decade several major studies have generated a small revolution in critical and scholarly attitudes toward Chaucer's poetry. What had become — following the achievements of Kittredge and other modern pioneers — almost a conventionalized mode of appreciative interpretation gave way in the 1950's to studies aimed more at objective elucidation of the bases of Chaucer's art than at persuasion of the rightness of particular interpretations. Charles Muscatine and Robert O. Payne, for example, in their different ways have shown how Chaucer's art developed out of his mastery of established modes of discourse and levels of style. And D. W. Robertson, Jr., has provided a primer of the iconographic principles which defined Chaucer's theological milieu. These studies point toward the attempt which I have made in the present book, that is, (to define the essential features of Chaucerian narrative and to provide an aesthetic rationale which is more relevant to the Chaucerian facts than are the precepts of narrative art which have generally prevailed in criticism since Henry James.) For example, I have found it very difficult to discern in Chaucer much trace of such values as organic unity or subtle structural balance of content and expression. On the contrary, analysis seems to me to reveal that Chaucer's narratives are often unbalanced and harshly angular, and that generally their construction is explicitly clear to the point of extreme simplicity and seeming naiveté. Indeed, the overt manipulation of fixed structural elements seems to impart a distinctly in-organic quality to Chaucerian narrative. The frequent tendency of modern readings is either to patronize these features of Chaucer's art as charming vestiges of medieval primitivism, or to overlook them in favor of Chaucer's more "modern" qualities.

I think it is important to recognize that these features are definitive, that they are Chaucer's means of solving medieval aesthetic problems in accordance with medieval principles of structure. Much of my effort in this book has been to develop a critical vocabulary adequate for the understanding of medieval aesthetic theory in general and of Chaucerian practice in particular. In this effort I have derived considerable guidance from non-Chaucerians, such as Erich Auerbach, whose *Mimesis* has shaped my thinking in ways too subtle to cite in my text and too pervasive to disregard in the Preface. I have also learned much, as my citations make at least partially clear, from art historians such as Edgar de Bruyne, Erwin Panofsky, and Otto von Simson, whose fine aesthetic discriminations have provided for me a yardstick for aesthetic studies in literature.

The order of this book does not recreate the order of my own experience. I began with Chaucer, and in seeking to understand what I saw and felt there I worked back to Plato and Pythagoras, following routes which had been well traveled in the Middle Ages and lay not far beneath the surface of today's cultural geography. In deciding to adopt for this book a historical order rather than the order of my own experience with Chaucer and his cultural milieu, I perhaps risk losing the interest of the reader intent upon getting directly to the poetry. But since the burden of my argument is the interplay of Chaucer's art and an aesthetic for which modern Chaucerians lack a satisfactory rationale, the only other mode of presentation would have been equally risky, that is, to start with Chaucer and move continually away from the literary work to the aesthetic forces and assumptions behind it. Primarily in order to allow for sustained critical discussion of the poetry I have separated the Chaucerian foreground from the historical and theoretical background and considered the latter first in an effort to establish a sense of milieu. The historical evidence I adduce in support of my argument concerning Chaucerian aesthetics is largely circumstantial, but it provides a conceptual framework and a critical vocabulary which I think fit the Chaucerian situation and therefore help us to understand what the poet was about.

I have emphasized documents which were seminal in creating the context of Chaucer's aesthetic imagination, his sense of the shape of creation and the mode of creating. I have paid particular attention to the *Timaeus* and pagan tradition partly in the hope of redressing an increasing emphasis on patristics in Chaucerian studies, but primarily because virtually all medieval thought about aesthetics — of which, strictly speaking, there was

PREFACE

not very much — either points back to the *Timaeus* or quotes it directly. ✓ That ubiquitous document not only crystallized the conception of creation as the rationally ordered disposition of measured quantities; it also established a "structural" dialectic which guided aesthetic theory throughout the Middle Ages.

My consideration of patristic thought differs from Robertson's more thorough and much more knowledgeable discussion in that I stress those elements of it which are common to the traditions of pagan aesthetics, as sustained in the *Timaeus,* while he stresses the elements of uniquely Christian doctrine. While the Fathers, Augustine in particular, decisively Christianized pagan aesthetics, the framework of their thought, that is, the concept of hierarchy and universal sacramentalism, remained essentially mimetic. Augustine understood the visible world to be a sign of invisible truth, and knowing that God had disposed all things in "measure and number and weight" Augustine employed the musico-mathematical language of the *Timaeus* — as did Boethius, Macrobius, and other major thinkers — to elucidate the rational order of divine creation.

My discussion of Gothic architecture views that great achievement as a literal realization, structured in stone and glass, of the principles of Creation, principles which had been formulated in the pagan language of proportion and revered by Christians for more than a millennium as the language of God. In tracing the Gothic builders' translation of the divine principles of hierarchy, analogy, and measured structure from theology and cosmology into art — iconographic art, to be sure — this discussion serves as a transition from medieval theory about the nature of Creation to medieval practice in the making of works of serious art.

What the making of poems has to do with the making of cathedrals is a difficult but legitimate question, and I do not press the analogy very far. But I do believe — both for medieval and for modern reasons — that an ✓ analogy exists between Chaucer's art and that of the Gothic builders. The evidence of Chaucerian narrative structure testifies that the poet to a considerable extent treated his materials as "inorganic" building units analogous to the sections and subsections of a Gothic floor plan or an elevation. The typical Chaucerian narrative is literally "built" of inert, self-contained parts, collocated in accordance with the additive, reduplicative principles which characterize the Gothic edifice. In the case of the *Canterbury Tales* and the

Troilus I think the iconographic function of the whole, the ultimate pointing toward God, adds a further architectonic dimension characteristic of the Gothic. Beyond this basic orientation to principles of structure the analogy cannot be drawn. Chaucer's poems are never as balanced or as mathematically proportional as a Gothic cathedral had to be if it was to stand up. On the other hand, I think we shall find that Chaucer was a builder in this very literal sense, and that he expressed his feeling for life — for this life and the other — through the inorganic materials and structures of Gothic art.

My concentration upon the quantitative values of Chaucer's art may seem to imply a denial of the humane values for which that art has always been cherished, but I think it will become apparent that architectonic and humane values are by no means inimical. Even though Chaucer approached the materials of his art much in the manner of a builder approaching bricks, the choice, discrimination, and disposition of those materials was entirely his own, which is to say that in the deepest and most meaningful sense Chaucer's art is his humanity; it is his personality, his mind, his sensibilities, his way of viewing both his materials and his life. To locate Chaucer's humanity in the humanity of his subjects — say, in the pathos and energy of the Wife of Bath — does only partial justice to the poet and does not significantly advance our understanding of his art. The implications of an architectonic approach to Chaucer are not to deny the poet's humanity but to locate it where it has not customarily been sought — in his artistry, rather than in the world he depicts. I think it will become clear that in working with fixed quantities — whether epithet, character, genre, or world — Chaucer plays delicately and masterfully upon such deeply human concerns as rhythm, proportion, perspective, and, ultimately, the human position in the order of Creation.

I have received help for this study in many forms from many sources, for which I wish to express my gratitude. The time necessary to initiate the work was provided by a Canada Council Fellowship and study leave from the University of British Columbia. Support for a summer's study of medieval science and mathematics — the background for Chapters Two and Three — came from the National Science Foundation's Institutional Grant to the State University of New York at Stony Brook. A grant-in-aid from the Research Foundation of the State University of New York assisted ma-

PREFACE

terially in meeting the costs of research and manuscript preparation. I am grateful to the editors of *ELH* for permission to reprint, with some changes, articles of mine which appeared earlier in that journal, and to the editors of *PMLA* for permission to reprint, again with changes, my discussion of the Merchant's Tale. I am indebted to many individuals for invaluable contributions of time and thought—to Bertrand Bronson for nurturing my early interest in Chaucer and for teaching me more lessons in scholarship and critical discernment than I have been able to learn; to Morton Bloomfield and Sidney Feshbach for reading and criticism of large segments of the text; to Donald Howard for a thorough and rigorous reading of the whole. Among those who have helped to bring the text to a readable and printable condition I wish to record special thanks to Joseph Juettner, Rowena Scarrow, Phyllis Reed, and my editors at the Harvard University Press, Mrs. Christine Ammer and Mrs. Natalie Frohock. Finally, a debt too deep for words is left unpaid by the dedication of this book.

Robert M. Jordan

Stony Brook, New York
March 1967

CONTENTS

ILLUSTRATIONS

CHAUCER AND THE SHAPE OF CREATION

ABBREVIATIONS

CL	Comparative Literature
ELH	[Journal of English Literary History]
JEGP	Journal of English and Germanic Philology
MP	Modern Philology
PL	Patrologiae cursus completus; series latina
PMLA	[Publications of the Modern Language Association of America]
PQ	Philological Quarterly
RES	Review of English Studies
SP	Studies in Philology
UTQ	University of Toronto Quarterly

ONE INTRODUCTION
CONCEPTS OF STRUCTURE

In the light of recent major studies of Chaucer, it is no longer satisfactory to celebrate the poet for his "modernity," for we are learning more and more about his medievalism — not only his literary sources, but the traditions and conventions that constituted his aesthetic language and the Christian assumptions that shaped his moral and spiritual outlook. Muscatine has emphasized literary uses of traditional levels of style and modes of discourse, Payne has underlined the importance of rhetorical tradition in shaping a medieval sense of poetics, and Robertson has stressed the body of Christian doctrine that pervaded the medieval consciousness and expressed itself in conventional iconography.[1]

[1] Charles Muscatine, *Chaucer and the French Tradition: A Study in Style and Meaning* (Berkeley, and Los Angeles, Calif.: University of California Press, 1957);

CHAUCER AND THE SHAPE OF CREATION

The difficulty of recovering Chaucer's aesthetic principles is compounded by the modern critical vocabulary, which expresses presuppositions that often are irrelevant or even antipathetic to the literature of the Middle Ages. In his admirable general appraisal of the contrast between medieval and modern approaches to literature, Robertson has pointed out how poorly we are served by the romantic and modern dialectic of "dynamic tensions" in appraising a literature composed in harmony with what he calls the "quiet hierarchies" of the Middle Ages.[2] The distinction is fundamental, and although Robertson implies more quietude than could have been present in medieval life he casts considerable light upon the differences between medieval and modern approaches to art. I have learned much from him and share many of his views, especially his appreciation of the central importance of the rational faculty in medieval art, but I must demur — for reasons which will become clear in due course — from his extravagant estimate of the importance of Christian exegetical tradition in the poetry of Chaucer.[3]

Although my discussions of Chaucer's poetry emphasize its visible and tangible structure, the central problem of this study is the relationship between the world Chaucer makes in his fiction and the world he knew in his cosmology and his theology. Though I

Robert O. Payne, *The Key of Remembrance: A Study of Chaucer's Poetics* (New Haven, Conn., and London: Yale University Press, 1963); D. W. Robertson, Jr., *A Preface to Chaucer: Studies in Medieval Perspectives* (Princeton, N.J.: Princeton University Press, 1963).

2 Robertson, *A Preface*, pp. 3-51.

3 See my discussion of the Wife of Bath, pp. 211-212 below. The principles of Robertsonian exegesis are discussed from different points of view by Robert E. Kaske and E. Talbot Donaldson in *Critical Approaches to Medieval Literature*, ed. Dorothy Bethurum (New York, 1960). See also Robert E. Kaske's judicious review of Robertson's *A Preface* in "Chaucer and Medieval Allegory," *ELH*, 30: 175-192 (1963); and Francis Lee Utley's less sympathetic but trenchant "Robertsonianism Redivivus," *Romance Philology*, 19: 250-260 (1965). On "allegorical interpretation" in general see Morton W. Bloomfield's important paper, "Symbolism in Medieval Literature," *MP*, 56: 73-81 (1958), which argues the significance of literal meaning and the limitations of multileveled systems of interpretation, even as understood by medieval exegetes.

CONCEPTS OF STRUCTURE

emphasize structure over doctrine, I try to make clear how closely the two are related, since medieval Christianity posits a rationally structured cosmic hierarchy whose parts are meaningfully disposed along the ascending way to God: the structure itself is divine. But I think we must place structure before divinity in studying the art of a secular poet; otherwise we risk confounding the obvious and turning matter into spirit, which only God — not even Chaucer — can do. We are guided here by Chaucer's very clear practice: for example, the Prioress' Tale is religious, the Miller's Tale is not; the ending of *Troilus* is religious, the body of the work is not. Without denying the poet's Christian bearings, I believe that to see Christian doctrine everywhere is to see too well. Perhaps it can be shown that I substitute one extreme view for another when I maintain that if doctrine is not universally pervasive, certain structural principles are. But I shall attempt to demonstrate what these principles are and how they shape Chaucer's narrative art, whether the instance be explicitly Christian, implicitly Christian, or secular.

Since the body of this book expounds what I mean by "structure" in medieval theory and Chaucerian practice, I should like to spend a moment here in making clear what I do not mean by that term. A few general observations about the meaning of "structure" in modern theory and practice can provide a useful negative orientation for our study of structure in medieval contexts.

René Wellek has formulated the modern consensus: "There is wide agreement today that the old distinction between form and content is untenable."[4] This is not simply a theoretical formulation but a conviction which has been developing since the eighteenth century and has decisively affected the basic assumptions of modern critical thought. The gradual collapse of "old distinctions" has been an increasingly pervasive condition of the general literary consciousness. The coalescence of form (or structure) and content is perhaps

---

[4] René Wellek, "Concepts of Form and Structure in Twentieth Century Criticism," *Neophilologus*, 42: 1-11 (1958).

3

no more central to the contemporary situation than, say, the coalescence of comedy and tragedy in the literature of black humor and the absurd. Particularly relevant to my concern with "structure" is the collapse of critical language itself, which seems to have drawn all the old key terms into a new homogeneous vocabulary. Thus, for example, Conrad Aiken's essay on Faulkner is subtitled, "The Novel as Form," which means, as Aiken observes with regard both to Faulkner and Henry James, that "it is practically impossible to make any real distinction between theme and form."[5] Mark Schorer speaks, in "Technique as Discovery," of the intermingling of artistry and life in the "achieved content" of the work of art.[6] Carrying the discussion to more fundamental levels, R. P. Blackmur sees the fusion of language (art and proto-art) and gesture (life): "Gesture, in language, is the outward and dramatic play of inward and imagined meaning. It is that play of meaningfulness among words which cannot be defined in the formulas in the dictionary, but which is defined in their use together; gesture is that meaningfulness which is moving, in every sense of that word: what moves the words and what moves us."[7] This is a critical dialectic which, using "as" for "is," answers the crucial questions with suggestive collocations: form as content as technique as language as gesture as illusion as truth.

The tendency of this mode of thought to obscure the old distinctions and fuse the old divisions into a new, organic unity finds its fullest literary expression in the post-Jamesian novel. Indeed it is the novel and novelistic theory which have decisively shaped the instruments and the perspective of modern criticism, even to a large extent that criticism whose object is medieval narrative fiction. Since it is unlikely that we can view medieval narrative exactly as it was

[5] "William Faulkner: The Novel as Form," in *William Faulkner: Two Decades of Criticism*, ed. F. J. Hoffman and Olga W. Vickery (East Lansing: Michigan State College Press, 1951), p. 143.

[6] *Hudson Review*, 1: 68-87 (1948).

[7] *Language as Gesture* (New York: Harcourt, Brace and Company, 1952), p. 6.

viewed in its own time, it is important to recognize our presuppositions so that we can reasonably appraise their utility and their limitations. Both in critical theory and in novelistic practice the pressure of the romantic and postromantic literary sensibility has been to break down lines of demarcation and thereby to achieve a communion between artist and art. Art thus becomes "alive" and ultimately responsive to its own nature rather than inert and submissive to externally imposed limitations, such as the rules of genre or the fixed outlines of structure. M. H. Abrams has charted the transition from "mechanism" to "plant" or "organism" as basic metaphors of mind in the formative stages of romantic thought.[8] How fully the novel was nurtured by the liberating impulses of the romantic imagination is strikingly evident in James's *apologia,* which articulates the transition from poety to prose fiction as the dominant literary vehicle for expressing the romantic sensibility in modern times: "Experience is never limited, and it is never complete; it is an immense sensibility, a kind of huge spider-web of the finest silken threads suspended in the chamber of consciousness, and catching every airborne particle in its tissue. It is the very atmosphere of the mind . . ."[9] Henceforth critical fiat could corroborate and dignify the new literary situation, in which the novel emerged as the dominant mode of exploration into the newly postulated infinity of experience. Traditional mimetic theory, which openly posited a distance — however skillfully disguised — between real object and artificial imitation, could no longer serve the new sense of intimacy, of interpenetration, between the artist's experience and his expression. The idea of narrative underwent a radical redefinition: "Life does not narrate but makes impressions on our brains. We in turn, if we wished to produce on you an effect of life, must not

[8] *The Mirror and the Lamp* (New York: Oxford University Press, 1958), pp. 57-69, 218-225. On the genesis of biological metaphors in historiography see George Kubler, *The Shape of Time* (New Haven and London, 1962), pp. 8-10.

[9] Henry James, "The Art of Fiction, "in *The Major Critics,* ed. C. S. Holmes, et al. (New York: Alfred A. Knopf, 1957), pp. 275-276; widely anthologized.

narrate but render impressions."[10] The imperatives of this mode of thought have led to a widespread mistrust of those narrative practices and critical attitudes that would inhibit the organic continuity between fiction and experience. As I shall be attempting to demonstrate, precisely such disruptive practices are at the very center of Chaucer's art, and they are integral to his sense of the inorganic discontinuity between fiction and experience. The primary artistic means of discriminating between art and life is the clear structural outline, the explicit indication of the limits of illusion.

This sense of structure has in recent times dissolved, not only in the language of criticism, as we have noted, but in the practice of novelists who have developed subtle techniques for the "rendering" of experience, techniques intended to exclude from the fiction the signs of an external, shaping hand. The absence of "explanations" and of explicit beginnings and conclusive conclusions indicates the importance for modern fiction of preserving the illusion that art is not "made" but *is,* that it is an organism rather than a mechanism. The organism is the criterion of verisimilitude, and consistency of illusion is its primary requisite. Though the illusion may be complex and multileveled, as in *The Sound and the Fury,* it is never broken; the only sign of a maker's hand is in the extrinsic sectioning of the book. Persuasiveness of the fiction depends upon the illusion of organic self-perpetuation. In pursuing this criterion of verisimilitude modern fiction has captured the imagination of the reader and sustained his empathy to an extent far beyond the possibilities of mimetic fiction. But this achievement has not been without cost. The literature of involvement, of commitment, of unqualified immersion in illusion, cuts itself off by its own nature from a wide range of human experience, from those impulses that are more rationalistic and less sensory, more given to detached appraisal than

10 Ford Madox Ford, *Joseph Conrad: A Personal Remembrance* (New York: Octagon Books, Inc., 1965), pp. 194-195.

6

to sympathetic union, more inclined to comedy and redemption than to tragedy and death.

When Dante spoke of poetry as a "beautiful lie" he was expressing one of the postulates of medieval literary theory that is least congenial to modern views. Modern theory places so high a premium upon the truth of literature, upon its closeness to life, and cares so little about its "beauty" that we are likely to regard Dante's phrase as a witticism. But it was a commonplace of his time and he meant it in all seriousness, as did Boccaccio and Petrarch in similar pronouncements. Though strongly secular in their persuasion, the new humanists of the late Middle Ages shared with the Church Fathers the understanding that poetic utterance is literally untrue. St. Jerome, for example, asserted that the poet's business, like the prophet's, was not to speak plainly but to speak in such terms as only the initiated could understand. It was understood that the obscurity of the surface and the need to penetrate it enhanced the value of the hidden truths and preserved them from vulgarization. In adopting this symbolic conception of poetry the humanists were borrowing the prestige of traditional Scriptural exegesis. But prior to the process of exegesis, prior even to the need for it, was the conscious awareness that the "literature," the visible data, being untrue, is distinctly separated from the truth, as the letter of Scriptures was known to be separated from the spirit. Not all medieval poets, and certainly not all their auditors and readers, were as knowledgeable as the Fathers and the later humanists in the subtle modes of relationship between surface and meaning, but even in less intellectual works medieval poets were predisposed to emphasize the untruth of their fictions.

Clearly a strong sense of the limitations of fiction motivated Chaucer's two most explicit and forthright pronouncements on his own art, the "Retractions" following the *Canterbury Tales* and the "Epilogue" of *Troilus and Criseyde*. In both of these statements the poet anxiously questions the bases of his art and condemns all

7

that is not openly conducive to piety and spiritual enlightenment. Chaucer's ultimate criteria define Christian instruction, not what later ages have come to call art. Mistrust of fiction permeates Chaucer's art and manifests itself in more subtle and, I think, more important ways, not only through such explicit statements, which, however fervent, are after all only statements, but also through the structure and style of the poems. Chaucer introduces his two major works, *Troilus* and the *Canterbury Tales,* not as fictions but as history and journalism respectively. And in both cases Chaucer's recurrent insistence upon the "truth" of his fictions — attested to by his unimpeachable "auctour" in *Troilus* and by his own unimpeachable eyes and ears in the *Tales* — imparts to the poems an artless "Chaucerian" quality, a quality that determines the essential nature of Chaucer's art. Of course, all fiction "pretends" in one way or another to be true, but Chaucer's artifices — and medieval practice in general — are easily misunderstood, for they do not spring from the assumptions that underlie modern concepts of artistic truth. Regarding his poems as finite, limited illusions, the medieval poet developed modes of formalism which in the light of modern theory will seem mechanical and artificial but which in truth express assumptions — about both art and life — which are fundamentally and enduringly human.

The irregularities and inconsistencies of a Chaucerian narrative, particularly the recurrent disruptions of illusion but also other overt evidence of the maker's hand — the exposed joints and seams, the unresolved contradictions, the clashes of perspective — are not simply the signs of primitive genius, as Sidney and Dryden were willing to believe; nor are they trivial stylistic blemishes, as modern advocates of psychological realism and dramatic unity have maintained. They are significant determinants of Chaucer's art, based upon an aesthetic which conceives of art not as an organism, a living plant, but as an inorganic material, a "veil," as Petrarch and Boccaccio understood it, or in more complex works such as *Troilus,*

CONCEPTS OF STRUCTURE

the *Canterbury Tales,* and, preeminently, the *Divine Comedy,* as a structure possessed of architectonic as well as planimetric dimensions. The role of the artist is not to express himself and not to express a new, unique way of viewing reality, but to shape and adorn the materials of his art. The organicist is likely to regard such an approach to art as frivolous, as lacking "inspiration" or "commitment" or "high seriousness." I hope this book can dispel such reservations and perhaps offer some insight into the possibilities of inorganic art and into the durable bases of such art in a fundamental human responsiveness to quantitative values. The fact that Chaucer still speaks vitally and delightfully to us — while displaying so many qualities antithetical to our organic idea of literature — justifies us to an extent in celebrating him as a "modern." But as I shall be concerned to show, even brief study of a Chaucerian narrative can reveal how much such a view leaves out of account. The critical truth must be that despite the immersion of our own culture in an aesthetic which regards "organic unity" as the measure of art, we are by no means numb to "inorganic" art, though we may be partially blind to it and largely inarticulate in our responses to it. This book attempts to contribute to an already developing rationale which can define the features of inorganic structure and which perhaps can lead to a more enlightened and conscious responsiveness, neither superciliously patronizing nor blindly admiring.

TWO   THE ELEMENTS OF MEDIEVAL AESTHETIC THEORY

Though the general outlines of a medieval "world view" are well known, its aesthetic implications are less familiar; the implications for literary art are less familiar still; and for Chaucer's literary art they remain almost totally unexplored. Robertson's *A Preface to Chaucer*[1] has made an impressive beginning, but as a study of aesthetic norms it is weakened by an ambiguous definition of the scope of the subject. For the Middle Ages the end and source of aesthetic principles was indeed God, as God was the end and source of all things, and the tradition of Scriptural exegesis everywhere enforced this commonplace. But in pursuing this patristic orientation, which invites a strong emphasis on the symbolizing process, Robertson is led to dwell much more extensively upon spiri-

[1] D. W. Robertson, Jr., *A Preface to Chaucer: Studies in Medieval Perspectives.*

10

tual and moral than upon aesthetic considerations. Thus his richly detailed three-part chapter on "Some Principles of Medieval Aesthetics" is concerned primarily with principles and instances of symbolic interpretation. The first section, "The Aesthetics of Figurative Expression," expounds and illustrates the Augustinian doctrine of *allegoria,* of saying one thing and meaning another, as the means to spiritual understanding in a fallen world. The second section, "The Use and Abuse of Beauty," is equally concerned with responses to signs, the proper response to beauty being to use it as a means of spiritual understanding leading to God, the abuse of beauty being the enjoyment of it for its own sake. The third section, "The Nature of Beauty," devotes somewhat less than half its length to those principles of harmony and proportion which can effectively distinguish aesthetics from apocalyptics, though indeed both are integral to the medieval concept of order. The rest of the section deals with spiritual and carnal, the "New Song" and the "Old Song," and similar problems in exegesis.

As Robertson expressly states (p. 52), he was interested in correcting imbalances in de Bruyne's *Etudes d'esthétique médiévale,*[2] which in Robertson's view slighted the contribution of St. Augustine. There is some validity in the criticism, although it should be apparent that de Bruyne defines aesthetics more rigorously than an Augustinian would, and in the field of aesthetics thus defined, the writings of the Fathers were more conventional than innovative. The balance of emphasis between aesthetics and spiritual exegesis is a delicate one, since the two spheres were so thoroughly intermingled in medieval thought. It is well for us to remember, however, that Chaucer was neither aesthetician nor churchman, and neither emphasis nor both together can claim definitive insight into the poet's imagination. Both aesthetics and church doctrine are elements of Chaucer's artistic inheritance. If I lay heavier stress on the Platonic

2 Edgar de Bruyne, *Etudes d'esthétique médiévale,* 3 vols (Bruges: De Tempal, 1946).

and Neoplatonic tradition of aesthetic theory than on patristic contributions, it is because the significance of the *Timaeus* for medieval aesthetics is less widely understood among Chaucerians than is the significance of Christian doctrine, largely, perhaps, because Professor Robertson has not addressed himself to that subject.

De Bruyne stresses the fact that medieval ideas of order and beauty, wherever they are purposefully worked out, depend upon the mathematical principles of proportion received from antiquity. De Bruyne begins with Boethius and emphasizes the combined traditional and seminal quality of his powerful influence on the Middle Ages. Directly relating Boethius' thought to that of Plato, Plotinus, and St. Augustine, de Bruyne summarizes the salient features of traditional aesthetic theory and at the same time indicates its universality and its continuity: "As did Plato, Plotinus, and St. Augustine, Boethius rises gradually from the beauty of changeable qualities to that of immutable proportions. From the beauty of simple relationships realized in the world and in the order of mathematics, he rises to the beauty of the divine Architect, in whose intelligence exists the mathematical exemplar of the universe."[3]

Learned tradition, to which learned poets such as Dante and Chaucer were heirs, continually repeated this basic concept and developed from it a body of common knowledge about the nature of Creation, common knowledge fixed in the detailed, unambiguous language of Pythagorean mathematics. The intimacy of mathematics, philosophy, and poetry in defining and sustaining a meaningful standard of order for medieval men is dramatized in Chaucer's relationship to the *Consolation of Philosophy*. Students of Chaucer will be familiar with the Boethian source of Theseus' stately discourse on cosmic order near the end of the Knight's Tale; I mean the celebrated song of praise to the Creator and his creation in Book III, Meter 9 of the *Consolation:* "Oh God, Maker of heaven and

[3] *Etudes d'esthétique médiévale,* I, 9.

earth, Who govern the world with eternal reason . . . It was the form of the highest good, existing with You without envy, which caused You to fashion all things according to the eternal exemplar. You Who are most beautiful produce the beautiful world from your divine mind and, forming it in your image, You order the perfect parts in a perfect whole. You bind the elements in harmony[4] so that cold and heat, dry and wet are joined and the purer fire does not fly up through the air, nor the earth sink beneath the weight of water . . ."[5] As introduced by Lady Philosophy, this moving poem is explicitly addressed to the God of *Timaeus,* and the essential elements of the poem are Platonic formulas of reason, exemplar, image, harmony, perfect whole, perfect parts. The cosmic structure envisaged in this poem is a virtual paraphrase of the first part of the *Timaeus.* The vision Boethius purveyed to the Middle Ages was of a perfectly harmonized, hierarchically structured universe. He also passed on the means of apprehending this complex yet perfect order, namely, the vocabulary and the mode of thought of mathematics, the quantitative language of pure reason. Restatements of this Hellenic concept of universal harmony are encountered again and again from Boethius to the fourteenth century and after. "From one end to the other medieval aesthetic forms a consistent whole, whose fundamental themes, always the same, are developed with infinite nuances and interminable variations."[6]

In the late Middle Ages, when the forces of the humanist revival enlarged the potentialities of art, and when the techniques of art had developed a high degree of flexibility and control over materials, the great works of the Gothic era, literary as well as

---

[4] The original is "Tu numeris elementa ligas." *Patrologiae cursus completus; series latina,* ed. J. P. Migne (Paris, 1844-1903), vol. 63, col. 759. Chaucer's rendering of "numeris" as "by nombres proporcionables" (*Complete Works,* ed. F. N. Robinson, 2nd ed. Boston, 1957, p. 350) is more literal than the modern English "in harmony" and indicates closer touch with the Pythagorean basis of the concept.

[5] Trans. Richard H. Green (Indianapolis and New York: Bobbs-Merrill Co., Inc., 1962), p. 60.

[6] De Bruyne, *Etudes,* I, viii.

architectural, found in this rationally ordered structure of creation the model for their artistic images of the world. This was a universe of fixed quantities, and in it values were readily apprehensible and measurable in relation to a fixed, eternal standard. Since the aesthetic values implicit in such an orientation are almost totally antithetical to those of modern times, it will repay us to cultivate our understanding of the aesthetic possibilities of fixity, divisibility, and juxtaposition, as distinct from those of limitlessness, continuousness, and coalescence.

We begin with Plato's *Timaeus,* which was one of the most widely respected and durable sources of medieval aesthetic theory; then we shall attend to some of the other voices which, throughout the Middle Ages, wove the "infinite nuances and interminable variations" on those fundamental themes.

Plato's Timaeus: *Reason, Ratio, and the Quantitative Bases of Order*

The credibility and persuasiveness of the Platonic account of the Creation is underscored by continuing attempts, culminating in the twelfth century in the School of Chartres, to harmonize the Platonic and Mosaic narratives.[7] The major obstacle to reconciliation is the idea of the Incarnation, but that mystery, being only remotely relevant to the architecture of creation, did not reduce the attractiveness of Plato's rational exposition of cosmic order. It was this meticulously detailed account of the complete rationality — and by that token the supreme beauty — of the

---

[7] Evidence of the continuing study of the *Timaeus* during the Middle Ages and of its interweaving with Christian teachings has been summarized by Raymond Klibansky, *The Continuity of the Platonic Tradition during the Middle Ages* (London: The Warburg Institute, 1939). Klibansky tells us (p. 28) that the first part of the *Timaeus* "was studied and quoted throughout the Middle Ages, and there was hardly a mediaeval library of any standing which had not a copy of Chalcidius' version and sometimes also a copy of the fragment translated by Cicero."

MEDIEVAL AESTHETIC THEORY

universe which carried the most profound implications for medieval ideas of aesthetic propriety. Throughout the intermingling of Platonic, Neoplatonic, and Christian thought from the time of Augustine onward, the *Timaeus* continued to exert this appeal. Its celebration of the visible world contrasts with the tendency of Christian doctrine to praise the harmony less fervently than the Harmonizer. For this reason the *Timaeus* and the literature of commentary and allusion to which it gave rise — even as it was absorbed into Christian teaching — is more germane to a study of aesthetic principles than is the Book of Genesis and its exegetical tradition.

In this detailed and comprehensive account of the origin and structure of the universe Plato develops an intimate parallel between the forms of creation and the perfection of the ideal forms which reside in the mind of the Creator. In accordance with this fundamental relationship, Plato shows human life, both physical and moral, to be a microcosm of the macrocosmic order. The human head, for example, is spherical in imitation of the heavenly exemplar, the spherical cosmos; since the latter contains the revolutions of the world-soul, it is fitting that the organ which contains the revolutions of the human soul should have the same shape.[8] Morality is defined by Plato as true harmony of the soul, the soul's harmony being not only analogous to but a counterpart of the harmony of the world-soul, which in turn is the exemplar of universal order, created by divine reason itself.

Following the teachings of the Pythagoreans, Plato envisioned the Creator as a master mathematician.[9] For Plato the universe

[8] *Timaeus*, 44d, in *Plato's Cosmology*, trans. F. M. Cornford (New York: The Humanities Press, Inc.; London: Routledge & Kegan Paul, Ltd., 1952).
[9] The broad cultural significance of the Pythagoreans is indicated by R. G. Collingwood, *The Idea of Nature* (Oxford, 1945), pp. 49-55. An authoritative technical description of Greek mathematics before and after Plato is Thomas L. Heath, *A History of Greek Mathematics*, 2 vols. (Oxford, 1921). For a brief, less technical account, see H. W. Turnbull, "The Great Mathematicians," in vol. I, *The World of Mathematics*, ed. J. R. Newman, 4 vols. (New York, 1956). On the twofold character of Pythagorean number theory see F. M. Cornford, "Mysticism and Science

possesses the ultimate mathematical virtue: it is a unity whose elements harmonize in perfect proportionality. Plato begins with a postulate of wholeness or finitude and proceeds to explain the cohesive and harmonious structure of things according to simple, unvarying laws of proportion. This principle underlies Plato's conception of both the world-body and the world-soul: ". . . the god, wishing to make this world most nearly like that intelligible thing which is best and in every way complete, fashioned it as a single visible living creature, containing within itself all living things whose nature is of the same order."[10]

Plato defends the assumption of finitude on rational and deductive, not empirical, grounds. The postulate of finitude, that is, of a perfection which is knowable and divisible, is central to Plato's mode of thought and has relatively little to do with direct observation and measurement of the cosmos. At this initial stage in the construction of the cosmology, rationalism is employed to preserve a logical consistency in the terms of the argument; later, rationalism in the pure form of mathematical reasoning is utilized to describe the constituent elements of the universe. Thus Plato here argues that the world, being a copy of the eternal model, should be, like it, unique. And it should embrace "all the living creatures that there are" so that there would be nothing left over to necessitate another agency equivalent to this world and similarly subservient to a model, because if there were another world there would then have to be postulated another model, which is impossible. From the premise that the model or exemplar must be unique and all-embracing Plato deduces the nature of the world.

When Plato begins to describe the composition of the "body of the world" his mode of thought reveals itself to be the pure rational-

in the Pythagorean Tradition," *Classical Quarterly,* 16: 137-150 (1922); 17: 1-12 (1923). A lively nontechnical account of Pythagoreanism and the modern implications of its mystical offshoot, numerology, is Eric Temple Bell, *The Magic of Numbers* (New York, 1946).

10 *Timaeus,* 30d.

ism of a mathematician proving a postulate. Starting from the assumption that the visible, tangible world is one complete whole, Plato proceeds to explain how all the constituent parts were formed into this unity. Pythagorean mathematics provides the language and technique for his demonstration.

Fire being the element of visibility and earth the element of solidity, these two were the basic elements of creation. A bond was necessary to unify them, and Plato attributes to the Maker a mind sufficiently Pythagorean to realize that "of all bonds the best is that which makes itself and the terms it connects a unity in the fullest sense; and it is of the nature of a continued geometrical proportion to effect this most perfectly."[11] Plato proceeds to define geometrical proportion in purely mathematical terms, which we may illustrate with the simple geometrical progression 2, 4, 8. The middle term, the mean, is a perfect bond for the following reasons: as the first term is to the mean (2:4), so is the mean to the last term (4:8); conversely, as the last is to the mean (8:4), so is the mean to the first (4:2). Thus "the middle becomes the first and last, and again the last and first become middle (4:2 = 8:4); in that way all will necessarily come to play the same part towards one another, and by so doing they will all make a unity."[12] That which unites earth and fire must, then, stand to them as the mean of a three-term geometrical progression stands to the extremes. But Plato must account not only for such a third element, to bind fire and earth, but also for a fourth, since he knows *a priori* that in addition to earth and fire the universe consists of water and air. Again mathematics provides the explanation, for it is known that while plane surfaces are united by a single mean, two means are required to unite solids. Hence the world requires two means. "Accordingly the god set water and air between fire and earth, and made them, so far as was possible, proportional to one another, so that as fire is to air, so air is to water,

11 *Timaeus,* 31c.
12 *Timaeus,* 32a.

and as air is to water, so is water to earth, and thus he bound together the frame of a world visible and tangible."[13] In a word, the universe is proportional; its unique structure is describable only in the quantitative and completely rational language of mathematics.

Throughout his discussion of the structure of the world's body, Plato uses the four elements of the real world as though they were the components of an abstract mathematical proportion. The interchangeability of substance and abstraction is a characteristic feature of Plato's metaphysical thought. It enables him to speak persuasively about abstractions, but also, and ultimately more significant for the development of aesthetic theory, it enables him to regard the real world as a structure possessed of all the clarity and rationality of a mathematical equation. Physical imperfections and irregularities, of the kind that empirical investigation would discover — such as the fact that the human head is not really spherical — can be safely disregarded.

Probably because the argument becomes more difficult as it becomes more abstract, Plato discusses the soul after the body, but he insists that despite his own order of treatment, "the god made soul prior to body and more venerable in birth and excellence, to be the body's mistress and governor."[14] The basic materials of the world's soul are the abstractions Existence, Sameness, and Difference, but Plato describes the god's shaping of them in the same mathematical terms he used to describe the making of the four physical elements into the world's body; that is, the abstractions are regarded as tangibles, which can be sliced, divided, and mixed, according to the mathematics of proportion, to produce the "fabric" of the world's soul.[15] From this "fabric" the maker produces the

---

13 *Timaeus*, 32b.

14 *Timaeus*, 34c.

15 I pass over the intermediate stage in which Plato adduces in the world's soul all the musical intervals from the octave (2:1) to the semitone (256:243); *Timaeus*, 35b-36b. The reader interested in the numerical details should refer to Cornford's full and lucid account in *Plato's Cosmology*, pp. 66-72.

physical structure of the cosmos. He cuts and fashions two concentric circles which he sets into contrary motion. The outer circle is of the Same, the inner of Difference. The latter is divided into seven unequal circles, corresponding with the double and triple intervals. ("Unequal" refers to radius and indicates that the circles form a nest around a common center.) It remains to fit the world-body into the world-soul, and finally to fix the heavenly bodies — sun, moon, and five other stars — into the seven circular motions of the world-soul. We need not recount the reasoning used to accomplish this, except to attest that it is scrupulously mathematical. The resulting structure is the cosmos as western European civilization was to know it for some seventeen centuries. It is a finite universe, utilizing in perfect fullness all the material there is and consisting of seven planetary orbits circling the earth at varying distances and at varying speeds — all calculated according to principles of proportion — with the entire system enclosed by an outer sphere, beyond which is nothing.

This is the cosmos that Ptolemy defined in the technical language of astronomy in the *Almagest*. In these essentials Aristotle concurred. Though he was critical of the high metaphysical value the Pythagoreans and Plato placed upon numbers, he nevertheless regarded the universe as one, unique and all-inclusive, and he could assert that "the sphere of the fixed stars is that which moves all the other spheres . . ."[16] But to medieval cosmology and its aesthetic implications Aristotle was of minor importance compared to Plato — scholastic Aristotelianism notwithstanding[17] — and Plato was known preeminently through the *Timaeus*.

[16] Aristotle, *Metaphysics,* 1073b-1074a, trans. W. D. Ross, 2nd ed. (Oxford: Oxford University Press, 1928). Earlier in the *Metaphysics* (985b-986a) Aristotle ridicules the abstract rationalizing procedures of the Pythagoreans: ". . . as the number 10 is thought to be perfect and to comprise the whole nature of numbers, they say that the bodies which move through the heavens are ten, but as the visible bodies are only nine, to meet this they invent a tenth — the 'counter-earth.' " But as the later passage, quoted above, makes clear, Aristotle is not challenging the essential shape of creation assumed by the Pythagoreans and Plato.

[17] See below, pp. 40-41.

CHAUCER AND THE SHAPE OF CREATION

The importance of the *Timaeus,* to sum up, is that it established the deductive principle and the quantitative mode of reasoning which are at the heart of medieval thinking about the nature of Creation. The *Timaeus* is a detailed mathematical demonstration of God's adherence to Pythagoreanism — which is to say, it demonstrates God's rationality in the quantitative language of pure reason. Further, by showing how the assumed perfection of the intelligible whole could serve analogically as a measure of the value of the visible parts, the *Timaeus* established both the principle and the pattern for a symbolic interpretation of the universe. That this marvelously intricate yet perfectly ordered concept should have gratified the minds of men for upwards of fifteen centuries is perhaps not remarkable. Nor is it fortuitous that in the later Middle Ages, when secular art began to emerge as a serious enterprise, men should attempt to shape their most highly valued works by the same aesthetic principles and the same quantitative procedures which — according to accepted presuppositions — order the works of God.

Boethius, Macrobius, and St. Augustine

The continuing meaningfulness of Plato's cosmic vision throughout the Middle Ages is evident in the persisting influence of Boethius and Macrobius, whose sixth-century commentaries were well known to Chaucer personally and to his age in general. Boethius, the "divine popularizer," was important to the late Middle Ages not only for the *Consolation of Philosophy* but also for two technical treatises, *De arithmetica* and *De musica,* which helped to keep alive the mathematical details as well as the grand design of Greek number science.[18] Macrobius followed the more mystical tributary of the Pythagorean mainstream and pursued the allegorical possibilities of numerology. In this respect the *Commentary on the*

18 Both appear in Migne, *PL,* vol. 63.

MEDIEVAL AESTHETIC THEORY

Dream of Scipio — Chaucer's "olde bok totorn" — reveals a Neo-platonic strain which echoes the theological speculations of the Church Fathers. Though the Fathers, and theologians in general, were not among Chaucer's particular intimates, patristic thought, as we shall presently see, reacted with the pagan doctrines of the transitional writers to affect significantly the basic assumptions of Chaucer's world, assumptions about God, Creation, and man, and about man's capacity to know and to create.

Boethius modeled his *De arithmetica* and *De musica* on such widely influential Neo-Pythagorean handbooks as the *Exposition of Mathematical Matters Useful in the Reading of Plato* by Theon of Smyrna and the *Introduction to Arithmetic* by Nicomachus of Gerasa, both of which were intended largely as guides to Plato's thought in the *Timaeus*.[19] For Boethius, as for his sources, music and geometry are the means for understanding both the structure of the universe and the meaning of that structure and the values it defines. Music comprehends all temporal movements, and geometry comprehends all spatial forms. But prior to both, providing the absolute principle to which both refer, is arithmetic, the science of numbers. This fundamental conviction is affirmed in the opening chapters of both treatises, prior to the technical exposition of ratio and proportion which forms the body of each.

In Macrobius' *Commentary on the Dream of Scipio* Chaucer and his contemporaries found a version of the *Timaeus* complementary to that of Boethius. Following his Neoplatonic sources, particularly Porphyry's commentaries on the *Timaeus* and the *Republic*,[20] Macrobius pursues the mystical branch of Pythagorean number theory. Unlike Boethius, who after eulogizing the divine

[19] F. E. Robbins, "The Development of Greek Arithmetic before Nicomachus," in Nicomachus of Gerasa, *Introduction to Arithmetic*, trans. M. L. D'Ooge (New York, 1926), p. 28.
[20] See the detailed discussion by William H. Stahl, ed. and trans., in Macrobius, *Commentary on the Dream of Scipio* (New York: Columbia University Press, 1952), pp. 23-39.

exemplar in the opening chapters of *De arithmetica* and *De musica* could return to dwell exclusively and exhaustively upon the image — that is, the arithmetic of ratio and proportion — Macrobius' primary interest is the symbolic properties of numbers. Macrobius concentrates on the continuous interplay between rational perceptions and divine essence, number being the linking phenomenon which participates in both. To "read" the world as number is Macrobius' aim. His discussion of the number seven illustrates both the continuity of the Platonic vision and the mode of symbolic interpretation characteristic of Neoplatonic numerology.

After a purely arithmetical discussion of the different combinations of numbers whose sum is seven, Macrobius proceeds to the qualities of the number seven: "It was by this number first of all, indeed, that the World-Soul was begotten, as Plato's *Timaeus* has shown. With the monad located on the apex, two sets of three numbers each descended on either side, on one the even, on the other the odd . . .[21] and the mixture arising out of these seven numbers brought about the generation of the World-Soul at the behest of the Creator."[22] Macrobius goes on to adduce additional reasons why the number seven is worthy of our reverence, a prominent one being the fact that the Creator, "in his constructive foresight, arranged seven errant spheres beneath the star-bearing celestial sphere . . ." Thus the perfection of the number seven is associated with the perfection of the universe.[23]

[21] That is, the first three products of 2 (viz., 2, 4, and 6) descend from 1 on one side, and the first three products of 3 (3, 9, 27) descend on the other. The two sets of three numbers, plus the monad at the apex, add up to 7.

[22] Macrobius, p. 109.

[23] In Macrobius' mind there is no contradiction between this statement and his earlier observation about the number eight, which also deserves to be called perfect, for "it is . . . without doubt intimately related to the harmony of the spheres, since the revolving spheres are eight in number" (Macrobius, p. 98). In this count Macrobius includes the celestial sphere, while in the count of seven he regards only the planetary spheres. Modern cosmologists might look askance at this reasoning, but Macrobius' purpose was to reveal the known, not to discover the unknown, and there-

MEDIEVAL AESTHETIC THEORY

Number lies behind not only the world's physical structure but also its moral structure. That is, Macrobius' symbolism is sufficiently thoroughgoing and pervasive to reveal that abstract qualities, too, are but the diverse external forms of unchanging numerical truth. Thus he regards the soul to be, "as wise men have not hesitated to proclaim . . . a number moving itself."[24] Macrobius does not reproduce the entire scheme of Pythagorean numerological derivations of other abstract qualities, though he does point out that the number eight is Justice: "Since it is the product of equal even numbers [$2 \times 2 \times 2$] and may be divided equally . . . it deserves to receive the name Justice."[25]

To summarize the comparison of Boethius and Macrobius, we can say, though the distinction is not absolute, that for Boethius the study of number was a science and for Macrobius it was a theology. These complementary versions of Platonic-Pythagorean number theory were kept alive throughout the Middle Ages, the one stressing the anatomy of the image, the other stressing the proximity of the Exemplar.

When we turn from pagan to Christian concepts of the structure of the world, we find differences of emphasis but substantial agreement on the fundamentals. Christian thought absorbed the patterns of both Platonic rationalism and Neoplatonic symbolism; indeed, in sanctioning these pagan modes of thought Christianity made its principal contribution to aesthetic theory. It is these aspects of patristic thought that I wish to emphasize, in contrast, for example, to Robertson's emphasis on the iconographic meaning of individual artistic images or literary allusions.

St. Augustine, having contended mightily with the enticements of pagan culture,[26] had thoroughly absorbed the mental habits of

fore his reason was free, even obliged, to deduce examples of the Creator's perfection, to which end all means were subordinate and contributory.

24 Macrobius, p. 100.
25 Macrobius, p. 99.
26 See *Confessions,* especially Books I-IV.

Platonic rationalism, and he was prepared to bring his knowledge of pagan number theory to the service of Scriptural interpretation: "Let no one be so foolish or so absurd as to contend that they [numbers] have been put in the Scriptures for no purpose at all, and that there are no mystical reasons why these numbers have been mentioned there. But those which I have given have been handed down by the Fathers with the approval of the Church, or I have gathered them from the testimony of the divine Scriptures, or from the nature of numbers and analogies."[27] So thoroughly immersed was Augustine in both pagan philosophy and Holy Scriptures that he not only brought number to the service of the Word, but he also found in Scripture authoritative support for antique number theory. In *The City of God* (XI, 30) he concludes a defense of number theory with an appeal to the authority of the Book of Wisdom: "Neither has it been without reason numbered among God's praises, 'Thou hast ordered all things in number and measure and weight.'" The passage from Wisdom reflects the sources of that book in sophisticated Alexandrine thought and indicates familiarity with the metaphysics of Pythagorean rationalism. In medieval Latin texts, as Curtius observes, "few Bible verses are so often quoted and alluded to as the phrase from the Wisdom of Solomon, 11:21: 'omnia in mensura et numero et pondere disposuisti' . . . Through this verse, number was sanctified as a form-bestowing factor in the divine work of creation."[28] As we shall see, this formula was to play an inspirational role in the practical as well as the conceptual aesthetics of the Gothic period.

St. Augustine, working from the premise that numbers contained in Scripture are symbolic, combines traditional Pythagorean ideas of the arithmetical qualities of numbers with Christian inter-

[27] *The Trinity*, IV, 6, trans. Stephen McKenna (Washington, D.C.: Catholic University of America Press, 1963).

[28] Ernst Robert Curtius, *European Literature and the Latin Middle Ages*, trans. Willard R. Trask (New York: Pantheon Books, Inc., 1953), p. 504.

pretations of their spiritual and moral qualities. For example, in *The Trinity* Augustine recounts the traditional view that six is a perfect number because "it is completed in its own parts, for it has these three: sixth, third, and half, nor is any other part in it which can be called an aliquot part. For its sixth part is one, its third two, and its half three."[29] Then, turning to the spiritual dimension of the number, Augustine employs Neoplatonic symbolizing procedures in the service of Christian doctrine: "And Holy Scripture commends to us the perfection of this number, especially in this, that God finished His works in six days, and on the sixth day man was made in the image of God."

This commentary on "six" illustrates not only Augustine's historic role as a mediator between pagan and Christian culture but also the composite quality of medieval Christian thought in general. If the Christian writers of the Middle Ages regarded the ancients as damned despite their virtues because Revelation was not granted them, Christianity nevertheless depended to a considerable extent upon the substance of antique thought — so far as it could be shown not to conflict with Revelation — and it depended even more heavily upon the rationalistic and symbolic mode of antique thought. Augustine's discovery of perfection in the number six is a deductive process which begins with the extramathematical assumptions that (1) the Bible is divine and Genesis is therefore Truth and (2) God is perfect. The second of these assumptions was also held by the Pythagoreans and gave rise, as we have seen, to the intricate rationality of arithmetic and geometry, the language of perfection.[30] Therefore

29 *The Trinity,* IV, 4. Cf. Macrobius, *Commentary,* p. 102: "Six . . . is a number with various and manifold honors and abilities: first, because it is the only number under ten that is equal to the sum of its parts. We may divide it by two, three, or six, a half being three, a third two, and a sixth one; the three added together make six."

30 The full range and potency of the idea of "perfection" in medieval thought is effectively demonstrated in the culminating chapter — *"Piers Plowman* and the Quest for Perfection" — of Morton W. Bloomfield's study of that poem. In interpreting Langland's complex vision Bloomfield makes clear that the stages of perfection are associated with the life of Christ, that monastic philosophy exemplifies this perfection

Augustine, discovering mathematical perfection in "six," could find gratification in the biblical association of "six" with God's work of creation. The mathematical lineaments of six's perfection — the "scientific" demonstration — Augustine found in Pythagorean tradition, as did Macrobius. And like Macrobius, Augustine understood that the mathematics was a direct manifestation of a higher perfection.

Though belief in the divinity of the Bible was not an element of the Pythagorean heritage, the Christian mode of implementing this belief was consistent with the symbolic rationalism of the Pythagoreans. Indeed, the symbolic interpretation of language is no less venerable than the symbolism of number. But antique studies of rhetoric did not give rise to a cosmic symbolism comparable to Pythagorean mathematics and number theory, the reason being inherent in the respective possibilities of number and language as images of perfection. Nevertheless, belief in the symbolic value of revered texts was part of the classical heritage of the Christian Middle Ages. Like number theory, textual symbolism began with the assumption that the text as perceptible object mirrored a higher, intelligible truth.

Interpretation of Holy Scriptures was the primary labor of medieval learning, and in recent years considerable scholarly effort has been devoted to illuminating its methods and its achievements.[31]

in social terms, and that the virtue of Temperance (or restraint and order) is man's and society's principle resource in the quest for perfection. Bloomfield indicates that Langland envisions perfetion of life as an integral part of the perfection of the universe: "Temperance is violated by men and especially clerics and religious, not only in the moral realm but also in the cosmological realm. The excesses of mankind, especially those of the friars, who should be in the vanguard along with the monks in the quest for perfection, tend to destroy the very basis of intellectual and ontological existence. They are turning the world into an undifferentiated hell which is the model for nothingness and infinite confusion." *"Piers Plowman" as a Fourteenth-Century Apocalypse* (New Brunswick, N.J.: Rutgers University Press, 1961), pp. 146-147.

[31] The major studies of medieval Scriptural exegesis are the following: Henri de Lubac, *Exégèse médiévale: Les quatre sens de l'Écriture*, 2 vols. (Paris, 1959-1961);

MEDIEVAL AESTHETIC THEORY

The field is as broad as medieval learning itself, and I shall attempt only to define some of the essential features of the exegetical mode of thought and to indicate how textual exegesis proceeds within the same imaginative framework that shapes mathematical symbolism and quantitative aesthetics.

The symbolic interpretation of the Bible was a rational process which proceeded logically from premise to conclusion. Logic was no less stringent in the Middle Ages than now, and the laws of valid reasoning, as Augustine affirmed, could be learned in the schools. But the truth of premises could be determined only from the sacred books of the Church. Augustine illustrates the principle and the method in a discussion of I Corinthians 15, wherein Paul, addressing skeptics, is preaching the resurrection of the dead. Paul reasons that "if there be no resurrection of the dead, then is Christ not risen." Augustine points out that Paul is deliberately adopting a false premise in order to reach a conclusion which, although logical, is so manifestly false that the premise must be condemned. Augustine sums up: "If there is no resurrection of the dead, neither was Christ resurrected. But Christ was resurrected. Therefore there is a resurrection of the dead."[32] The articles of faith provide the basis for certitude. Knowledge of any kind — even profane or pagan — that was consistent with faith was adopted, whereas, as Aquinas said of Augustine and as he observed in his own labors, "those things which he found contrary to faith he amended."[33]

Acceptance of the faith resulted in a form of intellectual absolutism, a mental attitude which, though uncongenial to modern relativism, is thoroughly characteristic of medieval thought. On this common belief in the existence of certitude, Pythagoreanism joined

Ceslaus Spicq, *Esquisse d'une histoire de l'exégèse latine au moyen âge* (Paris, 1944) ; Beryl Smalley, *The Study of the Bible in the Middle Ages,* 2nd ed. (Oxford, 1952).

[32] *On Christian Doctrine,* II, 32, trans. D. W. Robertson, Jr. (Indianapolis and New York: Bobbs-Merrill Co., Inc., 1958).

[33] *Summa theologica,* trans. English Dominican Fathers, 2nd ed. (London: R. and T. Washbourne, Ltd., 1922), I, Q. 84, art. 5.

with Christian sacramentalism; both adopted the ancient distinction between the intelligible and the perceptible, the exemplar and the image, and upon this distinction based the unshakable assumption that symbolic relations connect the two. It was the task of active rationality to discern and articulate these relations. The role of reason is stressed by Robertson in his discussion of Augustine's demonstration of "how far reason may progress from the visible to the invisible, ascending at the same time from the temporal to the eternal."[34] Augustine's rationalism, as Robertson rightly emphasizes, tends always to refer the visible — whether letter, number, or object — to the invisible essence in the Godhead, but it should be observed, as Robertson reminds us, that this progress toward God does not imply a casual or careless attitude on Augustine's part toward the visible surfaces of creation. Augustine's attentiveness to Ciceronian principles of rhetoric and verbal style in his "handbook" of Scriptural interpretation, *On Christian Doctrine,* illustrates his concern for the visible and tangible. Nevertheless, the emphasis of patristic practice — St. Jerome's labors as a philologist and translator notwithstanding — leans heavily toward the Neoplatonist sense of the proximity of the exemplar and its ready accessibility through rational interpretation of the image.

The continuity of the Christian symbolic world view is illustrated by twelfth-century Victorine restatements of Augustinian principles. It is clear that Hugh of St. Victor, for example, is charting Augustine's universe when he proclaims, "This entire perceptible world is as a book written by the finger of God, that is, created by divine power, and individual creatures are as figures within it, not invented by human will (placito) but instituted by divine authority (arbitrio) to make manifest the wisdom of the invisible things of God."[35] And Adam of St. Victor complies with Augustine's injunction that we should use the things of this world

34 *A Preface,* pp. 65-66.
35 *Eruditionis didascalicae,* VII, cap. 4 (*PL,* vol. 176, col. 814).

28

rather than enjoy them when, in a well-known exegesis, he reasons his way from a walnut to the Godhead: "What is a nut if not the image of Jesus Christ? The green and fleshly sheath is His flesh, His humanity. The wood of the shell is the wood of the Cross on which that flesh suffered. But the kernel of the nut from which men gain nourishment is His hidden divinity."[36]

An understanding of the common imaginative bond between Christian and pagan sacramentalist concepts of universal harmony brings us to the matrix of medieval aesthetic principles, that is, to those conceptualizing habits and predispositions from which the secular art of the late Middle Ages derived its sense of shape and structure. In the remaining pages of this chapter I shall attempt to indicate the significance for literary art of the recurring patterns of sacramentalism and rationalism I have been thus far considering.

Quantitative Aesthetics and Literary Theory: Medieval Humanism, Dante, and the New Poetry

Augustinian theology, echoed in Christianized natural science, shares with Platonic and Neoplatonic Pythagoreanism the fundamental mode of thought which differentiates the medieval from the modern imagination, a mode of thought which is likely to strike us — the heirs of Galileo and Newton — as disturbingly "unscientific." It is a thoroughgoing deductivism, which begins by attributing to God, the divine architect, the qualities of perfection and truth and the status of exemplar of all things. Reasoning from this assumption, medieval man would always know the conclusion as a truth (not guess it as a hypothesis) before he began intellectual investigation. When the purpose of study is thus to corroborate old truths rather than to discover new ones, the mind works within a closed system

---

[36] Quoted by Emile Mâle, *The Gothic Image: Religious Art in France of the Thirteenth Century,* trans. Dora Nussey from 3rd French ed., 1918 (New York: Harper's, 1958), p. 30.

of thought and endeavors to work out new connections, new equivalences, between perceptible phenomena and the source of all. Theology and natural science so conceived express their equivalences in metaphors and in nominalism of varying kinds and degrees of extensiveness. Mathematics expresses its equivalences in equations. Thus Pythagoreanism begins with a unity, a whole, and proceeds rationally to deduce relationships among parts variously designated but always constituting an aggregate equal to the whole. Patristic thought, though not occupied primarily with the precise language of number, nonetheless expresses itself within a similarly firmly fixed framework of primary presupposition: Christianity specifies a divinely shaped and enclosed universe, whose purpose and end are known by the Maker, and whose constituent parts all play meaningful participating roles, which can be "read" by reason as tangible signs of the ineffable divine order. The guidelines which St. Paul set down for this world view parallel those established by Plato in the *Timaeus.* The assurance of fulfillment, that is, of completeness of that divine creation which is presupposed to be ultimate totality, is implicit in Paul's preachings of the coming fulfillment of Christ's promised Law: "For we know in part and we prophesy in part. But when that which is perfect is come, then that which is in part shall be done away" (I Cor. 13). The Platonic counterpart of this harmonious unification in perfect wholeness is pictured in the *Timaeus,* where, as we have seen, the frame of the universe is described as taking up all there is of each of the four elements to form "a body whole and complete." Within the fixed limitations of known truth — whether the Pythagoreans' truth of divine harmony or the Christians' truth of Revelation — the mind moves freely, guided by reason, in the search for new evidence of the perfection of Creation and harmony of all things.

Medieval literary art and aesthetics developed within these patterns of deductive reasoning. But before human makers — as distinct from the Maker — could develop a language of metaphors

MEDIEVAL AESTHETIC THEORY

for truth which could be accommodated within the domain pre-empted by Holy Scriptures, certain conditions had to obtain. Above all, a place had to be found for human creations within the closed, theocentric system visualized in the medieval picture of the world. The mode of accommodation was defined by the allegorical poetry which appeared in the early Middle Ages. The decisive innovation offered by this poetry was the use of personified abstractions as primary structural materials. Being tangible representations of abstract qualities, personifications related allegory naturally and intimately with the imitative, analogical, rationalistic processes of the medieval imagination.

Allegory, to borrow Huizinga's definition, is properly regarded as a servant of symbolism. It serves the belief in the reality of abstract conceptions by imbuing such conceptions with life, that is, by personifying them. "Symbolism expresses a mysterious connection between two ideas, allegory gives a visible form to the conception of such a connection. Symbolism is a very profound function of the mind, allegory is a superficial one. It aids symbolic thought to express itself . . ."[37] In discussing the *Psychomachia* of Prudentius, the first "fully fledged allegorical poem," C. S. Lewis stresses the moral revolution and the sense of inner conflict which "forces men to personify their passions."[38] He also points out the more palpable influence of Scriptural exegesis and the concurrent practice, among

[37] J. Huizinga, *The Waning of the Middle Ages* (London: E. Arnold and Co., 1924), p. 186. C. S. Lewis draws the distinction in a similar fashion: "Symbolism is a mode of thought, but allegory is a mode of expression." *The Allegory of Love* (Oxford: The Clarendon Press, 1936), p. 48. Lewis' campaign to recapture for allegory some of the value sacrificed to the modern romantic love of "symbolism" seems now to have been successful. Edwin Honig, *Dark Conceit: The Making of Allegory* (Evanston, Ill. 1959); Angus J. S. Fletcher, *Allegory; the Theory of a Symbolic Mode* (Ithaca, N.Y., 1964); Rosemond Tuve, *Allegorical Imagery* (Princeton, N.J., 1966). Two important discussions of the limits and the possibilities of medieval symbolism and allegory are Robert W. Frank, Jr., "The Art of Reading Medieval Personification Allegory," *ELH*, 20: 237-50 (1953); Morton W. Bloomfield, "Symbolism in Medieval Literature," *MP*, 56: 73-81 (1958).

[38] *The Allegory of Love*, p. 63.

the Stoics and others, of the exegesis of Greek mythology to bring the old tales of the gods into accord with current beliefs and sensibilities. For example, the story of Saturn eating his children was interpreted "allegorically" as representing Time bearing all his sons away.[39] Exegesis of this kind is no less imaginative and "creative" than a deliberately composed moral allegory of the kind produced by Prudentius. Prudentius depicts the conflict between sin and virtue, a conflict which he sets forth in the trappings and clangor of Virgilian epic encounters, but whose protagonists are Anger, Patience, Courage, Humility, and other abstract qualities. There is no doubt about the meaning of Prudentius' allegory, that virtue can triumph over temptation and bring happy concord to the troubled breast. The discovery of this truth beneath the surface requires little effort and no ingenuity. As a secular form of serious imaginative utterance the *Psychomachia* must have been much less impressive than a "nonfictional" commentary such as the *Virgiliana Continentia* of Fulgentius, in which "the *Aeneid* is treated as an image of life, and the travels of Aeneas as the symbol of the progress of the human soul, from nature, through wisdom, to final happiness."[40] Yet the allegorical mode of expression demonstrated by Prudentius retained its vitality and attractiveness for later poets largely because of its association with the spiritual and mystical efficacy of symbolic exegesis.

Naming and concretizing abstractions in the making of allegories was a procedure which mixed naturally with the procedure of symbolically interpreting "temporal things" to discover the abstract truths behind them. For the Middle Ages, the nature and the extent of literature were defined by the twin progeny of mimetic symbolism: allegorical interpretation and allegorical expression. Thus Curtius can point out that from the meeting and mingling of

[39] *Ibid.*, p. 62.
[40] J. E. Spingarn, *A History of Literary Criticism in the Renaissance* (New York: Columbia University Press, 1925), pp. 7-8.

MEDIEVAL AESTHETIC THEORY

Biblical and Virgilian exegesis in the Middle Ages, "allegory becomes the basis of all textual interpretation whatsoever . . . not only in the 'moralizing' of Ovid and other authors through allegorical interpretation, but also in the fact that personified beings of a supersensual nature . . . could become the principal personages of poetic creations: from Prudentius' *Psychomachia* to the twelfth-century philosophical epic; from the *Romance of the Rose* to Chaucer and Spenser . . ."[41] Both allegorical interpretation and allegorical expression are rooted in the symbolic predisposition, which Curtius traces to a basic quality of Greek religious thought, "the belief that the gods express themselves in cryptic form — in oracles, in mysteries."[42]

We may well wonder at Curtius' inclusion of Chaucer among the company of Prudentius, the *Romance of the Rose,* and Spenser in the allegorical tradition, for it is plain that whereas personified abstractions are essential to the other three they are rare and peripheral in Chaucer. Sophisticated efforts to read Chaucer as though he were practicing allegorical expression, as though his characters were as simplified as, say, Guillaume's Deduit, and as though he were as industriously devoted as Augustine to "using" all temporal things as means to eternal Truth have proved to be unconvincing.[43] But to say that Chaucer does not customarily express himself allegorically is not to say that he transcends or revolts against the allegorical tradition and its conceptual framework of aesthetic directives. Rather, it is from within this framework and its structural implications that Chaucer derived the techniques of his art, as we shall presently see.

From the symbolic tradition and its capacity to nurture allegory the new humanism of the late Middle Ages derived its concept of

[41] *European Literature,* p. 205.
[42] *Ibid.*
[43] See, for example, the questions raised by E. Talbot Donaldson, "Patristic Exegesis in the Criticism of Medieval Literature: The Opposition," in *Critical Approaches to Medieval Literature,* ed. Dorothy Bethurum (New York, 1960).

poetic structure. Alan of Lille, for example, discussing the nature of poetry in *De planctu naturae,* enforces the conventional quantitative differentiation between "false exteriors" and "secret truths" and then goes on to indicate how poets employ deliberate, palpable means to beautify these "false exteriors" or "veils." "Poets combine historical events with fictional entertainments to form an elegant structure, so that from a suitable joining together of the narrative itself a more elegant picture may result."[44] In this view the art of poetry is primarily a manipulative art, consisting in the conscious, deliberate disposition of clearly delimited parts. Art so conceived is properly regarded as "structure" rather than "expression." Its elements are "inorganic," and its natural modes of development are defined in such quantitative terms as amplification, division, embellishment. The strong sense of a separation between the superficial veil and the true essence beneath made it natural to speak of poetry as a "lie." The humanists from Alan's time onward attached eulogistic connotations to this "lying" kind of utterance — as in Dante's "bella menzogna" — and by this means helped to enlarge the prestige of literary art. Though there is no evidence for attributing this sentiment to Aristotle's praise of Homer, "who taught other poets the art of telling lies skillfully,"[45] since the *Poetics* remained unedited and virtually unknown until the sixteenth century, the sense of poetry as a lie or veil is inherent in the mimetic-symbolist framework of thought. The contribution of the poets and theorists of the late Middle Ages was to renew the possibility that poetry other than that of the ancients and other than that of God could rise to moral and aesthetic stature. Petrarch, for example, finds complete concord between poetry and religion, symbolic language being the bond between them: "Poetry is in no sense opposed to Theology. I might almost say that theology is poetry which proceeds from God. When Christ is called now a 'lion,' now a 'lamb,' and now a 'worm,'

---

44 *De planctu naturae, PL,* vol. 210, col. 451.
45 *Poetics,* XXIV, 8.

MEDIEVAL AESTHETIC THEORY

— what is that if not poetic? . . . What are the Saviour's parables but allegories? . . . The Bible treats of God and divine things, poetry of gods and men, wherefore we read in Aristotle that the poets were the first to practice theology . . ."[46] The same idea is expressed by Boccaccio, in almost the same way: "Then it seems clear, not only is poetry theology, but also theology is poetry."[47] The close association of poetry and theology in humanistic thought of the time, and the wide currency of the metaphor, antique in origin, of the *Deus artifex*[48] make clear the source of Alan's image of the poet as an artificer analogous in his limited field to Plato's Artificer of the world. From the exemplary concept of the cosmic art of God the newly prestigious art of poetry derived its aesthetic rationale.

Dante's literary criticism sounds strange to modern ears because it is based in the quantitative conception of poetic art. Dante's version of the "veil" metaphor, which he uses in defining a poetic fiction, reflects the quantitative basis of his concept of poetry. Dante regards a poetic fiction as a material substance which can be deliberately "woven," then draped over the truth, and, at will and with the requisite cunning, removed. Dante's formulation is typical: ". . . great embarrassment would come to one who, having written things in the dress of an image or coloring of words, and then, having been asked, would not be able to strip his words of such dress in order to give them their true meaning."[49]

This general concept gives rise to a method of close critical analysis similarly quantitative and similarly alien to most modern approaches to close reading. Dante's critical commentary on his own works makes it clear that he regards a poem as an artful col-

[46] *Le Familiari,* X, 4; quoted in Curtius, *European Literature,* p. 226.

[47] *Life of Dante;* quoted in *European Literature,* p. 226.

[48] The development of the medieval topos of the *Deus artifex* from pagan and Christian elements is sketched, with appropriate examples and citations, by Curtius, pp. 544-546.

[49] *La Vita nuova,* XXV, trans. Mark Musa (New Brunswick, N. J.: Rutgers University Press, 1957), p. 55. (Reprinted, Bloomington: Indiana University Press, 1962.)

location of inorganic parts and that he discerns meaning primarily in quantitative terms. In the *Vita nuova* and the *Convivio*, as well as in the more mature commentary on the *Commedia* contained in the dedicatory Letter to Can Grande, Dante heavily stresses the critical procedure of "dividing" a poem, that is, getting at the meaning by delineating the parts of the whole, the parts of parts, and so forth.

Dante's method is illustrated by his commentary on the Canzone "Donne, ch'avete intelletto d'amore," a poem which he regards more seriously than the sonnets which precede it in the *Vita nuova* and which he therefore analyzes with particular care:

In order that this *canzone* may be better understood, I shall divide it more carefully than the previous poems. Therefore, I first divide it into three parts. The first part is a preface to the words that follow; the second is the intended subject; the third is a sort of handmaiden to the words which precede it. The second part begins: *The mind;* the third: *My song, I know that you.* Now the first part subdivides into four. In the first I declare to whom I wish to speak about my lady and why I wish to speak; in the second I tell in what condition I seem to find myself whenever I think of her worthiness and what I would say if I did not lose courage; in the third I tell how I intend to speak of her in order not to be hindered by baseness . . . When I say, *The mind,* then I begin to deal with this lady, and this part is subdivided into two. In the first I tell how she is thought of in heaven; in the second I tell how she is thought of on earth, beginning here: *My Lady is desired.* This second part divides further into two. In the first I speak of her in respect to the magnificence of her soul, relating examples of the wondrous powers that proceed from her soul; in the second I speak of her in respect to the magnificence of her visible qualities, mentioning some of her beauties with the words, *Love says of her.* This second part is further divided into two . . .

The two parts into which the poet divides the beauty of the lady's body are the whole person and a definite part of her person, the latter being divided in turn into eyes and mouth. Then follows a paragraph alluding to the envoi of the poem, which is "easy to understand" and hence requires no more divisions. The concluding paragraph of the analysis refers once more to the subtlety of the poem and to the efficacy of this mode of interpretation: "Certainly, to make the meaning more apparent, I should have to make my divisions more extensive; nevertheless, if there be those who have not wit enough to understand it by the divisions already made, it would not displease me if they would leave it alone; for certainly I fear I have communicated its meaning to too many through the divisions I have made, if it should come about that many should hear them."[50]

How antithetical these views are to modern critical sensibilities need hardly be pointed out. Plainly Dante understands literary art to be a process of construction, in the most literal and unsubtle sense of the term. In these early love poems Dante apparently finds no spiritual levels of meaning, and his interpretations are confined to quantitative analysis of what in the learned tradition of Scriptural and classical exegesis is simply the surface, the literal meaning. But after Dante turns to the courtship of Wisdom in the *Convivio* his discussions of interpretation take account of the symbolic as well as the literal dimension. Despite the enlargement of scope, however, Dante's more mature commentaries are still based upon the concept that a poem is a fixed, tangible structure, whose meaning is available to reason. This is the concept that Dante would naturally appropriate from his study of the philosophers and theologians from Macrobius and St. Augustine to Bernard Silvestris, Alan of Lille, and Thomas Aquinas. The interpretation of poetry, like that of all things, is an exercise of reason in the discernment of stages and divisions within a clearly delimited field of inquiry.

Dante's Letter to Can Grande, in which he explains the *Paradiso* and its relation to the total poem, provides further insight into the quantitative approach to literary structure. Dante defines, in Section 9, two aspects of form, the form of the treatise and the form

[50] *La Vita nuova*, XIX, pp. 35-36.

of the treatment.[51] "Treatment" refers to the symbolic ramifications of the poem's literal meaning; that is, the "treatment" is the symbolic realization of what he earlier (Section 7) refers to as the poem's "polysemous" quality.[52] The hierarchical range of meanings thus defined indicates verticality, or depth, of structure. The "treatise," on the other hand, is the literal meaning, contained in the surface or "veil," and its form is determined by the pattern in which the sections of the poem are composed, or, in Alan's terminology, "joined together." The "treatise," then, is the lateral dimension, or breadth, of the poem, the "treatment" its depth.

The dimensionality of breadth and depth imparts to the poem a finite, tangible quality. Within this conceptual framework it is natural to seek meaning and clarification in the procedure of analysis by quantitative division, as Dante does when he defines the form of the treatise: "The first division is that whereby the whole work is divided into three cantiche; the second, whereby each cantica is divided into cantos; and the third, whereby each canto is divided into rhymed lines."[53] The quantitative approach makes it possible thus to separate substantive content from structural form.

Dante follows a similar analytic procedure in clarifying the divisions of vertical structure. Here the method is more familiar, being that of traditional allegorical interpretation. Dante makes implicit acknowledgment of his debt to the tradition of Scriptural exegesis by using a four-level interpretation of a Scriptural text to

---

[51] "Forma vero est duplex, forma tractatus et forma tractandi." "Epistle X," *Dantis Alagherii Espistolae,* ed. and trans. Paget Toynbee (Oxford: Clarendon Press, 1920) p. 174.

[52] My interpretation of the "form of treatment" (*forma tractandi*) is somewhat conjectural. The only explanation Dante offers in the immediate context is one sentence, which is merely a series of epithets: "Forma sive modus tractandi est poeticus, fictivus, descriptivus, digressivus, transumptivus; et cum hoc definitivus, divisivus, probativus, improbativus, et exemplorum positivus." The nature of the terms, taken together with the earlier discussion of the "polysemous" quality of the poem, justifies, I think, the connection I have drawn between "treatment" and the hierarchy of symbolic meanings.

[53] *Dantis Alagherii* p. 200.

illustrate what he means by "polysemous," the quality he attributes to his poem. But despite his adherence to the "polysemous" principle in theory, Dante's actual interpretation is "duosemous." After explaining the literal, allegorical, moral, and anagogical meanings of the passage from the Scriptures, he reduces the concept to its simplest symbolic form, which is twofold: "Although these mystical meanings are called by various names, they may one and all in a general sense be termed allegorical, inasmuch as they are different from the literal or historical." He then (Section 8) provides a twofold interpretation of "the subject round which the alternative senses play." Literally, the subject is "the state of souls after death." Allegorically, it is "man, as by good or ill deserts, in the exercise of the freedom of his choice, he becomes liable to rewarding or punishing justice." The discrepancy between Dante's stated critical assumptions, in which he defines four levels of meaning, and his actual critical performance, in which he settles for two, is instructive, for it suggests the limitations encountered by medieval exegetes in efforts to adapt the traditional methods of Scriptural exegesis to new poetry. Whereas received doctrine provided the materials for an elaborate, multilevel interpretation of a text which was known to be sacred, there was no such storehouse of possibilities for texts which were merely the products of human reason, however seriously they may have been intended as guides to salvation. The kind of rationalistic superstructure of interpretation which Holy Scriptures and the traditionally admired classics could support was neither readily available to new poems nor easily adaptable to them.[54] Dante's introduction to his poem, like his commentaries on the *Vita nuova* and the *Convivio*, was no doubt intended to enhance

[54] It is interesting to observe that before the end of the fourteenth century the *Commedia* was itself a "classic" and therefore susceptible to the effort of Benvenuto da Imola to "unravel the web of its fictions, elucidate the mysteries veiled by its various figures, find out the meanings hidden in its multiple senses." Richard H. Green, "Dante's 'Allegory of Poets' and the Medieval Theory of Poetic Fiction," *CL,* 11: 122 (1957).

the prestige of the work, composed as it was in the untraditional vernacular tongue. That he does not in fact move beyond the second level of interpretation, either in the Letter or in the *Convivio,* does not alter the fact that in Dante's mind quantitative complexity was associated with value. The form of the theoretical scheme is meaningful in itself.

The new Aristotelianism of the twelfth and thirteenth centuries did not, of course, diminish the impulse to formalize, and we know how deeply Dante's approach to problems of literary analysis was influenced by Thomas Aquinas and the methods of scholastic logic. That the impact of Aristotle was as revolutionary and decisive as many students of the period have maintained is, I think, doubtful. The suddenness and thoroughness of Aristotle's penetration of the schools did indeed generate a rivalry between his thought and that of Plato, and since then historians of philosophy have tended to emphasize the disparities between "Platonism" and "Aristotelianism." Among literary scholars, too, there has been a tendency to polarize the two. Wicksteed, for example, pointed out that Dante's initial analysis of his odes into "divisions" was copied from the method of Aquinas' Aristotelian commentaries, "where they are more in place."[55] The implication here is that the Aristotelian influence was not only new and unaesthetic but actively inimical to poetic art. (It should be remembered that the Aristotelian corpus at this time did not include the *Poetics.*) A similar view is more fully expressed by C. S. Lewis. With undisguised distaste Lewis characterizes Aristotle as "the philosopher of divisions," and he looks back with nostalgia at the "humane" Platonism of Chartres.[56] The proper response to this challenge is not a defense of Aristotle — who doubtless is more rigorous and less humorous and therefore perhaps less "humane" than Plato — but rather a reminder of the character of

[55] *The Convivio,* ed. Philip H. Wicksteed (London: J. M. Dent Co., Ltd., 1903), p. 70n.
[56] *The Allegory of Love,* p. 88.

40

MEDIEVAL AESTHETIC THEORY

Chartrian Platonism. The masters of Chartres learned their Platonism from the *Timaeus* and William of Conches' commentary.[57]
As we have seen, the vision of the universe which the *Timaeus*
transmitted to the Middle Ages is based entirely upon the concept
of divisions, that is, the exact, mathematically defined proportioning
of the elements of creation — animate, inanimate, and incorporeal
— into the supremely harmonious structure of the cosmos. What
the Middle Ages admired most in Plato and found most meaningful,
both ontologically and aesthetically, was the comprehensive, rationally ordered structure of his thought. It is true that Aristotle's
strong empiric sense effectively challenged some of the too facile
deductions of Platonic and Pythagorean reasoning,[58] but recent
studies of the influence of the *Timaeus* affirm that "Aristotle's
agreement with Plato is far greater than his divergence."[59] Werner
Jaeger has stressed the fact that Aristotle "stands wholly on ground
prepared by Plato . . . and his works on physics and cosmology are
essentially discussions within the academy."[60] Within the Platonic
and Pythagorean schema the Aristotelian emphasis upon division
and classification is not an inconsistent or incongruous development.
It, too, devolves from the fundamental postulate of a finite, universal whole, which is the cosmic unity. From this unity Plato and
Aristotle rationally deduced the infinite divisions of intelligible and
perceptible reality.

If Dante's literary commentaries lack the charm and the idealism characteristic of the Platonic dialogue, it is not because his approach is unpoetic. It is because for him poetry shares with all things
this side of faith the quality of rational structure. For Dante the

---

[57] The principal documents in the transmission of the *Timaeus,* i.e., Platonic
thought, through the Middle Ages, from Chalcidius to the School of Chartres, are
surveyed by Klibansky, *The Continuity.*

[58] See above, n. 16.

[59] George S. Claghorn, *Aristotle's Criticism of Plato's "Timaeus"* (The Hague:
Nijhoff, 1954), p. 135.

[60] *Ibid.,* pp. 134-135.

41

road to understanding poetry is the road of reason, and the method of composing poems is essentially quantitative, part by part, both in the lateral disposition of rhetorical sections and in the vertical division of levels of meaning. Commentary is essentially a process of taking apart what the poet has put together.

The humanists' emphasis upon the verbal surface of poetry, that is, upon the composition of the "veil," was congenial to a rhetorical approach to the art of poetry. The revival of Ciceronian and Horatian precepts in the popular rhetorical handbooks, such as the *Poetria nova* of Geoffrey of Vinsauf and the *Ars versificatoria* of Matthew of Vendôme, substantiated and enlarged the concept of poetry as a quantitative or "inorganic" art, that is, an art concerned with the management and disposition of the fixed elements constituting a preconceived whole. A characteristic metaphor for the poet is articulated by Geoffrey of Vinsauf near the beginning of the *Poetria nova.* In a passage which Chaucer was to include almost verbatim in *Troilus,* Geoffrey admonishes the poet to learn from the builder how best to dispose the parts of his work.[61] Like a builder, he should work out his plans beforehand. He should not embark on his composition before he has carefully considered each of its parts, assigned appropriate qualities to each, and balanced all in relation to one another and in relation to the whole.

Geoffrey of Vinsauf makes explicit the medieval assumption that poetry is possessed of "structure," that it is tangible and quantitatively measureable. His aim is to circumscribe the procedures of composition and enumerate its fixed elements. He treats these verbal components in the same manner that a builder would treat stones. The largest division of his treatise concerns the problem of size, conceived in abstract, quantitative terms, exclusive of any considera-

---

61 "Si quis habet fundare domum, non currit ad actum Impetuosa manus: intrinseca linea cordis Praemetitur opus." *Les Arts poétiques du XIIᵉ et du XIIIᵉ Siècle,* ed. Edmond Faral (Paris: Champion, 1924), p. 198. Chaucer adapts the passage to a discussion on the building of an intrigue, *Troilus and Criseyde,* I, 1065-71.

tion of content or substantive meaning. Here he enumerates the devices of amplification and those of abbreviation. Practices such as personification, description, repetition, and, contrariwise, their suppression, are regarded by Geoffrey as a builder regards his techniques of adjusting materials to specifications. The other major division of the *Poetria nova* deals with ornaments of style. Here, too, though the elements are more minute — such as metonymy, hyperbole, asyndeton — the approach is entirely quantitative. In all, Geoffrey enumerates and illustrates sixty-three ornaments of style and fifteen methods of amplification and abbreviation.

Undoubtedly medieval theorists entertained a notion of literary theory quite different from our own, and when medieval poets such as Alan of Lille and Dante discussed their art, they did so within the framework of assumptions made familiar in the mimetic tradition. I have tried to draw attention to some of the salient features of that framework of assumptions in this brief survey of Pythagorean rationalism and its ramifications in medieval modes of perceiving and defining the nature of things. In literary theory in the late Middle Ages this mode of thought eventuates in the idea of a poem as an edifice composed of prefabricated parts. This inorganic conception of art, with its concentration on quantity and structure, does not sit well with the modern interest in vital inner relations and organic interpenetrations. Rather than attempt to bend medieval art to our particular predispositions, it is of course more prudent to explore the aesthetic possibilities of inorganic structure. To attempt to disguise the quantitative character of medieval literary art would be futile, and to deemphasize it would be misleading. Therefore we shall examine the structure of medieval art in its most tangible manifestations — in architecture, the form which provided Geoffrey of Vinsauf with his exemplar for poetry — in order to establish an appropriate vocabulary and frame of aesthetic reference for a discussion of medieval poetry.

THREE   THE GOTHIC CATHE-DRAL: SALVATION THROUGH STRUCTURE

More fully and more clearly than any other form of expression, Gothic architecture transmuted the basic ordering principles of the medieval world-view into the substance and structure of art. In splendid, awe-inspiring fashion the Gothic cathedral fulfilled the imperatives of mathematical rationalism and Christian revelation. In studying Gothic solutions to problems of adapting palpable materials to the expression of a complex abstract vision, we discover a vocabulary for talking about inorganic properties in artistic forms in general. The relevance of such a study to literary scholarship can be inferred, I believe, from our brief examination of Dante's concept of poetic art, a concept in which a poem emerges as a dimensioned structure of individually articulated quantities. This manner of aesthetic thinking is as "architectural" as it is

44

"poetic," and while the differences between a poem and a cathedral require no demonstration, such differences should not obscure our awareness of fundamental aesthetic similarities. The problem is to define valid terms of aesthetic comparison between arts whose materials are so different.

One of the major achievements of the Gothic, which added immensely to its prestige in its own time, was its demonstration that man could create in accordance with God's own aesthetic principles. Thus for this most serious of all of man's creative endeavors — to build a mansion of God on earth — the mathematical rationalism of harmonious order provided the theoretical basis. From this starting point — the assumption that mathematics is the divine ordering principle — proceeds the quantitative mode of Gothic construction, the measuring of proportions and the additive and cumulative repetition of basic geometrical figures to form the total structure.

Narrative art, too, is adaptable to complex patterns of mathematical proportion. Curtius has surveyed the ways in which medieval writers consciously applied principles of number symbolism to literary composition. The idea of "numerical composition" as Curtius discusses it relates literary works to the general background of number symbolism — stemming from Pythagoras and the apocryphal Book of Wisdom, as we have seen — but does so only in a limited way, that is, by counting the number of lines, stanzas, cantos, or other units of composition and referring the result to the theory of symbolic numbers. Thus Curtius cites several works, such as Augustine's *Contra Faustum,* which are divided into thirty-three parts, the number sanctified as the years of Christ's life. "The wonderful harmony of Dante's numerical composition is the end and the acme of a long development . . . the elaborate numerical structure of the *Commedia*: $1 + 33 + 33 + 33 = 100$ cantos conduct the reader through 3 realms, the last of which contains 10 heavens. Triads and decads intertwine into unity. Here number is no

45

longer an outer framework but a symbol of the cosmic *ordo*."[1] The fact that no such recondite symbolism is to be found in Chaucer does not mean that his art is dissociated from the "cosmic *ordo*" and the milieu of quantitative aesthetics. Any work of art which seriously concerns itself with a representation of the world, as Chaucer's major works do, is necessarily shaped by the creation it represents. The world of the Gothic builders was also Chaucer's world. Chaucer did not have to contend with gravity, and he did not choose to adhere to mathematical imperatives, but his poems display everywhere the signs of overt structuring, in the sharply articulated manner of the Gothic. Muscatine and Robertson have made important efforts to relate Chaucer's poetry to the ideals and techniques of the Gothic. While Robertson's *A Preface* develops at length the possibilities of literary iconography, my own effort follows the rather sketchy but provocative lead of Muscatine, who has emphasized structural characteristics, particularly the principle of juxtaposition.[2] The present chapter stresses the essentials of Gothic theory and foregoes the attempt to take account of the infinite variety of individual Gothic structures. My interpretation of Gothic theory rests upon the careful investigations of such art historians as Erwin Panofsky and Otto von Simson,[3] whose findings are on the one hand consonant with the principles of medieval aesthetics as we traced

[1] Curtius, *European Literature*, p. 509.

[2] Muscatine, *Chaucer and the French Tradition,* pp. 167-169, 245-247.

[3] Erwin Panofsky, *Gothic Architecture and Scholasticism* (Latrobe, Pa.: Archabbey Press, 1951) ; Otto von Simson, *The Gothic Cathedral,* 2nd ed. (New York: Pantheon Books, Inc., 1962). A salutary reminder of the limits of a mathematically and symbolically neat theory of the Gothic is James S. Ackerman, " 'Ars sine scientia nihil est' ; Gothic Theory of Architecture at the Cathedral of Milan," *The Art Bulletin,* 31: 84-109 (1949), which stresses the "imperfection" of Gothic theory and shows how technical considerations (*ars*) often modify the theory (*scientia*) of the whole. Other valuable studies of the Gothic are two works by Paul Frankl, *Gothic Architecture* (Baltimore, Md., 1962) and *The Gothic* (Princeton, N.J., 1960). See also Nikolaus Pevsner, *An Outline of European Architecture* (London, 1948), pp. 31-76.

46

them in the preceding chapter and on the other analogous to literary practice as we shall observe it in succeeding chapters. In stressing the fact that the Gothic represents a human adaptation of divine principles of order, I intend to highlight principles and techniques which Chaucer naturally adopted — probably without forethought, and certainly in less exacting and less thoroughgoing fashion than was demanded of the Gothic builders — in the two works which demanded the full-bodied and sustained evocation of a world, *Troilus and Criseyde* and the *Canterbury Tales*.

For the Middle Ages the church was a sacred symbol, in two important senses. As an icon the church in many ways could direct the faithful from the material bonds of this life to the contemplation of divine Truth: *ecclesia materialis significat ecclesiam spiritualem.* But in the Gothic period the church developed another, more integral kind of symbolic relationship with the Celestial City. The physical construction of the cathedral was designed in accordance with the laws that governed the cosmic harmony of creation. The Gothic cathedral, in other words, was conceived and constructed as a visible embodiment of divine order. Thus, in addition to being an icon in the traditional symbolic sense, it also became an analogue of creation itself, a concrete microcosm of the abstract, musico-mathematical perfection of the universe.

It is the iconographic concept of the church which underlies Abbot Suger's ecstatic response to the opulence of his abbey church of St.-Denis: "Thus, when — out of my delight in the beauty of the house of God — the loveliness of the many-colored gems has called me away from external cares, and worthy meditation has induced me to reflect, transferring that which is material to that which is immaterial, on the diversity of the sacred virtues: then it seems to me I see myself dwelling, as it were, in some strange region of the universe which neither exists entirely in the slime of the earth nor entirely in the purity of Heaven; and that, by the grace of God, I can be transported from this inferior to that higher world in an anagogical manner."[4]

This sense of the church as the visible and tangible representation of God on earth is based on the authority of the Scriptures. The Christian imagination, as von Simson points out, had always regarded the Temple of Solomon, as well as the Temple of Ezekiel, as an archetype of the Christian sanctuary.[5] ("Thou hast commanded me to build a temple upon thy holy mount . . . a resemblance of the holy tabernacle, which thou hast prepared from the beginning." Wisdom of Solomon 9:8.) But the primary source of the iconographic interpretation of the church was the Revelation of St. John: "And I John saw the holy city, new Jerusalem, coming down from God out of heaven, prepared as a bride adorned for her husband. And I heard a great voice out of heaven saying, Behold the tabernacle of God is with men, and He will dwell with them, and they shall be His people, and God himself shall be with them, and be their God."

Some of the iconographic features of the church building are quite recondite, and were so even for medieval communicants. The cruciform ground plan, for example, was not readily perceptible to be symbolic of Christ crucified, the Ascension, the Resurrection, and ultimately Salvation. But the symbolic efficacy of other features was more immediate. The west façade, for example, containing the central portal, was understood to form the threshold leading from this world to eternity. As in St.-Denis, the representation of the Last Judgment on the tympanum above the central portal often added vivid support to this idea. And further, as von Simson points out, around the jambs of the door of St.-Denis is represented the parable of the wise and foolish virgins, the former already admitted to the

---

[4] *Abbot Suger on the Abbey Church of St.-Denis and Its Art Treasures,* ed. and trans. Erwin Panofsky (Princeton, N.J.: Princeton University Press, 1946), pp. 63-65.

[5] See *Gothic Cathedral,* pp. 11, 37-38.

THE GOTHIC CATHEDRAL

Celestial City, the latter in despair at finding the gate locked.[6] As if the meaning were not clear, Suger, in his scrupulous zeal, inscribed on the golden door of St.-Denis verses cautioning the admiring observer that the splendor of these doors should not be misunderstood, "but, being nobly bright, the work should brighten the minds, so that they may travel . . . to the True Light where Christ is the true door."[7]

In contrast to the iconographic symbolism of the church, which *represents* or *illustrates* the Celestial City, the structural symbolism of the Gothic cathedral *reproduces,* in analogical fashion, the harmonious order of Creation. As a microcosm the cathedral is linked to the macrocosm by the laws of proportion, which are understood to be common to both. The Gothic style incorporates into the physical structure of the cathedral the abstract principles of the aesthetics of musical proportion, and it does so in so thoroughgoing a fashion that virtually every element of a very complex structure can be seen to play an integral part in the total harmony. As is true of the iconographic symbolism of the church, the structural symbolism is not entirely new with the Gothic; for example the Scriptural description of the Temple of Solomon (I Kings 6) reflects an awareness of the principles of proportion and musical consonance, the given dimensions being 60, 30, and 20 cubits. What differentiates the Gothic cathedral from the Temple of Solomon and from early forms of Christian church architecture is the extent to which it fulfills the possibilities of musico-mathematical aesthetics. We have observed how important number and the idea of proportionality was in patristic thought, but in the Gothic period the seminal verse from Wisdom — "Thou hast ordered all things in number and measure and weight" — emerged from abstract, eulogistic dogma into practical architectural realization. Von Simson has gathered evidence to

---

[6] *Gothic Cathedral,* pp. 113-115. See also Hans Jantzen, *High Gothic,* trans. James Palmes (London, 1962), pp. 179-180.
[7] *Abbot Suger,* pp. 47-49.

show how deeply aware Gothic architects and builders were of the Pythagorean implications of this passage.[8] It was invoked in the late Middle Ages not only as a guide for architects. Thomas Aquinas, for example, referring to St. Augustine, discerns the threefold evidence of the Trinity in every created thing, which evidence he finds to be a reduction of "the three characteristics mentioned in the Book of Wisdom, namely number, weight, and measure."[9]

The Abbot Suger is one of the most articulate apologists for the musical, and hence divine, character of the Gothic. As von Simson aptly expresses it, Suger's writings indicate clearly that he wished to be understood as an architect who *built* theology.[10] That is, Suger saw the church not only as an icon of the Heavenly Jerusalem but also as an embodiment of the laws of divine harmony. Von Simson demonstrates that Suger was fully aware of the musical link which bound his sanctuary to the Celestial City in a close analogical relationship. In doing so, von Simson offers further testimony to what de Bruyne and others have shown to be the homogeneous character of medieval aesthetic doctrine. As might be expected of Suger, who considered Denis his patron saint, the opening of his book *On the Consecration of the Church of St.-Denis* is particularly indebted to the Christianized Neoplatonic cosmology of the Areopagite, as conveyed to the immediate milieu of Suger through Scotus Erigena's translation of and commentary on the Dionysian Corpus. The Dionysian *Celestial Hierarchy* echoes through the pages of Suger's *Consecration,* whose opening sentences are a tribute to that "one unique and supreme reason" which bridges the disparity between things human and things divine and binds all together "by the single, delightful concordance of one superior, well-tempered harmony."[11]

---

[8] *Gothic Cathedral,* pp. 22, 25, 28, 32, 36n, 39, 156, 188.

[9] *Summa theologica,* I, Q. 45, art. 7.

[10] *Gothic Cathedral,* p. 133.

[11] *Abbot Suger,* p. 83. For a modern commentary on the Dionysian Corpus see

THE GOTHIC CATHEDRAL

The doctrine of celestial harmony was an integral part of the philosophical and theological atmosphere of twelfth-century France, considerable impetus being provided by the influential Platonists of Chartres. In addition to the Neoplatonism of Scotus Erigena, the most notable Chartrian contribution to Platonic cosmology was the commentary on the *Timaeus* by William of Conches. Alan of Lille, toward the end of the twelfth century, disseminated the thought of Chartres in works which were still to be widely read for three centuries. In the *De planctu naturae* Alan describes the "invisible chains" of musical consonance which harmonize the universe (*ad unitatem pluralitas, ad identitatem diversitas, ad consonantiam dissonantia, ad concordiam discordia*) and maintain the unity of all creation.[12] Alan also describes the Creator as the skillful architect of the cosmos (*mundi elegans architectus*).

The Gothic architects and builders were able to translate this grand theoretical vision into the actuality of the cathedral. "The first Gothic, in the aesthetic, technical, and symbolic aspects of its design, is intimately connected with the metaphysics of 'measure and number and weight.' It seeks to embody the vision that the Platonists of Chartres had first unfolded, no longer content with the mere image of truth but insisting upon the realization of its laws."[13] The bridge between concept and physical actuality was geometry, which Pythagoreanism had defined as the science which made visible the invisible laws of cosmic harmony. Geometry enabled the Gothic builders to construct in stone an analogue of the cosmos.

We have glanced at some of the most important figures in the transmission of antique number science to the Middle Ages. Boethius, for example, though concerned more with the mathematics than the aesthetics of number, nevertheless freely employs geometri-

Joseph A. Mazzeo, *Medieval Cultural Tradition in Dante's "Comedy"* (Ithaca, N.Y., 1960), pp. 13-30.

[12] *PL,* vol. 210, col. 453. See *Gothic Cathedral,* pp. 31-33.

[13] *Gothic Cathedral,* p. 39.

cal figures, in both *De musica* and *De arithmetica,* to give visible body to principles of proportionality. The more mystical Macrobius, as we have seen, stresses the primacy of number before all perceptible reality. In the later Middle Ages the geometry of proportions takes on practical meaning in the design and construction of important buildings and thereby becomes the language of structure, articulating the assumption that structure is a quantitative idea, that a whole consists of numberable and measurable parts disposed according to fixed mathematical principles of order. The application of mathematical theory is illustrated in a ground plan for a cathedral contained in the sketchbook of Villard de Honnecourt (Fig. 1).[14]

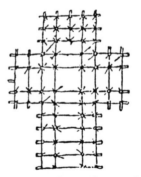

Fig. 1.   Ground plan for a cathedral

Such a plan embodies in visible form all of the attributes of Pythagorean number theory. The basic unit in this case, corresponding to *one* in Pythagorean arithmetic, is the square. The whole consists of multiples of the unit, built up according to a specific, unvarying pattern. In this instance the basic ratio is 3:2. Thus the whole ground area, before reduction at the corners to form the cross, is three square units in length and two in width. The area is subdivided into smaller squares, which constitute the basic module. In terms of

14 Cited by Edgar de Bruyne, *Etudes d'esthétique médiévale,* I, 22-23; III, 257.

the module, the ratio of length to width is then expressible as 12:8. The parts of the church are then apportioned as follows: The total length of twelve modules is divided into the nave (five modules), the crossing (four modules), the choir (three modules). The total width of the aisle is four modules, giving ratios of 5:4 (nave), 4:4 (crossing), and 3:4 (choir). The total breadth of the transept is eight modules, which is divided into two for each arm and four for the crossing. The width of the transept is four modules, giving ratios of 8:4 (total transept), 2:4 (each arm), and 4:4 (crossing). As de Bruyne points out, all of the ratios of music are found here: the octave (4:2) in each arm of the transept; the unity (4:4) in the crossing (the central, unifying area of the church); the fifth (12:8) in the ratio of the total dimensions (aisle to transept); the fourth (4:3) in the choir. These are, of course, the proportions contained in the Pythagorean perfect harmony, 6:8 = 9:12.

Villard's ground plan accords in every respect with the thoroughgoing rationalism of Pythagorean theory. Like the World-Soul of the *Timaeus,* the whole is divided and subdivided into units and subunits, all of which are analogous to one another; that is, they are of the same pattern but different magnitudes. There are no "unexplainable" parts; every unit is directly accountable as an element of the whole. Construction is an additive process which consists in the patterned disposition of finite elements, namely the basic module, repetitions of it, and multiples of it.

Not only the ground plan but also the elevation of the cathedral was achieved according to the simple ratios of proportion. The skilled architect was able to develop all of the magnitudes of his structure by means of linear proportions, using a single polygon, usually the square, as his module. All of the measurements of every part of the well-made cathedral — from the base of a single interior pier to the side of a pinnacle — are related proportionally to a single basic dimension.[15] Knowledge of this method of working

[15] See *Gothic Cathedral,* pp. 13-20.

out architectural proportions from a single given dimension was so highly valued that it remained the secret of the professional lodges until the fifteenth century.

The geometry of the Gothic is not a gratuitous indulgence in number-play. Gothic architecture developed as a balanced interplay of functional and visible elements. The physical supports are all exposed, and it is these visible sinews of the edifice that form the richly harmonized pattern of geometrical configurations which is the Gothic interior. The total pattern consists of varied repetition, in varied proportions, of a basic geometrical figure. The individual wall section, for example, is outlined by piers which begin at the floor and soar upward to come together at the ceiling to form the arched vault of the bay. Within this configuration the wall section of the "classic" Gothic cathedral, such as Chartres and St.-Denis, divides into three subsections, the arcade, triforium, and clerestory, which repeat on a smaller scale the arched configuration of the whole. At Chartres, for example (Fig. 2), above the single large arch of the arcade, the triforium is formed by a span of four smaller arches, and above it the clerestory consists of two arches, topped by a circular window at the point where the outlining piers join at the apex. The widths of the arches on the three levels of elevation are "proportional"; that is, each of the arches of the clerestory is one-half the width of the arcade (which equals the total width of the bay), and each of the arches of the triforium is one-half the width of each clerestory arch and one-fourth the width of the arcade. The heights of the elements of wall elevation are also proportional, to one another and to the total height of the church, and actual measurement has yielded the ratios of the perfect proportion.[16]

This rough indication of the proportional relationships which exist among the elements of a single wall section is perhaps sufficient

---

[16] *Gothic Cathedral,* p. 209.

THE GOTHIC CATHEDRAL

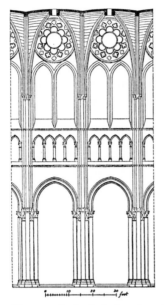

Fig. 2.   Chartres Cathedral, interior elevation

to suggest something of the geometric harmony of Gothic. This complex harmony is multiplied seemingly without end throughout the structure of the cathedral. And the interior configurations are reflected in the exterior. The cathedral is a vast system of divisions, subdivisions, and multiplications — a mighty maze, but clearly not without a plan. A definitive feature of the Gothic is that the plan is distinctly visible in the completed structure; in fact it is deliberately accentuated. Piers, shafts, ribs, and buttresses are fully exposed, and lines of stress can be visibly followed out. Inspection reveals that each line is not only significant but doubly so. Aesthetically it plays an independent, necessary part in a harmonic pattern. Architecturally, it plays a practical role in contributing necessary support to the total structure. The full exposure of the joints and seams renders the processes of construction fully visible. We shall find this im-

55

portant feature of the Gothic — explicit articulation of the elements of construction — to be equally important in the structure of Chaucerian narrative.

While earlier modes of church architecture shared with the Gothic the impulse to symbolize the Heavenly City, the Gothic alone embodied the very laws of the universe in its own structure. The Gothic builders undertook to perform an awesome task, one which broached upon the prerogatives of God. If Alan of Lille could praise God as the *mundi elegans architectus,* it is no wonder that Suger should feel a Godlike exhilaration as he plans and oversees construction of the Heavenly Jerusalem in Paris. The uniqueness of the Gothic, then, is not exclusively iconographic; it is also structural. Through its multiform concrete, physical attributes, the cathedral symbolizes the abstract truths of sacred doctrine. But by incorporating iconographic elements within a system of order which is itself cosmic, the cathedral moves beyond representational symbolism to sacred reality. Thus could Suger, after passing through the Celestial Portal of St.-Denis, undergo a transfiguration as he experienced the "delightful concordance of [that] one superior, well-tempered harmony" that gathered up the human into the divine. The God-given means which enabled men to reproduce the cosmic harmony in earthly materials was, as Suger affirmed, "unique and supreme reason."[17] Medieval architects praised reason not only because it enabled them to build a building that would stand up, but because it enabled them to approach holiness.

The rational basis of Gothic architecture — like that of Pythagorean mathematics and Platonic cosmology — imparted to the structural system certain distinctive aesthetic characteristics. First of all, proceeding from the absolute presupposition that the perfection of Creation is mathematical, the Gothic architect deliberately set about to imitate the exemplar; that is, he worked deductively,

[17] *Abbot Suger,* p. 83.

THE GOTHIC CATHEDRAL

beginning with the fixed pattern of the Heavenly City in mind. The next stage, still theoretical, was to divide that harmonious whole into parts, according to just proportion. Actual construction, reversing the analytical procedure, was an additive process, in which parts would be built up until a predetermined, outlined whole was completed, which in turn would be added to equal and similarly achieved wholes to form a larger, proportionally predetermined magnitude.

The method of the Gothic architects and builders is closely analogous to that of the Creator as described in the *Timaeus*. Both depend on the rationalistic, Pythagorean assumption that structure begins with the preconception of a whole. Then it is possible to divide all matter into parts and parts of parts according to preconceived principles of proportion and harmony. The rationalistic approach to construction is based upon unquestioning confidence in first principles. It adheres to patterns and to modes of procedure which are external to the individual maker, which are "natural," divine; moreover, and happily for man, they are perceptible to reason and explicitly formulable. Therefore the well-ordered structure — man-made Gothic or divine cosmos — can convey a deep sense of assurance, an awesome calm. Because the maker is so certain of what he is doing and certain that what he is doing is right, the structure will tend to emphasize its pattern of organization to a greater extent than will an internally motivated work, one which is more subjective in impulse and does not adhere to a fixed, "structured" set of first principles. Hence in Gothic the deliberate, proud exposure of structural outlines. The effect of weight and massiveness which the fortress-like walls imparted to the earlier Romanesque structure gave way in Gothic to lightness and transparency. In the transition to Gothic the Romanesque wall seemingly dissolved into bare structural supports, outlines of stress and thrust. And it was these exposed seams and joints which were deliberately capitalized. In them the processes of construction became explicitly clear. Because they were

intricately rational as well as fully visible to reason, structural outlines assumed unusual moral and aesthetic significance.

The unabashed nakedness of Gothic represents a general interest in the way things were put together, an interest which seems
to have attributed more importance to the *how* than to the *what*
of creation. Technique and process were at the very center of the
aesthetic sensibility of the Middle Ages. Erwin Panofsky emphasizes
this quality of "visual logic" which is so prominent in the Gothic
edifice: "Ultimately, the flying buttress learned to talk, the rib
learned to work, and both learned to proclaim what they were doing
in language more circumstantial, explicit, and ornate than was
necessary for mere efficiency." Panofsky goes on to compare Gothic
architecture and Scholasticism in this respect: "A man imbued with
the Scholastic habit would look upon the mode of architectural
presentation, just as he looked upon the mode of literary presentation, from the point of view of *manifestatio* . . . But he would not
have been satisfied had not the membrification of the edifice permitted him to re-experience the very processes of architectural composition just as the membrification of the *Summa* permitted him to
re-experience the very processes of cogitation. To him, the
panoply of shafts, ribs, buttresses, tracery, pinnacles, and crockets
was a self-analysis and self-explication of architecture much as the
customary apparatus of parts, distinctions, questions, and articles
was, to him, a self-analysis and self-explication of reason."[18] This
concern for technique and process is conveyed in the tradition of
Pythagorean-Platonic cosmology. Gothic architecture provides a culminating, concrete realization of these persisting proclivities toward
clarifying the nature of things in terms of the structural relationships
of independent, constituent parts. As Plato justified the shape of excellence by analogical reference to an assumed perfection — the
roundness of man's head, for example, being analogous to the shape

18 *Gothic Architecture,* pp. 58-59.

of the universe — and as musical consonances were regarded as analogues of the mathematical harmony of heaven — so was the Gothic cathedral regarded as an analogue of Creation, the shape of the whole and of the parts being articulated in accordance with the presupposed shape of the Heavenly Exemplar.

Like most major undertakings of medieval man, Gothic architecture was a testament in praise of Creation. We have seen how the Gothic, enacting the truism that imitation is the highest form of praise, embodied the laws of Creation in its own structure. The physical materials of the cathedral made possible a more richly textured and more highly articulated mode of cosmic imitation than was possible in any other medium, though music, because of its similarly close affiliation with mathematics, also achieved considerable structural complexity. Sacred music, particularly motets, developed very subtle techniques of proportional imitation in rhythmic structure and contrapuntal imitation in melodic structure, and always favored the perfect ratios, namely the consonant intervals of octave and fifth, at important cadential points.[19]

The structure of verbal expression, because it is so impalpable, is more difficult to define than the structure of architecture, but a sense of the structural principles of the Gothic can guide us toward an adequate definition. When modern critics speak of literary structure they generally do not mean anything so concrete, palpable, and physically measurable as the ground plan of a Gothic cathedral or the lengths of phrases in a contrapuntal motet. We have seen how mercurial is the concept of structure in modern theory, as represented by such critics as Blackmur and Schorer, and how closely the term resembles form, style, technique, vision, and similar counters, all of which tend to stand for the total unity of a literary work. The organicist presuppositions of modern criticism preclude the possi-

---

[19] On the isorhythmic motet of the thirteenth and fourteenth centuries see *Early Medieval Music* (New Oxford History of Music, vol. 2, ed. Dom Anselm Hughes (London, 1954), pp. 390-395.

bility that "structure" can have a meaning independent of "content" or "texture" or any and all other qualities of the unified literary organism. But the Middle Ages held no such presuppositions. If my exposition of the rationalistic and quantitative bases of medieval aesthetics has served its purpose, it should be possible now to see how literary structure could participate in the universal vision of rational order that governed other modes of expression.

The burden of the preceding chapters has been to lift the onus from "structure" and reveal structure to be a definable and essential element of order, both in the divine exemplar and in man-made images. Awareness of the meaning and significance of structure in medieval thought in general can make Chaucer's poetry more fully accessible. For the medieval artist structure did not limit, it liberated. In the Gothic period writers discovered new resources and a new flexibility comparable to the technical advances of the masons and engineers who built the great cathedrals. And though the Italians were the preeminent literary craftsmen — the proportion and symmetry of the *Commedia* being the supreme example — the French and English also followed the inorganic mode, if less rigorously. The medieval writer looked upward and outward to find the fixed bases of life, the fixed principles which gave meaning and moral value to existence. The modern writer, in contrast, is much less certain that the sources of truth lie outside himself.

On the basis of what we know of Chaucer's intellectual and aesthetic milieu we may assume that he regarded his materials — his characters and his plots as well as his moral sentences — as relatively fixed quantities, which were to be disposed according to recognized canons of structural propriety. It remains now to test this assumption, to examine Chaucer's art from a Gothic point of view and attempt to discover how the poet's sense of inorganic structure could enable him to resolve the serenity of Truth and the tumult of its images.

60

FOUR TROILUS AND CRISEYDE: CHAUCERIAN GOTHIC

That there should exist a meaningful analogical connection between architecture and literature plainly does not go without saying. Our mistrust of analogy, as reflected in T. S. Eliot's assertions that analogy is "lazy evasion of thought," and that ". . . nothing in this world or the next is a substitute for anything else . . ."[1] militates against superficial comparison and easy generalization. And rightly so. But it is important to distinguish between modern and medieval analogy. The latter accorded with established belief that every created thing is unique but at the same time is like every other created thing because all things participate in the divine *ordo.* Thus

---

[1] See René Wellek and Austin Warren, *Theory of Literature,* 3rd ed. (New York: Harcourt, Brace and Company, 1962), p. 31; Bonamy Dobrée, *English Literature in the Early Eighteenth Century* (Oxford: Clarendon Press, 1959), p. 122.

for the Middle Ages analogical relations were inherent in all things. Our own reluctance to generalize and synthesize — our tendency to feel safer if we regard every literary work as unique, and literature as fundamentally distinct from other arts — is consistent enough with the metaphysical assumptions of our time. In a relativistic age, where there is no universal frame and standards are obscure, every case seems to define its own terms, and analogies are *ad hoc* inventions of men rather than eternal attributes of the order of Creation.

For the Middle Ages analogies were not invented but discovered. Etienne Gilson, referring to St. Bonaventure's scrupulously precise and seemingly infinite concatenation of similitudes, points out that these are not simply verbal classifications but "the very structure of the universe we inhabit . . . analogy is the law according to which creation is fixed."[2] Aquinas employs the law of universal analogy to sustain the principle that every created thing is unique and also related to every other created thing by a common participation in the fundamental trinity of qualities: ". . . a trace of the Trinity is found in every created thing, according as it is one individual, and according as it is formed by a species, and according as it has a certain relation of order."[3] Aquinas goes on to relate these three qualities to the Scriptural basis of all order, the "measure, number, and weight" according to which God disposed all things.[4] The Scholastic *Summa* is essentially an exhaustively deduced support for medieval man's feeling that all things have their source in God. As medieval theology subsumed the work of science in studying the numerical and musical principles underlying God's disposition of the universe, medieval architecture and fine art pursued the application of analogies, equations, and similitudes to the end of reproducing or extending the divine *ordo* in the works of men.

[2] Etienne Gilson, *La Philosophie de saint Bonaventure* (Paris: J. Vrin, 1924), p. 169.

[3] *Summa theologica,* I, Q. 45, art. 7.

[4] Wisdom of Solomon 11:21. The importance of this Scriptural formulation to the Gothic builders is discussed above, pp. 48-50.

TROILUS AND CRISEYDE

There is no reason to regard literary art as uniquely exempt from the universal order. Though we tend to divide medieval literature into religious and secular — and to disallow the latter from relevance to man's supraterrestrial destiny — the distinction is in fact obscure. The literary career of Dante is too distinguished to be typical, but it illustrates the possibility for all men of an easy congress between the secular and the sacred. More germane to the strictly literary point is the evidence of Dante's commentary on his love odes in the *Convivio.* Line by line, even word by word, he moves, by a reasoned sequence of analogies, from the "secular" text to contemplation of the branches of learning, then to the angelic hierarchies, and, finally, to the order of the heavens.

Chaucer is less learned than Dante, and he wears his learning more lightly. Also, Chaucer is able to regard the social and natural world for prolonged periods without experiencing the awesome truth of its limitations. But if Chaucer did not produce, even in his major works, a cosmic edifice permeating middle earth and reaching to the extremities of Creation, he was nevertheless very much aware of the hierarchy and of man's place in it. The poem "Truth" is a brief, explicit, and fervent statement of the truth which Chaucer in his unsystematic, un-Dantesque way incorporated into his major poems. If *Troilus* and *The Canterbury Tales* are secular poems, they are also sustained examinations of the human condition by a sensitive poet and an orthodox Christian, and therefore they are concerned with the totality of truth. Chaucer expressed his vision of man and God not only through explicit statement but also — and more unequivocally — through technique and structure. In exploring the connections between Chaucer's poems and medieval aesthetics we shall be less concerned with what the poems say than with how they say it, not only because the how is more properly an aesthetic concern but also because it has been much less fully explored.

In this effort the discovery of analogies with Gothic architecture can prove illuminating, because while the uniquely literary qualities of *Troilus* have long been recognized and appreciated — the richness of its plot and characterization, the nobility of its themes, its wit and its humanity — the more abstract principles of aesthetic order have remained obscure. Consideration of structure as such has been discouraged by the prevailing modern bias we discussed earlier, namely, the organicist assumption that the best structure is the least structure. An understanding of medieval canons of form, as outlined in the preceding chapters, should lead us to anticipate a fundamentally different situation, one in which structure is not only separable from content but in its own way expressive of positive values.

Vertical Structure

The signs of structure in *Troilus* are not disguised. They stand out prominently as those elements of the narrative which the novel-oriented critic is most likely to regard as awkward appendages that interfere with the story. These are the numerous and often lengthy and flamboyant comments, explanations, and exclamations of various sorts which continually accompany the narration of the love story. This commentary is sufficiently substantial to constitute an extrinsic framework for the story of Troilus and at the same time to provide a kind of running indication of the parts and divisions of the poem. Until recently critics paid relatively little attention to these obtrusions and therefore tended to read the poem as a "modern novel," that is, as an organically unified fiction which maintained a consistently intimate rapport between the reader and the fictional characters. In such a view it was necessary to lament, if not to ignore, the digressions of the narrative. The extreme of such an interpretation, as urged by Curry and Tatlock, reached the conclusion that the most extensive and troublesome of these obtrusions, the so-called epilogue, is a grandiose irrelevancy.[5] For them this diffuse mixture of sententiousness, clownishness, and piety violates not only the spirit but the very subject of the love story, and, because it follows the story, they conclude that it must have been "tacked on" and so may be safely disregarded. Other commentators, such as Patch and Shanley, have defended the ending and offered Christian interpretations of the poem.[6]

The sustained controversy over the ending is a concentrated and aggravated symptom of the problem presented by the poem as a whole. The last fifteen stanzas are fraught with comments extrinsic to what might be called the story proper. These remarks range over a wide area, including both inane and pious moral comments on the meaning of the story, a farewell to the completed work, a dedication to certain contemporaries of the poet, a joke about women in love. The effect is complicated, but its predominant result is to enlarge the distance between the reader and the poem and to emphasize the delimited, constructed quality of the work. These stanzas are not detached, however; they are part of the prosodic texture of the poem. Moreover, in the total context of the poem they are not unique, either in substance or in effect. They are part of the framework of digressive commentary which is superimposed upon the narrated action. For these reasons and others, most recent commentators have discarded the "tacked-on" theory of the ending, and E. T. Donaldson's expressed dislike of the term "epilogue"[7] reflects widespread critical opinion that the ending is an essential part of the poem. Even within this area of agreement readers are bound to have varying ideas about the meaning of this complicated

[5] See especially J. S. P. Tatlock, "The Epilog of Chaucer's *Troilus*," *MP*, 18: 625-659 (1920-21); W. C. Curry, "Destiny in Chaucer's *Troilus*," *PMLA*, 45: 129-168 (1930).

[6] Howard R. Patch, *On Rereading Chaucer* (Cambridge, Mass., 1939), pp. 104-122; J. L. Shanley, "The *Troilus* and Christian Love," *ELH*, 6:271-281 (1939).

[7] E. Talbot Donaldson, "The Ending of Chaucer's *Troilus*," in *Early English and Norse Studies*, ed. Arthur Brown and Peter Foote (London, 1963), p. 35.

peroration and its relationship to the poem as a whole. My own concern is to locate the ending in a total structure which in its way consistently accommodates digressiveness and which moves ultimately, in the Gothic fashion, toward direct participation in the total harmony of Creation.

Against the modern aesthetic standards of organicism and expressionism it will sound harsh to speak of Chaucer's poem as a gathering of inert materials deliberately put together according to preconceived plans. But from the very beginning and throughout the poem forthright statements by Chaucer invite precisely such an approach. Initially our interest is captured not by Troilus or Criseyde or any of the fictional (or historical) characters, but by an "extrinsic" speaker explaining to us the difficulties of transmitting an old tale of lovers: "The double sorwe of Troilus to tellen . . . my purpos is, er that I parte fro ye." Though initiating a long preamble to the love story proper, a preamble mainly expository and therefore seemingly dissonant with the kind of narrative we anticipate, the opening lines cannot be rushed over or patronized. They are a part of the total poetic creation, and their prominence places certain demands upon us. We must approach the poem from a point of view which can regard the tangential and the central as equivalent elements in a larger frame of relevance.

Primarily by so prominently displaying a concern for the procedure of narration, but by other means also, the seven opening stanzas establish the structural mode of the poem. The speaker assumes such prominence at all the major junctures in the course of Troilus' adventures, sometimes setting forth a full-scale *exordium,* as at the beginnings of books of the poem, at other times assuming a more informal tone to comment on the events or simply to change the scene, as in the typical locution, "Now lat us stynte of Troilus a stounde." The complex *peroratio* at the end of the poem is, of course, a major instance of the superimposition of the speaker's presence upon the illusion of Troy. The illusion thus assumes independent status, and the poem contains both it and its maker.

Since the speaker so often rends the texture of the fiction, it was not unusual for critics interested in the "modern," psychological, and novelistic aspects of the poem to underestimate his role in the poem in the interest of preserving the consistency and "dramatic" quality of the story. More recently the countertendency has been to emphasize the narrator's role in the poem, so much so, in fact, that B. H. Bronson could say, not entirely without justice, that "nine-tenths of this talk is misguided and palpably mistaken."[8] Part of this dispute over the nature and significance of the narrating "I" is superficial, a simple enough matter of terminology. It is relatively unimportant whether the "I" of the poem is identified as some form of *persona* (such as the speaker, the narrator, the pseudo-Chaucer) or simply as Chaucer mischievously posturing. In an earlier study I apparently overstressed the term and created the impression that the narrator should be regarded as a character as deliberately formed by Chaucer as are Troilus, Criseyde, and Pandarus.[9] I did not mean quite that, and I am happy to profit from Bronson's thoughtful criticism. The narrating "I" *is* Chaucer, Chaucer displaying the great range of his expressive resources. The extent to which I regard the narrator as a "separable fiction" (Bronson's term) is determined by Chaucer's practice: until the very end Chaucer preserves the fiction that the narrating voice he uses in the poem is dissociated from a poetic sensibility, from the kind of sensibility which we know is behind the poem and to which we attach the name Geoffrey Chaucer. I think it is easier for us to use the term "narrator" than continually to say "Chaucer speaking ironically" or "Chaucer pretending to be naïve" or "Chaucer acting as though he were a simple

[8] Bertrand H. Bronson, *In Search of Chaucer* (Toronto: University of Toronto Press, 1960), p. 26.
[9] "The Narrator in Chaucer's *Troilus*," *ELH*, 25:237-257 (1958).

chronicler of actual historical events." That Chaucer was an ironist no reader would deny, and Bronson describes very well the ironic style Chaucer so masterfully practices: ". . . the audience neither takes the speaker at his literal word nor jumps to the conclusion that the discrepancy between what it hears and what it sees and knows signifies that someone else is being talked about. The remarks, indeed, gain their effect by virtue of the fact that all the while a tacit comparison with another image is proceeding. This silent process is the very core of irony. At this ironic game Chaucer was a master, and it is a pervasive and constant element in the social tone of his poetry."[10]

Irony describes the relationship between the Chaucerian "I" and the image behind this surface, and Bronson is right in saying that recognition of this play, this "tacit comparison," is essential to an understanding of Chaucer's art. In presuming to call one of these elements the narrator or Chaucer-the-commentator and the other one Chaucer-the-poet or Chaucer-without-irony, I do not seek "to deprive him and us . . . of the source of our keenest enjoyment." Allowing a distinction between narrator and poet — or between the visible and the invisible "I" — enables us to discuss *Troilus and Criseyde* as a poem rather than as a visible and audible presentation by the man Chaucer. Bronson would prefer to effect an imaginative shift from a reading experience to a listening one. We would then imagine ourselves an audience of Chaucer's contemporaries attending a court recitation by the poet and comparing what we witness — the ironic posture — with what we know of Geoffrey Chaucer, wise, urbane, artful poet. The difficulty of this approach, although it recognizes Chaucer's ironic manner, is that it clutters the imagination with matter which primarily interests the social historian and which does not affect our appreciation of Chaucer's literary artistry. As readers we are more concerned with the enduring poem than

[10] Bronson, *In Search*, p. 30.

with the passing social circumstances which contributed in many ways to making the poem what it is.[11] The poem as we have it contains all the elements we associate with Chaucer's manner, including an "I" whose voice and attitudes are clearly at ironic odds with the sensibility behind the poem.

The primary warrant for approaching the poem in this direct literary way is that the many prominent passages in the first person, though differing stylistically among themselves, in general define an attitude distinctly *unlike* that of a poet consciously engaged in composing a complex, large-scale poem. The unliterary "I" of the narrative continually plays against our sense of what *Troilus and Criseyde* is. This ironic play is part of the poem; it is there for the reading, whether or not we imagine ourselves part of an audience listening to Chaucer read the poem and knowing him to be a wise and witty man and a successful, sophisticated poet. Chaucer's audience need not be limited, even imaginatively, to a certain time and a certain place. Robert Payne has pointed out that Chaucer's audience is as timeless as his poems: ". . . the kinds of roles Chaucer creates for his narrators almost necessarily imply complementary roles for an audience which is nearly as much a created fiction within or around the poem as the narrator is . . . the manner of the narrator's self-deprecatory ironies is such that any reader is

---

[11] On the significance of oral presentation, see Bertrand H. Bronson, "Chaucer's Art in Relation to His Audience," *Five Studies in Literature* (Berkeley, Calif., 1940). On the vestiges of oral tradition in written narrative, see Ruth Crosby, "Chaucer and the Custom of Oral Delivery," *Speculum,* 13:413-432 (1938). Neither of these studies takes sufficient account of the differences between oral and written narrative as the latter was developing, with surprising suddenness, in the late Middle Ages in Western Europe. For a perceptive appraisal of the artistic implications of the transition from the orator of oral tradition to the narrator of written literature, see Robert Scholes and Robert Kellogg, *The Nature of Narrative* (New York: Oxford University Press, 1966): "The sudden acquisition by medieval narrative artists of the new role of authorship found them unprepared and somewhat ill at ease . . . The most natural course was found to be a fairly straightforward imitation of a teller reciting his story to an audience. But even this emergency measure opened the Pandora's box of irony, giving such masters as Chaucer, Wolfram, and (in the Renaissance) Rabelais and Cervantes new fields to conquer" (p. 55).

made to feel specifically included in the audience . . ."[12] It would seem that the insistence that we constantly bear in mind the conditions of oral delivery when we read Chaucer is somewhat off the mark.

It should also be borne in mind that Chaucer's circumstances were quite different from those of the Anglo-Saxon singer of noble songs. Even though printed books were undreamed of in Chaucer's time, he did compose on paper and in solitude. He did not improvise before an audience. As he wrote he no doubt visualized an audience, as all writers have done, both before and after the invention of printing. But that it was a specific audience, or even one limited to his contemporaries, we must certainly doubt, especially in the light of the *envoi* (V, 1793-98). Also, Chaucer knew that he himself would not be the only person to present his poem orally, even in his own lifetime, and of course he also knew that his poem would be read silently as well as listened to, as his *envoi* and his dedication to Gower and Strode make clear.[13] It may be said, I think, that there is ample evidence, both textual and circumstantial, that Chaucer regarded *Troilus* primarily as a poem, a finite work made by him and launched upon the waters of time and literary tradition. Only secondarily, if at all, did he regard it as an opportunity to exercise his talents as a wise and entertaining raconteur. *Troilus* is a finished, sophisticated, and complex work of literary art, and part of its sophistication and complexity is the illusion — which is integral to the poem — that it is a conversational, naïve, simple work of non-art. The poem represents a quantitative approach to literary art — which is not to say that it lacks wit, wisdom, and irony. Efforts to treat the poem as an organic extension of the author's personality run the risk of depending upon assumptions which were antithetical

12 Robert O. Payne, *The Key of Remembrance* (New Haven, Conn., and London: Yale University Press, 1963), p. 228.

13 Passages such as the following indicate that Chaucer had in mind the absent reader as well as the present listener: "Thow, redere, maist thiself ful well devyne . . ." (V, 270).

to Chaucer's art. The Chaucerian narrator is an important means of maintaining those clear distinctions of organization, structural outline, and point of view which characterize nonorganic narrative.

The nonorganic, quantitative mode of the poem is further defined by the presentation of the love story as a finite, preconceived whole. Unlike organicist fiction, whose evolutional quality demands that the reader know no more than the characters and that he learn with them as the narrative progresses, Chaucer's poem places the reader outside the action and indeed summarizes the entire tale for him in the opening stanzas:

> For now wil I gon streght to my matere,
> In which ye may the double sorwes here
> Of Troilus in lovynge of Criseyde,
> And how that she forsook hym er she deyde. (I, 53-56)

The story as a complete entity is not only known by the narrator but foretold to the reader, and hence the principal concern is not what happens but how it happens. From the narrator's point of view the problem is the effective disposition of the elements of a known totality. And since the narrator is the reader's means of contact with the poem, the reader establishes himself, at least initially, in this position external to the impending story.

But despite the elaborate evocation of the circumstances of the presentation, and despite the emphatic imposition of a point of view external to the hero's love-adventures, every reader of the poem knows how readily he loses himself in the story. It is impossible to measure exactly the extent of our immersion in the Trojan scene, but a rough negative guide is the extent to which we are aware of the voice and presence of the extrinsic narrator. The more conscious we are of the narrator, the less are we immersed in the affairs of the story-characters. Morton W. Bloomfield's tabulation of actually "felt" appearances of the narrator indicates that about 12 percent of Book One centers on him; the percentage is somewhat lower in

Books Two and Four and somewhat higher in Book Three.[14] Following the first sixty-three lines, in which the narrator absorbs all of
our attention, he appears at irregular, unpredictable intervals, but,
as the simple figures indicate, and as the reading experience con-
firms, he plays a major part in shaping our responses to the poem.

The episode in which Troilus falls in love offers a ready
illustration of the poem's "compound" quality, its ability to maintain two separate and dissonant levels of interest in a kind of running counterpoint with one another. The characteristic formula
"And so bifel" (I, 155) signals the beginning (or the resumption)
of the story proper. And almost immediately Chaucer has removed
us from the perspective of historical summary (where the narrator
had been instructing us to read the authorities if we want to learn
more about the Trojan War) and immersed us in Troy's festive,
highly social observances for Pallas Athena. Among the celebrants
in the temple stands Criseyde, somewhat apart in her widow's black.
On this scene enters Troilus, distinguished by the bold confidence
of his demeanor. His mind and his eyes are on the ladies and his
purposes are predatory, not amatory. Our interest is centered not
only on Troilus but in him, and as his thoughts are articulated our
absorption in the scene is complete — the narrator and his pre-
occupations are far outside our awareness:

> "I have herd told, pardieux, of youre lyvynge . . .
> Ther nys nat oon kan war by other be."
> And with that word he gan caste up the browe,
> Ascaunces, "Loo! is this naught wisely spoken?" (I, 197, 203-05)

The answer comes, of course, not from Troilus' admiring followers
but from the God of Love, goaded and intimidated beyond endur-

---

[14] Morton W. Bloomfield, "Distance and Predestination in *Troilus and Criseyde*,"
PMLA, 72:15, n. 2 (1957). Also see below, n. 20, for specific attributions of passages
to the narrator in Book III. Henry Lüdeke's attributions, based upon a more rigid
definition of functional first-person forms, are more conservative: "Die Funktionen des
Erzählers in Chaucers epischer Dichtung," *Studien zur englischen Philologie*, 72:
12-13 (1928).

ance. The abruptness of Cupid's reaction — "sodeynly he hitte hym atte fulle" — is matched by the abruptness of the narrator's return. He is unable to restrain himself, and from the outer fringes of our consciousness his cry of anguish suddenly descends fully upon us:

> O blynde world, O blynde entencioun!
> How often falleth al the effect contraire
> Of surquidrie and foul presumpcioun;
> For kaught is proud, and kaught is debonaire.
> This Troilus is clomben on the staire,
> And litel weneth that he moot descenden;
> But alday faileth thing that fooles wenden. (I, 211-17)

Now for fifty-six lines the poem focuses our attention upon the narrator — his reactions, his wise advice, his concern about keeping to the point of his story. Although the narrator is not always an agent of comedy, it should be noted that the mock-epic effects of this stanza depend for their effectiveness upon our awareness of the narrator as an embodied presence assuming an epic stance. And seeing him is to see beyond him, for we perceive that the elevated choric tonality is far more calamitous than the circumstances warrant. The event is not Troy falling in flames and carnage, but gay and lusty young Prince Troilus falling in love. Nor can it be argued that the speaker is activated by prophetic knowledge of the doom that awaits Troilus when Criseyde will betray him. All the narrator has in mind is the present event and the chance it offers him to display his moral wisdom, which he does finally in the banal observation, "And alday faileth thing that fooles wenden." But the irony of the limited narrator produces only part of the humor. The bathetic descent from the epic "O blynde world" to the homely last line of the stanza provides the *coup de grâce*. The true epic singer, in contrast to Chaucer's narrator, is sustained by the significance of his matter and maintains appropriate loftiness of tone and formality of diction, never revealing peasant garb beneath his formal robes. The present stanza, however, is an unassimilated mixture of the lofty and the common. In the light of the final line, with its country wisdom couched in country accents, the opening four lines, with their epic tonality, inverted diction, and stately rhythms, seem clearly to be a mere display by the narrator of his mastery of the rhetorical arts. The techniques of the rhetorician he has, but the sensibilities and the natural art of the poet he lacks, as indicated not only by the initial impropriety and excess of his outburst but by the sudden falling off of his verbal style at the fifth line of the stanza, "This Troilus is clomben on the staire." We might say the same of the speaker himself, who likewise seems unaware "that he moot descenden." At the next line, the end of the stanza, he hits bottom: "But alday faileth thing that fooles wenden."

What ensues in the following seven stanzas is equally entertaining and equally remote from the locus of the love story, but we find the narrator and his foolishness thoroughly engaging. First, concerned lest we miss the point, he spins out an elaborate simile, epic in form and in verbal style but barnyard in content, to describe the power love exerted over Troilus:

> As proude Bayard gynneth for to skippe
> Out of the weye, so pryketh hym his corn,
> Til he a lasshe have of the longe whippe;
> Than thynketh he, "though I praunce al byforn
> First in the trays, ful fat and newe shorn,
> Yet am I but an hors, and horses lawe
> I moot endure, and with my feres drawe";
> So ferde it by this fierse and proude knyght:
> Though he a worthy kynges sone were . . . (I, 218-26)

It would be hard to imagine a more woeful failure of taste or a less fitting context for the appearance of Bayard the horse, "ful fatte and newe shorn." Of English poets, only Pope could match Chaucer at such graceful gaucherie. And of course it is the grace behind the awkwardness that makes the narrator's performance delightful rather than offensive or embarrassing.

In the next several stanzas the narrator protrudes increasingly

74

TROILUS AND CRISEYDE

from his matter as he reaches out to us — "Ye wise, proude, and worthi folkes alle" — and delivers a eulogy on love and a warning that none of us can escape its influence. For this passage the speaker discards his epic manner and assumes an air of knowledgeability combined with deference toward his audience. He is now the jongleur performing before his superiors, digressing from his tale to deliver these patronizing preachments.

Though in a sense this long passage is a digression — beginning with the explosive "O blynde world" and ending fifty-six lines later as the narrator turns himself back to business, "For I it gan, I wol therto refere" — it is misleading to call it such. It is a digression only from the viewpoint of the narrator, whose purpose it is to tell Troilus' story. From our viewpoint and Chaucer's the "digression" is very much a part of the poem. It constitutes, within the poem, a plane of action entirely independent from that of the Trojan scene. However deeply engrossed we become in the "lower" plane of Troilus' experience, we find ourselves, at the caprice of the narrator, shifting our attention completely to the "upper" plane and the very different kind of action going on there. There are many aesthetic ramifications of the fact that the poem contains within its wholeness two such distinct levels of action, not the least of which is the incongruity of the two areas, one predominantly serious, the other predominantly humorous, one the story and therefore demanding our acceptance of illusion, the other reality and therefore intruding upon and breaking the illusion. That this reality is ultimately revealed also to be illusory is a matter to be considered later. All I wish to stress at the moment is the verticality or elevation of perspective which the narrator's actions impart to the poem.

Horizontal Structure

In addition to delineating the two planes of action, the narrator articulates the sequential or horizontal progress of the story. From

75

the beginning of the poem, through the exordial addresses at the beginnings of the books of the poem, to the complex peroration at the end, the narrator is at pains to specify the stages in the movement of the action "fro wo to wele and after out of joie." This kind of explicitness, as we have seen, is characteristic of Gothic structure. Although the characters and episodes of a poem — especially a Chaucerian poem — lack the fixity of stone and glass and therefore cannot be reduced into the mathematical regularity of a Gothic interior, nevertheless *Troilus* exhibits the same impulse to clarify structure by delineating individual parts of the whole. The function of line in the Gothic interior, dividing the whole into parts and parts of parts, is approximated in *Troilus* by the voice of the narrator. To an extent bound to trouble the reader who prizes organic continuousness of texture, *Troilus* moves in an irregular sequence of starts and stops and thus follows in its literary way the architectural advice Chaucer took from the rhetorician Geoffrey of Vinsauf:[15]

> For everi wight that hath an hous to founde
> Ne renneth naught the werk for to bygynne
> With rakel hond, but he wol bide a stounde,
> And sende his hertes line out fro withinne
> Aldirfirst his purpos for to wynne. (I, 1065-69)

Before considering the organization of the narrative as a whole, let us return to the episode in which Troilus first falls in love in order to illustrate the additive mode of construction. The narrator serves here not only to interpose himself and objectify a viewpoint external to the story but at the same time to articulate divisions of the narrative into more or less self-contained sections. It will be recalled that the long disquisition beginning "O blynde world" follows immediately upon the stanza in which Troilus falls, shot

[15] See above, p. 42.

TROILUS AND CRISEYDE

"atte fulle" by the vengeful Cupid. This is a way of saying, quite unmistakably though figuratively, that Troilus has fallen in love with Criseyde. The ensuing remarks of the narrator — underscoring the triumph of Love over "this fierse and proude knyght," lamenting for those who scorn love, advising us to bow to the yoke of love — all arise from the stated and known fact that Troilus has fallen in love. Yet when the narrative resumes, at line 267, it is as though Troilus' fall had not been narrated at all. Following the conclusion of the narrator's comments, the narrative retrogresses in time and presents a second and independent narration of the fall:

> And al his werk, as touching this matere,
> For I it gan, I wol thereto refere.
>
> Withinne the temple he wente hym forth pleyinge,
> This Troilus, of every wight aboute,
> On this lady, and now on that, lokynge,
> Wher so she were of town or of withoute;
> And upon cas bifel that thorugh a route
> His eye percede, and so depe it wente,
> Til on Criseyde it smot, and ther it stente.
>
> And sodeynly he wax therwith astoned,
> And gan hir bet biholde in thrifty wise.
> "O mercy, God," thought he, "wher hastow woned,
> That art so feyr and goodly to devise?"
> Therwith his herte gan to sprede and rise,
> And softe sighed, lest men myghte hym here,
> And caught ayeyn his firste pleyinge chere. (I, 265-80)

This rendition, more direct and detailed than the first and less figurative, nevertheless goes back over the same ground and the same moments in time without betraying any sense of relationship, either syntactical or substantial. "Withinne the temple he wente hym forth pleyinge" (267) does not follow from the point to which the narration had brought us before the narrator's interruption;

77

rather, it begins again at a point corresponding to this from the earlier version:

> This Troilus, as he was wont to gide
> His yonge knyghtes, lad hem up and down
> In thilke large temple . . . (I, 183-85)

What we have are two distinct narrations of the same event, separated by the long commentary from the narrator; one is figurative, the other direct. Nor are they rendered, as William Faulkner might do it, from different points of view. Both are presented from the same objective standpoint, and hence, strictly speaking according to the demands of narrative economy, one of the passages is superfluous. But economy is not Chaucer's aim. This sequence provides a good indication of the essential nature of *Troilus* as a narrative poem. We see here that Chaucer does not simply relate that Troilus fell in love and then pass on to what he did next. Unlike the simpler forms of romance, *Troilus* is a narrative with a subject as well as a verb. Its subject is love, and the dilatory and retrogressive mode of the narration provides a means of modifying the subject, or revealing the fullness of its nature. In the present instance the first statement that Troilus fell in love is brief, but the emotional quality of the event and some of its philosophical implications are conveyed impressively by the figurative form of the expression — the wrathful god cutting down the proud and heedless human. The second statement that Troilus fell in love is concrete, not merely stating, however impressively, that the event occurred, but dramatizing it and showing how it occurred, even to the point of quoting the astonished Troilus' thoughts as the beauty of Criseyde penetrates his consciousness. The sacrifice of sequential narrative allows the poet to amplify his presentation of this crucial moment in the experience of love. The figurative and the concrete, each with its particular kind of effectiveness, parallel one another in a form of varied repetition. Standing between them and acting to delay and

78

dilate the narrative as well as to separate and articulate the two sections is the lengthy performance by the narrator. His commentary, being on an entirely different plane, as we have noted, dramatically expands the range of illumination by making love the subject of explicit discussion as well as of exemplary representation.

If this analysis of a brief passage has served its purpose we should be in a position to see how a quantitative aesthetic defines the structure of the poem as a whole, and also to appreciate the richness and variety which can be attained within such a structure. The narrator's voice, simply by becoming prominent at certain places, divides the narrative of Troilus into more or less discrete parts, and the poet is able to amplify his subject at will by such aggregative means. The will to elaborate is at least as strong as the will to progress, and therefore repetition and dilation become significant positive elements of narrative construction. In addition to articulating this kind of horizontal or lateral organization of the narrative, the narrator's voice, when extended, imposes a tangible external point of view upon the story and thus provides a second dimension to enlarge the poem vertically. It is this tendency to articulate its structure as a composition of individuated elements, and to do so with unabashed explicitness, that defines the poem's quantitative character. Since the narrator is the principal means of clarifying the structure, it follows that his role must loom large in a structural analysis of the poem.

The clearest narrative divisions are the books of the poem. The narrator begins each of these — Book Five being an exception which I shall consider below — with an elaborate and structurally distinct introduction, and ends each with a similarly formal if less elaborate conclusion. Lesser parts of the poem, like that in which Troilus succumbs to love, are similarly enclosed by first-person utterances of the narrator and thus constitute parts within parts, all of which are delineated by the same means. Although the poem does not fulfill this pattern in a rigidly regular way, the governing principle is clearly the Pythagorean and Platonic one that is so widely evident in medieval thought, namely, that the whole serves as a macrocosmic model for its inner parts.[16] The wholeness of the poem, as delineated by particularly elaborate framing statements — the proem to Book One and the peroration that concludes the poem — is reflected in the wholeness of the component parts. The relationship is analogous to that between the wholeness of Plato's cosmic exemplar and the wholeness of its constituent parts.[17] The same relationship is evident in a Gothic wall section, the whole arch being the model for the constituent arches deduced from it. In all cases the structural integrity of the part precludes a continuous, organic relationship among the parts and between parts and whole. The principle of creation is not growth but aggregation.

As the controlling element in the rhetorical organization of the poem, the narrator's voice states the subject at the beginning and clearly articulates the stages of its development in the course of the poem. This careful attention to the thorough and ordered presentation of a stated subject imparts to the love story an expository character. A resemblance to the mode of allegory has been observed by Dorothy Everett, who maintains that in writing the early part of *Troilus,* "Chaucer had at the back of his mind the course of love as it had been allegorically depicted in the *Roman de la Rose.*"[18] I would extend this thought and suggest that not only Troilus' wooing but the entire story depicts the course of love, "Fro wo to wele, and after out of joie." In the case of Guillaume's *Roman* we can readily enough recognize the expository purpose as set forth near the beginning of the poem:

> Ce est li Romanz de la Rose
> Ou l'Art d'Amors est toute enclose.

16 Dante, who — unlike Chaucer — was a theorist as well as a poet, was implying this principle when he pointed out in the Epistle (X) to Can Grande (Sec. 12) that the form of the part is determined by that of the whole work.

17 See above, p. 15.

18 *"Troilus and Criseyde,"* in *Essays on Middle English Literature,* ed. Patricia Kean (New York: Oxford University Press, 1955), p. 125.

TROILUS AND CRISEYDE

The subject is love, and the technique of exposition is to anatomize the subject. Love is seen as a system or art whose essential nature can be displayed in a more or less fixed configuration of figures and situation. It is possible to over-psychologize the *Roman* — as I think C. S. Lewis does in *The Allegory of Love* — and read it as modern psychological fiction. Such an interpretation tends to obscure the quite unsubtle expository nature of the poem. Conversely, it is possible to under-allegorize *Troilus*. Although this poem is obviously less allegorical than the *Roman* — using human figures and being more dramatic and less pictorial — it nevertheless shares with the *Roman* the impulse to anatomize its subject, and in both cases the subject is love. Chaucer's narrator echoes the *Roman* in stating that his purpose is

> . . . to shewe, in som manere,
> Swich peyne and wo as Loves folk endure,
> In Troilus unsely aventure. (I, 33-35)

The narration is undertaken as an effort to imitate in poetic terms a known truth, the nature of love. The rationalistic approach dictates that the elements be deduced from the whole and consequently precludes the inductive technique more characteristic of narrative fiction, particularly of modern novelistic fiction.

At the beginning the story is displayed as a whole, with middle and end:

> The double sorwe of Troilus to tellen,
> That was the kyng Priamus sone of Troye,
> In lovynge, how his aventures fellen
> Fro wo to wele, and after out of joie,
> my purpos is . . . (I, 1-5)

The speaker is more explicit at the close of his exordial address:

> Now herkneth with a good entencioun,
> For now wil I gon streght to my matere,
> In which ye may the double sorwes here
> Of Troilus in lovynge of Criseyde,
> And how that she forsook hym er she deyde. (I, 52-56)

CHAUCER AND THE SHAPE OF CREATION

Thus the story is told as a whole at the outset. The ensuing narrative is a part-by-part dilation of the generalized rendering thus presented in the introduction. At the end of the poem the narrator returns to this level of generalization:

> But for that I to writen first bigan
> Of his love, I have seyd as I kan . . . (V, 1768-69)

These words are part of the extensive peroration which concludes the poem and which together with the equally extensive introduction forms a frame of first-person commentary delineating the boundaries of the love story. The pillarlike quality of these delimiting passages emphasizes the enclosed, finite form of the story.

Within this framework the books of the poem dilate separately the stages in the course of love. Book One amplifies the "wo" of love-longing and develops this phase of Troilus' "aventures" in a series of lyric plaints, dramatic displays of anguish, and sententious commentaries by the narrator on the power of love. Its closing stanza affirms the narrator's control over his material and by the imposition of his point of view recalls the general purpose which governs his narration:

> Now lat us stynte of Troilus a stounde,
> That fareth lik a man that hurt is soore,
> And is somdeel of akyngge of his wownde
> Ylissed wel, but heeled no deel moore . . . (I, 1086-89)

Book Two arrests the movement of the story between "wo" and "wele" and shows "how Troilus com to his lady grace" (II, 32). It opens with a typically elevated introduction, in which the narrator describes a troubled sea, and then comments upon his story:

> This see clepe I the tempestous matere
> Of disespeir that Troilus was inne;
> But now of hope the kalendes bygynne. (II, 5-7)

Book Two deals chiefly with Pandarus' preparations for the union of the lovers and ends in typically perorational style as the narrator appeals to his audience:

> But now to yow, ye loveres that ben here,
> Was Troilus nought in a kankedort . . . (II, 1751-52)

Book Three, in rendering the episode of consummation, achieves a grand dilation of "wele," of "the gladnesse of Troilus, to Venus heryinge." Again the subject is explicitly stated; the action is foretold by the narrator in an introductory statement, and the book is concluded with similar formality: "My thridde book now ende ich in this wyse . . ." Books Four and Five combine to comprise an attenuated display of the hero "out of joie," and complete the treatment of the subject, "aventures" in love.

As a whole the narrative progresses in a spasmodic mode of statement and development; the expository purpose of the poem continually impedes forward movement by stopping to define particular stages and to develop them. Thus we frequently encounter in the body of the poem statements which have the character of beginnings, and often a minor episode is introduced within an exordial statement similar in form to that which prefaces the story as a whole. Individuated parts relate to the whole in a way which Erwin Panofsky has observed to be characteristic of Gothic architecture. He discerns in the High Gothic a structural principle which assures "arrangement according to a system of homologous parts and parts of parts." The exemplary pattern is the arched rib vault, which appears in varying dimensions but fixed form throughout the structure. As Panofsky makes clear, "this principle of progressive divisibility (or . . . multiplicability) increasingly affected the entire edifice down to the smallest detail."[19] Plainly Chaucer's poem does not and could not exhibit structural uniformity to the extent possible in an edifice of stones, but it does seem to partake of the same structural principle, the narrative pattern of enclosed expository unit corre-

---

[19] *Gothic Architecture*, pp. 45-48.

sponding to the architectural pattern of the clearly delimited rib vault.

"Progressive divisibility" as a structural characteristic of *Troilus* is most readily demonstrable in Book Three, both in the distinctness of the structural outlines of the book as a whole and in its internal organization. Since the narrator is the principal instrument of structure, it is not surprising to find that in this most highly articulated book of the poem he plays a particularly prominent part.[20] The subject of Book Three, the weal that follows the woe of love-longing, is stated at the outset in an extensive introduction which is analogous in structure, style, and function to the introduction to Book One. The narrator's voice is intoned in high oratorical style, and for forty-nine lines our attention is in rapport with the speaker and centered on him and his immediate compositional problem. Characteristically he appeals for aid, first to Venus:

> . . . techeth me devyse
> Som joye of that is felt in thi servyse — (III, 41-42)

and then to Caliope:

> . . . sestow nought my destresse,
> How I mot telle anonright the gladnesse
> Of Troilus, to Venus heryinge? (III, 46-48)

Also characteristically, he defines the substantive scope of this section of his presentation, the happiness of achieved love. He does so not only explicitly, as in the lines cited immediately above, but also indirectly in the luxuriant eulogy of Venus. This address, it may be noted in passing, itself exhibits the additive structure characteristic of the poem as a whole. It presents in consecutive narrative order

---

20 About 13 percent of the text of Book III is devoted to the narrator. My attributions of passages to the narrator are as follows: 1-49, 90-1, 218-19, 234, 238, 344-6, 435, 442-52, 470, 483, 491-511, 553, 575-8, 593, 599, 604, 617-21, 701, 1058-64, 1117, 1146-8, 1156, 1161-2, 1191-7, 1199, 1204, 1212-18, 1223-25, 1246, 1310-37, 1369-70, 1373-93, 1400, 1408-10, 1576-83, 1677, 1681-3, 1688-94, 1727, 1774, 1795, 1804, 1807-20.

the several qualities of Venus, moving downward from the cosmic through the superhuman or mythological to the social and human. The first two stanzas, beginning "O blisful light, of which the bemes clere / Adorneth al the thridde heven faire!" pays tribute to the spirit of love that permeates creation and gives life to all things "in hevene and helle, in erthe and salte see." The third and fourth stanzas praise, respectively, Venus' role in activating Jove to love mortals and in moderating the fierceness of Mars. Stanza five, "Ye holden regne and hous in unitee," is a tribute to love's power to harmonize human diversities. Finally the base of the hierarchy of Venus' powers is reached at the end of stanza five, and it is specified more concretely in stanza six:

> Ye folk a lawe han set in universe,
> And this knowe I by hem that lovers be,
> That whoso stryveth with yow hath the werse. (III, 36-38)

Such is the metaphorical elaboration and the structural integrity of the introduction to Book Three.

The conclusion recalls this beginning: it returns the narrator to prominence, presenting him again addressing praise to Venus, and again clarifying the process of narration, now by explicitly closing "my thridde bok." Though shorter than the introduction, the conclusion is clearly of the same order of form and structural function, and in conjunction with the introduction it serves completely to enclose the matter of the lover's "wele":

> Thorugh yow [Venus, Cupid, the muses] have I
>   seyd fully in my song
> Th'effect and joie of Troilus servise,
> Al be that ther was som disese among,
> As to myn auctour listeth to devise.
> My thridde bok now ende ich in this wyse,
> And Troilus in lust and in quiete
> Is with Criseyde, his owen herte swete. (III, 1814-20)

The narrator's sharp delineation of the subject of Book Three accentuates the self-contained character of this section and de-emphasizes its connections with the preceding and following sections. Structurally "wele" is independent of the woe of love-longing and the woe of betrayal. Despite these tendencies toward separateness of parts and consequent instability of the whole, unity is maintained. But it is not the kind of unity which organicist presuppositions lead us to believe is the only kind. The inorganic unity of *Troilus* is maintained by a kind of forced accommodation. The parts do not "grow," they are "made." Holding them in juxtaposition with one another is a firm, definable framework. The parts relate to one another and to the whole by the principle of structural analogy, or homology, which we have seen to be so prominent a feature of medieval aesthetic theory and practice. The wholeness of "wele," its self-contained structure, is analogous to the firmly objectified structure of love — "aventures in love" — as the poem as a whole projects it. Thus a micro-macrocosmic relationship between the whole and the parts maintains a structural consistency. Substantively the "wele" of Book Three is coordinated with the whole through the agency of the narrator. It is his voice which explicity recalls in the introduction to the part the broad generalization of the whole. The narrator is the guide who in the forward movement of the narrative maintains contact with the governing expository purpose of the poem by relating the individuated stages of a love adventure to the universalized concept of love.

Before examining the narrower divisions within Book Three — its "progressive divisibility" — a word may be said about the relationship between Books Three and Four. The abruptness and completeness of the transition clarifies the separation between the two sections and at the same time indicates their common relevance to the major subject. The guide to these structural clarifications is again the narrator. His method is the same as that employed at the beginning of Book Three; placing himself and his editorial problems and emotional travail in the foreground, he foretells the action

of this book and establishes the emotional context for the lover's
fall from grace:

> But al to litel, weylaway the whyle,
> Lasteth swich joie, ythonked be Fortune . . .
>
> From Troilus she gan hire brighte face
> Awey to writhe, and tok of hym non heede,
> But caste hym clene out of his lady grace,
> And on hire whiel she sette up Diomede;
> For which right now myn herte gynneth blede . . . (IV, 1-2, 8-12)

Appropriate to the new subject, he now calls upon the Furies and
upon Mars, rather than Caliope and Venus:

> O ye Herynes, Nyghtes doughtren thre . . .
> Thow cruel Mars ek, fader to Quyryne,
> This ilke ferthe book me helpeth fyne,
> So that the losse of lyf and love yfeere
> Of Troilus be fully shewed heere. (IV, 22, 25-28)

These activities of the narrator set up Book Four as a self-sufficient
unit of the larger whole, equal in function and structural independence to Book Three. Though the stage of love here to be
"fully shewed" is different from the "gladnesse" of Book Three,
relevance to the larger subject is maintained because the narrator
explicitly coordinates these two elements of his exposition. From
this point forward the text is to be the lover "out of joie." Time
past in the life of Troilus and stages past in the exposition of love
will play no further part in the narrative, whose direction is constantly forward, though the pace is irregular, and whose concern
is to display as fully as possible the nature of the subject immediately in focus.

Immediacy of this kind is sustained largely by the "progressive
divisibility" of the sections of the narrative, as I have been suggesting. To view this pervasive characteristic in narrower focus let us
return to Book Three, the center of the five-book structure and the

pinnacle of the thematic cycle from woe to weal to woe. The most prominent phase of the gladness of love is, of course, consummation. Consistent with the narrative mode we have already observed to govern the larger divisions of the poem, the consummation scene is clearly framed by first-person pronouncements by the narrator. By this means it is accorded structural self-sufficiency, and at the same time the narrator, both by his unifying presence and by his explicit statement, connects this element with the whole. Following upon a phase of love-gladness which may be called the gladness of assured anticipation,[21] the consummation scene begins as Troilus finally takes Criseyde into his arms. The narrator effects an explicit and typically elevated modulation to the new subject:

> What myghte or may the sely larke seye,
> Whan that the sperhauk hath it in his foot?
> I kan namore, but of thise ilke tweye, —
> To whom this tale sucre be or soot, —
> Though that I tarie a yer, somtyme I moot,
> After myn auctour, tellen hire gladnesse,
> As well as I have told hire hevynesse. (III, 1191-97)

A few lines later, following a brief but fervent exchange of dialogue between the lovers, the rendering of the consummation comes to an apparent close with a moralization: "Thus sondry peynes bryngen folk to hevene" (1204). This brief comment grows into an expansive peroration as the speaker turns outward, addresses all women on the theme of joy through pain, and concludes with an exhortation:

> For love of God, take every womman heede
> To werken thus, if it comth to the neede. (III, 1224-25)

---

21 This section is introduced several hundred lines earlier in characteristic fashion: the narrator, in an exordial address extrinsic to the action, clarifies the substantive meaning of the change in Troilus' situation engineered by Pandarus:
> Who myghte tellen half the joie or feste
> Which that the soule of Troilus tho felte,
> Heryng th'effect of Pandarus byheste? (III, 344-46)

Thus the commentary of the teller encloses a rhetorically complete rendering of "consummation." This, however, is but one of several successive presentations of the same idea. Those that follow develop the subject according to the rhetorical technique which determines the larger divisions of the poem. For example, it is stated that Criseyde "made hym swich feste, it joye was to sene" (1228), and then, to amplify the statement and complete the rhetorical unit, it is shown that the lovers "gan ech of hem in armes other wynde" (1232). The succeeding stanza is rhetorically parallel to this one and is at the same time syntactically and dramatically independent of it. In different though similarly figurative language it expresses the same idea; "made hym swich feste" (1228) is now expressed as "opned hire herte" (1239), and the new simile compares the yielding lady to a nightingale. Another individuated rendering of the action informs the following stanza, which redirects attention to Troilus. He is compared to a condemned man granted reprieve, and then we are told, in a statement parallel to the two I have pointed out,

> For al this world, in swych present gladnesse
> Was Troilus, and hath his lady swete. (III, 1244-45)

The narrator's enclosing comment occurs in the next line: "With worse hap God lat us nevere mete!" We may observe in passing how easily the narrator moves between the idiom of the fabliau and that of the epic.

The following stanza effects another new beginning ("Hire armes smale, hire streghte bak and softe . . ."), describes Troilus embracing Criseyde, and declares that "in this hevene he gan hym to delite" (1251). There ensue seven stanzas of dialogue which are not interrupted by commentary from the narrator. These stanzas form a rhetorical section which amplifies by dramatic means the subject that we saw developed in a series of parallel and thematically equivalent descriptive units, all coming, incidentally, *after* the teller

has protested, "I kan namore." At the close of the dialogue section
the idea of consummation is expressed in the words of Criseyde:
"Welcome, my knyght, my pees, my suffisaunce!" (1309) This line
is climactic within the context of the dialogue, but within the larger
context of "consummation" it is one of several equivalent renderings
of the idea. The dialogue is thus the last in a succession of statements of consummation. The elusive moment of fulfillment is in
this way arrested and dilated into a series of independent and vividly
detailed rhetorical structures.

Following the dialogue the narrator reappears to articulate
the resumption of narrative movement, the transition to a new
phase of the subject. His words, including the exact repetition of
the "I can namore" formula, connect directly with the words in
which he first introduced the consummation section. I quote both of
these widely separated passages in order to illustrate the continuity
between them:

> I kan namore, but of thise ilke tweye, —
> To whom this tale sucre be or soot, —
> Though that I tarie a yer, somtyme I moot,
> After myn auctour, tellen hire gladnesse,
> As wel as I have told hire hevynesse. (III, 1193-97)

> . . . .

> Of hire delit, or joies oon the leeste,
> Were impossible to my wit to seye;
> But juggeth ye that han ben at the feste
> Of swich gladnesse, if that hem liste pleye!
> I kan namore, but thus thise ilke tweye,
> That nyght, bitwixen drede and sikernesse,
> Felten in love the grete worthynesse. (III, 1310-16)

In both passages we also notice — and this is characteristic of all
the teller's appearances — that he steps forward to address his
audience directly, and as he does so the illusion of Troy is necessarily dispelled. The locus of action becomes the here and now of
the recitation, and the subject changes from the love of Troilus and

TROILUS AND CRISEYDE

Criseyde to the circumstances of the presentation. Of the latter effect, the shifting of illusion, I shall have more to say shortly, for this has to do with the displacement of perspectives in the vertical structure of the poem. With respect to the horizontal structure, the passages above illustrate further the narrator's function as articulator of narrative progress. Within this framework "consummation" is dilated in the same way as the speaker's theme, presented at the beginning of the poem, is dilated throughout the spasmodic forward movement of the narrative.

Though the narrator's frequent interventions in the course of the story advance the Gothic ideal of clarification, they naturally impede the movement of the narrative. The result is the spasmodic and dilatory mode of the poem, a mode which, as I have suggested, takes on the quality of exposition. This mode of narration is not primarily concerned with simulating the "natural" flow of organic form. It invites amplification at all stages of its forward progress, and the way a poet responds to this invitation measures not only his narrative skill but also his concern with story as against his concern with doctrine. With a poet such as Jean de Meun, amplification clearly becomes digression as the rose-quest fades from sight for long periods. But with Chaucer amplification is integral to narration. This mode of narration makes possible a vividness and completeness of elucidation that are not attainable in the more economical mode of organic narration. Not only the story as a whole, as introduced by the narrator at the beginning, but the individuated parts and parts of parts, analogously presented in the course of the narration, release continually the energy and immediacy of new beginnings. Each part is made and presented new and fresh, and the effect is one of perpetual renewal. The reader can move among the finely fashioned parts of *Troilus* much as he can move within a Gothic cathedral, admiring the parts individually and admiring the capacity for order which unites them into an ordered, aggregative whole.

CHAUCER AND THE SHAPE OF CREATION

In this discussion of the poem's horizontal or rhetorical structure, I have tried to define the pattern of the poem as a whole and its microcosmic reflection in Book Three, both in that book as a whole and in the consummation section, as well as in that section's several individual renderings of the climactic action. I do not think it requires detailed analysis to demonstrate that the rest of the poem accords with the narrative mode exemplified by Book Three and its relation to the framework of the whole poem.

Although Book Three is representative of the narrative organization of the rest of the poem, there occurs in Book Five a significant departure from the norm. The change has to do with the basic question of our emotional rapprochement with the poem. Whereas in the earlier books of the poem our involvement with the action is continually mitigated by the obtrusions of the narrator in the role of the commentator and guide, in Book Five the narrator remains withdrawn for an unprecedentedly long period, and as a consequence we experience a kind and degree of emotional intensity unmatched elsewhere in the poem. The philosophical and emotional detachment so prominent in the earlier parts of the poem — even when the hero is as anguished as he is in love-longing — gives way to deep involvement in the overwhelming poignancy of Troilus' suffering as he awaits Criseyde's expected return to Troy. Troilus' period of anxious waiting is presented "straight," as the narrator attends strictly to the business of narrating and refrains from expounding, expatiating, or otherwise drawing attention to himself. Throughout most of Book Five Troilus' suffering is unrelieved, and since the narrator does not intercede the reader's involvement is not mitigated in the usual way.

This crisis in the hero's experience of love forms a transition between "wele" and "out of joie." It is beautifully appropriate — however inconsistent with the narrative mode of the poem — that the painful dissolution of the lover's ideal should be rendered in a mode which consistently involves the reader directly with the hero.

TROILUS AND CRISEYDE

The narrative follows Troilus day by day through the ten-day period. The expounding narrator last appears on the first day of Criseyde's absence to set forth the subject of the lover's pain:

> Who koude telle aright or ful discryve
> His wo, his pleynt, his langour, and his pyne?
> Naught alle the men that han or ben on lyve.
> Thow, redere, maist thiself ful wel devyne
> That swich a wo my wit kan not diffyne.
> On ydel for to write it sholde I swynke,
> Whan that my wit is wery it to thynke. (V, 267-73)

Until the ninth day there are no interruptions from the narrator, no explanatory comments or commiserations. Then the narration of Troilus' suffering is suspended altogether as the rendering of Criseyde's actions in the Greek camp is interposed. I shall consider this important episode below, but the point to be stressed here is that when the area of interest again becomes Troy and Troilus (at line 1100) the narration continues in the same unabating fashion, although the interposed episode of Criseyde's infidelity displays the dilatory and spasmodic mode more characteristic of the poem. Except for a quick "as I bifore have told" to mark the resumption of the Troilus segment of the action at line 1100, the narrator recedes and we look through him to the agonizing Troilus, struggling through the supposed last night and day of his wait.

After the twelfth day the tension — ours as well as Troilus' — diminishes as Troilus' doubts and anxieties move toward resolution, however unhappily for him. And at this juncture the voice of the teller begins subtly to reassert itself and resume control of the narrative movement:

> The thridde, ferthe, fifte, sexte day
> After tho dayes ten of which I tolde,
> Bitwixen hope and drede his herte lay,
> Yet somwhat trustyng on hire hestes olde. (V, 1205-08)

Though the extensive rendering of Troilus' experience of disillusionment is exceptional in many ways, it does not violate the basic rhetorical order of the poem, the order defined by the recurrent appearances of the narrator. The episode expresses an aspect of loving, and it is clearly set forth and delimited by the controlling voice of the narrator. But because the narrator is for so long a period so selfless and impalpable a medium, his return to prominence makes strikingly clear how fully we had suspended disbelief during this period. We are relieved when after the twelfth day our attention is redirected to the speaker and the "real" circumstances of the presentation. The worst is over, and it remains only to seal the unhappy lover's fate. We see him lamenting *in extensio* — in forms ironically comparable to his plaints of love-longing in Book One — first to Pandarus and then by letter to Criseyde. At first his lament is based on the impalpable proof of his dream of Criseyde and the boar, and then on the more palpable proof of Criseyde's letter, and finally the irrefutable evidence of the brooch he had given Criseyde, found on Diomede's coat of arms seized in battle. The end is near, and the narrator spells it out for us:

> Criseyde loveth the sone of Tideüs,
> And Troilus moot wepe in cares colde.
> Swich is this world, whoso it kan byholde:
> In ech estat is litel hertes reste.
> God leve us for to take it for the beste! (V, 1746-50)

> . . . for that I to writen first bigan
> Of his love, I have seyd as I kan . . . (1768-69)

> And thus bigan his lovyng of Criseyde,
> As I have told, and in this wise he deyde. (1833-34)

In guiding us through the linear ordonnance of the story the narrator fulfills one of the major requirements of the Gothic — the clarification of structural design. His apparent gaucherie and frequent overstatement only increase our awareness of how closely the poem follows the Gothic penchant for "clarification for clarification's sake."[22] Not only structurally but also with reference to content and meaning, the narrator's explicitness maintains the poem's close association with principles of medieval aesthetics. It is he who makes clear that Troilus' adventures represent "swich peyne and wo as Loves folk endure" — that the individual case is merely an instance of universal truth, an image of the exemplar. Thus, as the earthly model of a golden portal or a cruciform ground plan represents heavenly truth, so does the limited individual experience of Troilus represent the true course of love. The process of composition, whether architectural or poetic, begins with a preconception of the nature of truth and proceeds deductively to represent it in exemplary fashion, disposing the parts within the controlling framework.

Cosmic Structure

Earlier in the discussion of *Troilus* I tried to define the verticality of the literary structure in terms of alternating viewpoints, that of the narrator being "above" that of the story characters, and concomitantly the perspective of the recitation in present time containing that of the historical story in the past. The narrative oscillates between these two levels throughout the course of the poem, imparting a characteristic restlessness of focus and abruptness of shift in viewpoint. At the end, however, in the closing stanzas of the poem, a third and superior level of perception is introduced, and the poem ends by reaching beyond the "reality" of the narrator's position to the truth of divine perspective. In this way the secular love story finally is given its place in the total disposition of reality within the divine cosmos. It will become apparent, I believe, how closely the poem parallels Gothic architecture not only in the clarity with which it articulates these stages of perception, but also in the way it

[22] Panofsky, *Gothic Architecture*, p. 35.

participates directly in the actual structure of the universe, carrying the reader and his seeming reality to the apex of creation and the viewpoint of God.

I am suggesting that the goal of the poem's movement is a level of perception from which the narrator — who has always represented the "reality" from which we viewed the Trojan fiction — is ultimately to be seen not as a historian, not as a commentator, a master of recalled events, but as a dupe of time, a sham authority — in sum, a mortal. The climactic nature of this transformation in the role of the narrator can best be appreciated, I think, if we attend carefully to the context out of which it arises and observe in particular how distinctly and palpably the poem establishes levels of being. Taking bearings in the narration of Criseyde's infidelity, I shall attempt to chart our course through what becomes an increasingly turbulent mixture of viewpoints as we move through the last book of the poem.[23]

After the rendering of the first nine days of Troilus' anxious wait for Criseyde, which we observed to be unusually free from interpolations by the narrator, the scene is very abruptly shifted. Following his long dormancy the narrator rather suddenly steps forward, this time not to comment upon Troilus or otherwise to distance Troilus' woe but simply to change the subject. The shift is peremptory: "Upon that other syde ek was Criseyde . . ." (687) Here the line of narration divides in order to follow the activities of Criseyde in the Greek camp.

From this point forward the narrator becomes increasingly more prominent in relation to the events of the story. Concomitantly, our attention is increasingly drawn to the procedure of narrating

---

23 A different sense of the "anarchy" of Book V has been suggested by Gerry Brenner: "Action and time both run pell-mell in the last book, in concord with the disunity of the lovers . . . In the first four books two lines of action, Troilus's and Criseyde's, make a unified pilgrimage, merge in Book III, and are tenuously sustained in the strained unity of IV. But in V the pilgrimage splinters." "Narrative Structure in Chaucer's *Troilus and Criseyde*," *Annuale Medievale*, 6:8 (1965).

and the social circumstances of recitation. After Criseyde's resolve
to return to Troy the narrator himself becomes the center of attention, and from his point of view we "foresee" the outcome of the
action:

> "For which, withouten any wordes mo,
> To Troie I wole, as for conclusioun."
> But God it wot, er fully monthes two,
> She was ful fer fro that entencioun!
> For bothe Troilus and Troie town
> Shal knotteles thorughout hire herte slide;
> For she wol take a purpos for t'abyde. (V, 764-70)

The prescience of the narrator reminds us of our superior position
with regard to the action of the story. Thus, in resuming the function of expositor the speaker is also reasserting the "reality" of his
level of vision, as contrasted with the "fiction" of his tale. In the
following stanza the teller begins to emerge more fully: "This
Diomede, of whom yow telle I gan, / Goth now . . ." After several
lines devoted to Diomede, the superior position of the teller is
firmly established in the presentation of the portraits of the characters, beginning with the line, "This Diomede, as bokes us declare
. . ." (799) These portraits are, of course, peculiarly belated, and
to the reader interested exclusively in the love story they must
appear an intolerable indulgence of the teller's fancy. It is discon-
certing that a storyteller should leave off in the midst of a crucial
campaign of seduction to relate his own feats of scholarship in
gleaning from books and other authoritative sources various bits
of information about the characters in his tale. But when we understand that the poem is about the teller as well as about the tale,
we recognize that such abrupt shifts of attention between "fictive"
action and "real" presentation are by no means inconsistent with
the narrative mode of the poem. Here as elsewhere in the poem the
shifts of focus are accompanied by harsh changes of tonality and
attitude, the naïveté and clownishness of the narrator clashing with
the seriousness of the events he relates. The effect is not simply

97

"comic relief." It is the kind of inconsistency or incongruity which in a nonorganic aesthetic merits full artistic sanction. It is comparable to the extraordinary diversity of subjects depicted in cathedral statuary; the holy image which is the Gothic sanctuary contains not only angels and saints and scenes from the Scriptures, but symbolic laymen and animals, quasinaturalistic flora and fauna, and monsters of various kinds — all of these often standing in close proximity to one another.

From this point forward in the narrative the turbulence increases markedly as the narrator impinges himself with increasing frequency upon the presentation of Criseyde's infidelity. His elevated viewpoint is embodied in such typical locutions as (V, 946) "What sholde I telle his wordes that he seyde . . ." Immediately following the first, and notably ambiguous, statement of Criseyde's submission to Diomede — "He refte hire of the grete of al hire peyne" — occurs an attenuated display of the narrator in his role of historian and raconteur:

> And after this the storie telleth us . . . (V, 1037)
> I fynde ek in the stories elleswhere . . . (1044)
> And that she took, to kepen hym, good hede;
> And for to helen hym of his sorwes smerte,
> Men seyn — I not — that she yaf hym hire herte. (V, 1048-50)

Then the center of attention moves abruptly from the teller's here and now to the tale's there and then to depict the poignant farewell of the fallen Criseyde to the absent Troilus. For the final leavetaking of Criseyde the focus shifts once more, and attention is directed to the "real" world of the narrator and ourselves; emphasis is concentrated upon the mental processes of the narrator and the procedure and circumstances of composition:

> But trewely, how longe it was bytwene
> That she forsok hym for this Diomede,
> Ther is non auctour telleth it, I wene. (V, 1086-88)

. . . .

TROILUS AND CRISEYDE

> Ne me ne list this sely womman chyde
> Forther than the storye wol devyse.
> Hire name, alas! is punysshed so wide,
> That for hire gilt it oughte ynough suffise.
> And if I myghte excuse hire any wise,
> For she so sory was for hire untrouthe,
> Iwis, I wolde excuse hire yet for routhe. (V, 1093-99)

The motivations of Criseyde's action are deliberately obscured in favor of a display of the *narrator's* responses. It seems to me that this circumstance — the shift of narrative focus at the crucial moments — is more likely to provide an explanation of the celebrated enigma of the lady's infidelity than is the attempt to construct a "psychology" for her. The question is one of art, not of life. Chaucer's art, as we are learning to see with increasing clarity, is historically very much closer to mimetic allegory than to modern realism, and for this reason his characters are generally to be read more as personified illustrations of broad, abstract meanings than as self-limiting centers of interest. What Scholes and Kellogg observe of the Wife of Bath is, I think, equally applicable to Criseyde. They distinguish between two kinds of meaning in narrative: the "representational" attempts to convey a total and convincing impression of the real world, whereas the "illustrative" attempts, by symbolic means, to remind us of selected aspects of reality. The Wife of Bath, they say, "is a creature with roots in illustrative tradition modified by the first stirrings of the wave of representationalism which culminated in the realistic European novel."[24] Sanford Meech's judicious summary of scholarly opinion on the question of Criseyde makes clear that the controversy has taken place almost entirely within the arena of realistic psychological motivation, majority opinion holding that the lady's change of allegiance is sufficiently motivated, minority opinion claiming not.[25] I am suggesting

---

[24] Scholes and Kellogg, *The Nature of Narrative*, p. 91.
[25] Sanford Meech, *Design in Chaucer's Troilus* (Syracuse, N.Y.: Syracuse University Press, 1959), pp. 117-120, 395-397. Meech takes his own stand within

that in the art of characterization as Chaucer practiced it psychological motivation was not a central concern at all but was rather a peripheral, occasional matter. One readily admits that Criseyde is an intriguing creation, tinged with realistic enigma, but the kind of readjustment in the critical balance suggested by Scholes and Kellogg improves our understanding of the character and of Chaucer's art in general. Speculation about Criseyde's motivations and her moral fibre is irresistible, and in the narrow view it is justifiable. But the individuated instance is part of the broad view, preconceived, clearly specified, and variously reiterated in the course of the narrative — namely, that the purpose is to represent, through the experiences of Troilus, the universal truth of love. Criseyde's primary role is to demonstrate an important aspect of that truth, the fact that human love is subject to chance and change, the inescapable limitations of the mortal condition.[26]

As an elucidation of love the story of Troilus comes to an end when the hero at last comes to recognize "a kalendes of chaunge." This final event of the love story is related in characteristic fashion. Troilus' achievement of awareness is stated by the teller in a way which again emphasizes his own presence and function:

> But natheles, men seyen that at the laste,
> For any thyng, men shal the soothe se.
> And swich a cas bitidde, and that as faste,
> That Troilus wel understod that she
> Nas nought so kynde as that hire oughte be. (V, 1639-43)

The next hundred lines are an expansion of this idea, in which, with the help of Pandarus, Troilus displays dramatically the condition

---

the arena, maintaining that Chaucer's treatment of Criseyde "is designed to achieve maximum dramatic effect and yet to keep her the same dividedly motivated person throughout . . ." (120).

26 Payne offers cogent commentary on the artifices of Chaucer's characterization in *Troilus*, in *The Key*, pp. 221-227. On the "iconographical" interpretation of Chaucer's characters in general see D. W. Robertson, Jr., *A Preface to Chaucer*, pp. 241-259.

of understanding. Then the narrator comes forth to deliver his closing peroration. It is a complex performance and must be considered in some detail.

Following Pandarus' final denunciation of Criseyde, the narrator articulates a full rhetorical close:

> Gret was the sorwe and pleynte of Troilus;
> But forth hire cours Fortune ay gan to holde.
> Criseyde loveth the sone of Tideüs,
> And Troilus moot wepe in cares colde.
> Swich is this world, whoso it kan byholde:
> In ech estat is litel hertes reste.
> God leve us for to take it for the beste! (V, 1744-50)

The narrator is "in character" as the sententious moralizer of his material. And he is not really finished. Resuming his story, he perfunctorily describes the hero's deeds of battle, and then protests, in typically histrionic fashion, that his real subject is the love, not the arms, of Troilus; once more he delivers a rhetorical close. Having already pointed out the moral of the love story, that in this world, governed by remorseless Fortune, there is "litel hertes reste," he this time concludes on a less sententious note. Now leaning more toward the role of public performer than that of historian, he concerns himself with a matter of immediate and pragmatic interest, the vexing question of male-female relations. After disclaiming responsibility for the deeds of Criseyde, he moves further to propitiate the ladies in his audience by reminding them that women are betrayed as often as men are. This excursion leads him to a manifestly irrelevant conclusion; he takes leave of his audience by warning them to beware of men: "And this commeveth me / To speke, and in effect yow alle I preye, / Beth war of men, and herkneth what I seye!" (V, 1783-5) Thus the love story is concluded, and concluded not once but twice, with proper rhetorical forms of peroration in which the narrator delivers two different comments on his tale. This effect accords with Chaucer's tendency to "parti-

101

CHAUCER AND THE SHAPE OF CREATION

tion" the elements of the poem and to juxtapose structurally complete narrative units, regardless of the repetitions and incongruities which may result. But in the present instance we are concerned less with these linear and planimetric effects than with the concomitant verticality imparted by the narrator's appearances.

We have observed that throughout the poem these incursions produce a more or less continuous restlessness of focus, the illusion of Troy alternating with the "reality" of the present rapprochement between the narrator and ourselves. In the closing stanzas of the poem this clashing of perspectives is resolved through a dramatic vertical extension of the hierarchy of viewpoints.[27] This movement begins in the envoi, which follows immediately upon the propitiatory words of the narrator to the ladies in the audience.

The envoi comes without transition, following very abruptly upon the preceding stanza. The unexpected change in tone coincides with an unprecedented shift in viewpoint. The glib self-assurance and convivial banality of the narrator ("Beth war of men, and herkneth what I seye!" — 1785) is suddenly displaced by the undisguised voice of the poet, the creator behind the creature, expressing a new kind of concern about the story of Troilus:

> Go, litel bok, go, litel myn tragedye,
> Ther God thi makere yet, er that he dye,
> So sende myght to make in som comedye!
> But litel book, no makyng thow n'envie,
> But subgit be to alle poesye;
> And kis the steppes, where as thow seest pace
> Virgile, Ovide, Omer, Lucan, and Stace.

[27] A similar view is presented by Siegfried Wenzel, "Chaucer's Troilus of Book IV," *PMLA,* 79:545-547 (1964). Though Boethian elements in Book IV, as Wenzel maintains, anticipate the spiritual realm into which the poem moves at the end, these elements are exclusively verbal and thematic; they do not prepare us for the enormous power of the ending, which utilizes the architectonic resources of the poem's structure to complete its effectiveness. On this question of the "vertical" structure of the poem, see Morton W. Bloomfield, "Distance and Predestination in *Troilus and Criseyde,*" *PMLA,* 72:14-26 (1957); also Robert M. Jordan, "The Narrator in Chaucer's *Troilus,*" *ELH,* 25:237-257 (1958).

TROILUS AND CRISEYDE

> And for ther is so gret diversite
> In Englissh and in writyng of oure tonge,
> So prey I God that non myswrite the,
> Ne the mysmetre for defaute of tonge.
> And red wherso thow be, or elles songe,
> That thow be understonde, God I biseche! (V, 1783-98)

Here for the first time the speaker calls the story of Troilus a poem, a tragedy, a book; and above all he calls it *his*. Suddenly, in other words, the "I" of the poem is not a historian and chronicler, not a scholar gleaning what he can of times past from "authorities," not a public performer anxious to ingratiate himself with the feminists in his audience. Chaucer here steps from behind his mask, so to speak, openly to acknowledge himself a man of letters, a serious poet conscious of the classical tradition, aware of the problems of linguistic morphology, and concerned for the integrity of his text. In addition to identifying himself thus, several stanzas later, in a second envoi, Chaucer localizes himself in time by dedicating his book to the contemporary and historically identifiable personages, John Gower and Ralph Strode. Again the tone is unmistakably distinct from anything characteristic of the erstwhile narrator, regardless of the histrionic versatility of that figure.

> O moral Gower, this book I directe
> To the and to the, philosophical Strode,
> To vouchen sauf, ther nede is, to correcte,
> Of youre benignites and zeles goode. (V, 1856-59)

The narrative mode of the poem has accustomed us to sudden and often dissonant changes, not only of subject but also of tone, attitude, and viewpoint. But the present instance is unique, for now we confront for the first time "the real Chaucer." It is difficult in these days of relativist psychology to speak authoritatively of the "real" anybody, and those who choose to read *Troilus* with an image of the performing poet always in mind will perhaps find it

103

difficult to regard the Chaucer of these closing stanzas as any more "real" than the Chaucer of the rest of the poem. A serious Chaucer is no less "real" than a playful Chaucer, the argument might go. But if our primary interest is the actual poem rather than the imagined poet, I think we must acknowledge at least this much: in the closing stanzas the narrating "I" speaks in a tonality he has not sounded anywhere else in the poem, and he adopts an attitude toward his matter which he has nowhere else expressed. These I take to be demonstrable facts, facts which must strongly affect our interpretation of the poem, even though they appear unexpectedly and close to the end. J. W. H. Atkins has commented on Chaucer's adherence to general practice in his concept of endings: "According to medieval doctrine special importance was given to the *Conclusioun,* or main purpose, of a poem; and Chaucer in one place definitely states that 'th'ende is every tales strengthe.' Hence the significance of the moral and didactic endings of many of his tales . . ."[28]

Some critics do not feel that the end is the strength of this tale. B. H. Bronson's distaste for the whole idea of a narrator has led him, I believe, to overlook the transformation that takes place in the speaker at the end, and, in a gently derisive comment, to underrate its significance: "And a solution has been found for the troublesome conclusion of *Troilus and Criseyde* . . . The whole poem is told by a fictional narrator, and Chaucer enters in his own person only at the end, correcting the wrong ideas gradually imbibed by us from the over-emphatic teller of the tale and setting ultimate values, at the last possible moment, to rights."[29] Again, I think it matters little how we designate what happens at the end, so long as we recognize that it is something important and something unprecedented in the poem. If it is not agreeable to say that Chaucer "in his own person"

[28] *English Literary Criticism: The Medieval Phase* (London: Methuen, 1952), p. 157.
[29] Bronson, *In Search,* p. 29.

displaces a "fictional narrator" we should be able to say that Chaucer becomes serious, that he speaks straight, free of ironic humor and of ironic seriousness as well, and that this happens for the first time at this point, less than a hundred lines from the end of the poem.

When the poem thus comes into direct, open contact with its maker, a decisive change occurs in our own attitude toward it. The conclusion is especially moving not simply because of the intensity and lyric grandeur of the language but also because of the way the poem involves us in a dramatic reappraisal of our mortal position. The poem does this by controlling our point of view, that is, by reorienting us among the stages of the hierarchy of perception. As in the course of the poem our attention had continually alternated between the Trojan scene and the extrinsic narrating viewpoint, at the end the range is enlarged and our attention moves past the narrator to the poetic and moral sensibility behind that role, a sensibility now embodied in the poem and even named. Once we are in contact with Chaucer thus distancing himself from his poem, we are carried with him in an imaginative upward projection toward the divine eminence where all such translations end. Chaucer abandons the artifices of his narrating manner not in order to disavow connection with a deliberately created "separable fiction" but in order to place himself along the way to salvation, the actual way, through the illusions and delusions of this world. Thus, at the end he stands looking downward at his creation and upward at the Creator of all. Placing himself firmly in the terrestrial reality in which he has his sentient being, Chaucer is able to contemplate redemption in celestial reality. Though the way is parallel to that of Troilus, the ways of hero and poet are analogous rather than the same, for Chaucer transcends his creature in the same way that Chaucer is himself transcended by his Creator. Troilus, rising in death to the "eighthe spere," achieves the vision which comprehends mortality. He moves from involvement to detachment, from passion to understanding, from temporal life to eternal life. "Swych fin hath, lo, this Troilus for love . . ."

The decisive readjustment of the hero's vision, though it concludes his story, does not conclude the poem. It remains for Chaucer to enclose himself and his world — which includes all of us — within the cosmos under God. Chaucer casts his lines upward:

> And loveth hym, the which that right for love
> Upon a crois, oure soules for to beye,
> First starf, and roos, and sit in hevene above;
> For he nyl falsen no wight, dar I seye,
> That wol his herte al holly on hym leye.
> And syn he best to love is, and most meke,
> What nedeth feynede loves for to seke? (V, 1842-48)

This stanza does not constitute a simple palinode, comparable, say, to that of Andreas Capellanus at the end of the *De amore,* for Chaucer is not rejecting human love in a dialectical turnabout. He is redefining love, or better, repositioning it within the context of universal Christianity, a context outside the range of the love story. The poem had all along insisted, in its explicit Gothic fashion, upon making clear the separation between fiction and reality, so that however absorbing the fiction became the narrator's voice would recall present reality. Although the narrator could see the love story whole and recognize its general, illustrative quality, his range of moral vision extended only as far as some commonplaces about the role of fortune in human affairs. Therefore the sudden evocation of the universal Christian perspective — because it does occur so suddenly and yet so conclusively — produces an ending whose power is that of revelation. That it is brief in relation to the long process of the love story does not reduce its importance, because this is the brevity of truth. In the Dantesque prayer of the final stanza Chaucer achieves the final abatement of fluctuation and the resolution of uncertainties, not merely by uttering an orthodox supplication but by incorporating the way to redemption within the poem's structure.

106

TROILUS AND CRISEYDE

The final stanza is the pinnacle upon which the structural forces of the poem converge. The ultimate shift of perspective brings the poem, the poet, and ourselves into communion with the divine order of creation. This is the ultimate upward thrust of the poem, where its vertical structure reaches completion. What Dante said of the *Commedia,* in the Epistle to Can Grande, is true of *Troilus and Criseyde:* "The work ends in God himself."

The conclusion necessitates a reevaluation of the entire reading experience. Our sense of the poem is not complete until we have looked backward and downward and have seen the poem tangibly complete in its temporal and spatial dimensions. We see then that the presentation of love, clearly articulated and rhetorically and conceptually complete though it is, exists within a larger poetic framework, which in turn comprehends a larger moral and spiritual vision. The conclusion brings together the horizontal and vertical dimensions of the poem and completes a magnificent testimony to the glory of God and the continuity of all His works. In the final resolution of identities, Chaucer the medieval Christian poet becomes, by virtue of his very mortality, a transient voice, himself a fictive narrator for the Author of creation. Recalling the envoi, we recognize that God has indeed sent the poet the power to transform his tragedy into comedy. For in the vision of God there can be no tragedy, since there is no change. The distinctions between past and present, life and death, man's fictions and his truths, dissolve in the eternal simultaneity of divine vision. Within this perspective the affairs of humanity — including loving and writing about lovers — can be contemplated only with cool, assured laughter.

Though in *Troilus and Criseyde* Chaucer did not deliberately set about to "build" theology in the manner of the Abbot Suger, and though he does not, in Suger's fashion, explicitly praise reason as the God-given means to enable man to reproduce the cosmic harmony in earthly materials, he does, as we have seen, dispose the elements of his poem according to the pattern of a rational, preconceived structure whose apex is divine truth and whose base is sentient life. The universe Chaucer knew provided an ordered scale of ascent along which man could realize his salvation, and it was according to this pattern that Chaucer shaped his poem. He did not employ mathematical theory and the divine ratios of the Gothic builders, nor did he organize his movement toward Truth in the systematic and exhaustive fashion of Dante's *Commedia*. But *Troilus* reflects in its own way the absolute presupposition underlying all of these works, the belief in the palpability of the Way, and in its own fashion it gives structural body to this belief. Chaucer's poem and the Gothic cathedral are analogous in the sense that both utilize the fundamental relationships of the universe to create structures which are in touch with Truth: the mathematical ratios which order the cathedral order creation and have their source in the perfection of the Creator, and the stages of perception which order the poem order man's ascent through illusion and lead upward to total perception, which is God. Throughout its course *Troilus* emphasizes the processes of construction, as does the Gothic cathedral, and the culmination of the continuing restless movement among its articulated parts and perspectives is the arrival in eternal stillness.

In his discussion of Dante, Charles Singleton has observed that "a poem does what all created things do in a Christian universe, a poem participates in true existence, in Being."[30] And thus Chaucer's *Troilus* ends in God, despite the fact that it is a very "human" and theologically disinterested love story. It is easy to overemphasize

---

[30] Charles S. Singleton, *Dante Studies I* (Cambridge, Mass.: Harvard University Press, 1954), p. 59. This capacity of the poem to move beyond its characters, that is, beyond the fictional world it embodies, is overlooked in Alfred David's thoughtful study; for this reason David sees the ending as a balanced paradox rather than a final resolution: "No man may have his heaven on earth, but that is not to say that he may not enjoy a glimpse of heaven. Troilus's celestial laughter recognizes at the same time the absurdity *and* the sublimity of human endeavor." "The Hero of the *Troilus*," *Speculum*, 37:566-581 (1962), p. 580.

TROILUS AND CRISEYDE

Chaucer's theological affinities, since in his world all things were theological. But Chaucer's art is not theology. It is an analogue of theology in the sense that in the God-centered Middle Ages all serious meditations upon the human condition are analogues of one another, ending in God. Chaucer no doubt understood the patristic interpretation of Holy Scriptures to be an archetypal formulation: human destiny is to move from the limited world of the Old Testament, through the New Law, to transcendence and completion in Revelation. But for Chaucer Boethius was evidently more congenial than St. Augustine. The *Consolation of Philosophy* was as close to pagan philosophy as to Christian theology, but it described the same universal frame. Chaucer's affinity for the *Consolation* indicates not so much his "paganism" as the multiplicity of analogues which could express the absolute presuppositions of the medieval world view. When fundamentals are fixed — as they were from the *Timaeus* to the scientific revolution of the seventeenth century — analogy is a useful and meaningful technique of discovery, and the analogical imagination of the Middle Ages was limitless. Thus Chaucer would have found in the *Consolation of Philosophy,* among many other things, an analogical equivalent of the Christian formulation of the Way. And his own poetic structure partakes of the same vision. In its vertical structure *Troilus* embodies the mode of knowing expounded by Boethius as a four-level hierarchy of perception. According to Boethius, and the rationalistic heritage he represents, understanding is attained by withdrawal from the matter addressed (V, Pr. 4). This movement is represented on many levels in *Troilus.* For example, Pandarus' superiority over Troilus is signified by his ability to distinguish between "game and ernest" (III, 253-6) while Troilus can see only the painful "ernest"; and the narrator is superior to them both, since he commands the broader field of vision in which their world is discernible as fiction within his actuality. Finally, the translation of the narrator-poet, the leap which transcends terrestrial reality itself, evokes the viewpoint that comprehends all. Boethius calls the apex divine Intelligence; beneath it descend the levels of Reason, Imagination, and the Senses. These levels are mutually exclusive, and yet they are related in a coherent, rational pattern of graded values. "The senses grasp the figure of the thing as it is constituted in matter; the imagination, however, grasps the figure alone without the matter. Reason, on the other hand, goes beyond this and investigates by universal consideration the species itself which is in particular things. The vision of intelligence is higher yet, and it goes beyond the bounds of the universe and sees with the clear eye of the mind the pure form itself."[31]

It is apparent both in Boethius' expository description and in Chaucer's poetic embodiment that the aesthetic principle controlling the structure is a quantitative one. Each of the four levels of the Boethian hierarchy must be absolutely self-contained and independent; the lower does not partake of the higher, and therefore the higher comprehends the lower absolutely. Communication between parts is by definitive leap rather than by subtle flow, and yet the parts are contained within a regularly shaped frame and ordered according to a rational gradation. These are the attributes we have observed in Gothic architecture — the homologous relations among sharply articulated parts, the supraterrestrial elevation through the divine ratios — and it is to this comprehensive quantitative concept of order that *Troilus* reveals essential affinities. In its linear ordonnance the poem is essentially an aggregation of self-sufficient narrative units, "outlined" by the extrinsic voice of the narrator. Similarly in its vertical structure *Troilus* depends — for its restless, sometimes jarring, effects — upon movement among the absolutely separated levels of illusion, reality, and suprareality.

---

[31] *Consolation of Philosophy,* trans. Richard Green, p. 111.

FIVE   THE CANTERBURY TALES: CONCEPTS OF UNITY

Modern criticism has struggled mightily for several generations to "unify" the *Canterbury Tales,* that is, to achieve a satisfying description which is both comprehensive enough to see this large and diffuse work as a whole and discriminating enough to give a just account of its diversities. The task is formidable, all the more so because the beauty, richness, and self-sufficiency of individual tales make it seem unnecessary. It is enough of a challenge to produce a meaningful study of, say, the Merchant's Tale, and success in such an effort is worthy enough of readers' gratitude. In this sense the *Canterbury Tales* differs from equally (but differently) complicated narratives of our own time. Despite the fact that parts of a novel such as *Ship of Fools* or *Herzog* can appear in magazines before publication of the entire book, criticism cannot completely isolate parts from one another once the work exists as a book. The *Canterbury Tales,* in contrast, invites piecemeal criticism; it also invites the total view. In the equality of these two claims on our attention lies much of the critical problem. I think commentators have failed to recognize the extent to which the claim of the whole and that of the parts interfere with and disarm one another, though the absence of a satisfactory critical rationale is implicit acknowledgment of the difficulty of the problem.

Before the appearance of Ralph Baldwin's monograph "The Unity of the Canterbury Tales,"[1] the major attempts at unifying the poem coalesced into the "roadside drama" theory, whose deficiencies we shall discuss presently but whose general nature we may note in passing. This theory arises naturally enough from data presented in the General Prologue and in various linking passages between tales. Chaucer here activates and to an extent sustains the illusion of a pilgrimage from London to Canterbury. From the circumstances that (1) each of the pilgrims presented in the General Prologue was to tell a story or stories along the road and (2) there occurred occasional altercations and other forms of interaction among the pilgrims both during and between tales, there arose the theory that the poem as a whole is a drama, the pilgrims its protagonists, and the tales speeches contributing to characterization and motivation of the protagonists.

Baldwin's contribution was to enlarge the sense of journey beyond the purely literal and terrestrial dimensions forming the materials of the "roadside drama." Turning away from the letter of pilgrimage — the time designations and place names which appear among the prologues and links and suggest the chronology and geography of a literal journey — Baldwin explores the spiritual overtones of pilgrimage and finds that the *Tales* is bound metaphorically in the same way that "the life of the medieval Chris-

---

1 *Anglistica,* V (Copenhagen: Rosenkilde and Bagger, 1955).

tian . . . was framed by Creation and Doomsday."[2] Thus the opening lines of the General Prologue establish the springtime setting of Creation, and the Parson's treatise on penitence and Chaucer's penitential Retraction culminate the work on the threshold of salvation: ". . . the destination of the pilgrimage becomes . . . not so much the Canterbury shrine as the Parson's Tale, because it unfolds the *wey* to Him who is the way, the truth, and the light."[3]

Baldwin has offered an important insight into the "spiritual dimension" of the *Tales,* but I think it should be observed that the "unity" he thus propounds is only frame deep. That is, he confines his symbolic explication to the framework of pilgrimage, which is embodied in the framework of the *Tales,* namely the General Prologue at the beginning, the Parson's Prologue and Tale and the Retraction at the end, and occasional linking passages in the middle.[4] As for the rest of the poem — the vast body constituted by all the individual tales — Baldwin appropriates without qualification the "roadside drama" concept: ". . . the tales actually are performances incorporated into the frame story; they are the subjects of conversation, and they are, in a sense, the converse of the pilgrims themselves . . . The drunken Miller, the rascally ecclesiastics, the Alisouns, the dutiful Parson and his brother — all are 'framed' in that common piety, a pilgrimage . . . they have been conjured into existence as wayfarers and they activate a drama that does not cease for each of them with his tale."[5] To assert that the "drama" does

---

[2] "The Unity," p. 27.

[3] "The Unity," pp. 92-93.

[4] The problem has been recognized by Paul G. Ruggiers, who addresses himself not only to the frame but also, and primarily, to "the great middle," which "yields, through the technique of the medley, a variety of points of view suspended between the secular and spiritual interests of man." *The Art of the Canterbury Tales* (Madison and Milwaukee, Wis.: University of Wisconsin Press, 1965), p. 15. In defining the "technique of medley," however, Ruggiers is less concerned with structure than with genre and theme, the former being Chaucer's means for variety, the latter his means for unity.

[5] "The Unity," p. 78.

not cease for each of the pilgrims with his tale is to beg the major premise, that a drama *begins* for each with his tale. What Baldwin attempts to do is to graft his own spiritual interpretation of the framework upon the literal interpretation of the framework formulated in the "roadside drama" theory. He uses the preformed drama theory as entree to those parts of the poem which he does not himself examine, that is, the parts which are not framework. What bulky and recalcitrant parts they are neither he nor the commentary he depends on have scrupled to see. A more inductive and critical approach to the substance of Chaucer's poem will reveal that at least as often as not individual tales bear no definitive internal connections with their designated tellers or with the idea of pilgrimage, either literal or spiritual.[6]

Baldwin's spiritual interpretation of the framing pilgrimage was a long overdue and able response to an invitation clearly offered by the poem. But to claim to have discovered "The Unity of the Canterbury Tales" is, I believe, to claim too much. Such a "unity" is more wishful than actual, resting as it does upon connections which are not demonstrated, and which are not demonstrable, as we shall see presently. Thus, for example, though Baldwin can rightly emphasize the impact of the Parson's Tale as the spiritual culmination of the pilgrimage, he has no basis for his claim that the pilgrims wince and blanch, each in turn, as the Parson exposes their respective sins.[7] The pilgrims simply are not part of the "scene" of the Parson's Tale. The Parson's disquisition on Glotonye, for example, could apply to the Franklin, as Baldwin claims it does,[8] but it could apply to most of the other pilgrims as well, and indeed to most of the human race. And who is to say that the Franklin is any more or less prideful than the Wife of Bath, or the Pardoner, or anyone else?

6 See Kemp Malone, *Chapters on Chaucer* (Baltimore, 1951), pp. 210-235, for a reasonable discussion of the limits of the idea of the tales as characterizations of their tellers.

7 "The Unity," pp. 101-104.

8 "The Unity," p. 103.

THE CANTERBURY TALES

Clearly the assumed audience of the Parson's sermon is mankind, such an assumption being, I think, coextensive with the essential idea of preaching. In the absence of specific personal designations, his sermon must be understood to apply to all the pilgrims and, more important, to all of us. The universality of the Parson's Tale, its transcendence of the particular and the "dramatic," is the insight which should emerge from Baldwin's analysis. To drag the *Tales* down into particularity seems to me a misguided effort in the interest of a concept of unity with which Chaucer evidently was not familiar. Baldwin conceives of the whole and the parts — the framing pilgrimage and the tale-dramatized pilgrims — fusing into the kind of unity which clearly would fulfill *our* prescription, but not, I think, Chaucer's: "Nor is the *Parson's Tale . . .* told in complete dissociation from the rest. Each pilgrim and his story combine with the Parson's homily to make a momentary — and moving — diptych, a story and gloss, action and passion. This confers a sense of completeness which such episodic fictions often lack. Though most is left unresolved, little is left 'unexplained.' "[9] The vision is an attractive one, but it belongs to the critic, not to the *Canterbury Tales.* It represents an attempt to bend the poem to an organicist theory of unity. What to do with the disparities present in the *Canterbury Tales* remains a problem, but surely the answer cannot be to ignore them.

The running controversy over the order of the tales offers further illustration of the distance between the nature of the poem and the aesthetic assumptions of modern commentary. Ever since the efforts of Furnivall, whose "Six Text" edition was published in 1868, modern editors have been obliged to face the problem of correlating the arrangements of tales as they appear in the varying extant manuscripts not only with one another but with the arrangement implied by the pronouncements in the General Prologue. That

9 "The Unity," p. 101.

this continuing discussion is largely academic has been satisfactorily enough indicated, I think, by Manly, who, after exhaustive textual study, was able to say that "none of the extant manuscripts exhibits an arrangement which with any probability can be ascribed to Chaucer."[10] Nevertheless, speculation continues as to what Chaucer would have done had he completed the work and revised it. Thus Baugh's recent edition (New York, 1963) reverts, with a small exception,[11] to the order finally adopted by Furnivall, an adjustment projected from textual allusions to time and place on the road between London and Canterbury. The editions of Donaldson (New York, 1958) and Robinson (Boston, 1933, rev. 1957) chose to avoid such speculation. Adopting the order of the best manuscripts, they are therefore left with such inconsistencies as, for example, in the Ellesmere-Hengwrt order, the pilgrims drawing close to Sittingbourne (W. B. Prol.), which is forty-five miles from London, before they reach Rochester (Monk's Prologue), which is only thirty miles from London.

It is, of course, impossible to know what Chaucer would have done about such inconsistencies had he been able or willing to revise the *Tales*. But we do know that he fully composed a beginning (General Prologue and three tales, plus the Cook's fragment), an ending (Parson's Prologue and Tale and the Retraction), and eighteen other tales, plus variously constituted prologues and links. We know that Chaucer intended to — and to an extent did — adapt the intermediary materials to the framework of pilgrimage. That is all we know, and judicious commentary must begin from that knowledge, just as, it seems to me, judicious editing should end there. The Furnivall-Baugh rearrangement fulfills the editors' desire to fulfill

10 *The Text of the Canterbury Tales,* eds. John M. Manly and Edith Rickert (Chicago: University of Chicago Press, 1940), II, 489.

11 Baugh places Group B_2 before the Wife of Bath's Prologue and leaves Group C after the Franklin's Tale in *Chaucer's Major Poetry.* His reasoning is based upon Robert A. Pratt, "The Order of the Canterbury Tales," *PMLA,* 66:1141-1167 (1951).

THE CANTERBURY TALES

Chaucer's intention. But the fact is that the *Canterbury Tales* circulated as a gathering of fragments, as an unfulfilled intention. The degree of artistic frustration suffered on this account by Chaucer we can never know, but I think we can assume it to have been very slight. At least such is the inference to be drawn from our knowledge of Chaucer's working methods, as elucidated by source studies. The important point is that Chaucer was a maker of tales, and in the present case he also made a framework. His method of reconciling the framework and the tales was, by and large, to adjust the external details of substantially complete artifacts. Thus a churl's tale would be brought into conjunction with a churl, and which one would go with which would be largely a matter of external choice rather than of inner inevitability. Though in some instances, notably the Wife of Bath's Prologue and the Pardoner's Prologue and Tale, Chaucer moves toward a more fully inner-motivated development of his material, the prevailing impression is one of sharp edges and unsewn seams. Within his framework Chaucer moved his tales around a good deal, shifting tales from one teller to another — from the Man of Law to himself (the *Melibeus*), from the Wife of Bath to the Shipman, and perhaps from the Friar to the Merchant.[12] Such imperfections of adjustment, and many others as well — some simply textual, others integral to Chaucer's artistic technique, as we shall see — reveal the essential character of Chaucer's art. It is an art of superimpositions, adjustments, accommodations. The Six-Text rearrangement of the Tales does not in itself challenge this view or distort the essentially "arrangeable" quality of the poem. However, the editors' desire to smooth the road to Canterbury eventuated in a journey Chaucer's pilgrims never made. And the "roadside drama," which is a further extension of the desire to

---

[12] Baugh offers an excellent summary of these and related problems of teller-tale adjustment in his introduction to the *Canterbury Tales* in *Chaucer's Major Poetry* (New York: 1963), pp. 228-235. See also Robinson's explanatory notes to the tales in question.

"unify" the pieces, eventuates in a poem Chaucer never wrote. Our study of the principles of medieval aesthetic theory and Gothic structure would rather suggest that the basis for a valid unified view of the *Canterbury Tales* is to be found not in the idea of "fusion" but in that of "accommodation." From a Gothic viewpoint the *Tales* can be understood both as a pilgrimage (literal *and* spiritual) and a compound of tales. The mode of relationship between whole and parts can be one which does not at any time rob the parts of integrity and completeness within their own formal outlines. Nor need the part, in its wholeness and complexity, detract from the integrity of the whole. In order thus to have it both ways, Chaucer's art must pay a price, or so it may seem to the modern reader; the price is hard outlines, imperfect resolutions, exposed seams, contradictory viewpoints — in short, conspicuous absence of the primary attributes of post-Jamesian fiction.

I think the most fundamental of these distinctions between Chaucerian and Jamesian canons of literary art concerns attitude toward fictional illusion. There is ample evidence to indicate that Chaucer was thoroughly indifferent toward a quality which modern theory has conditioned us to regard as indispensable to good fiction, namely, consistent, unbroken illusion. In fact, we have seen that illusion-breaking is as essential to Chaucer's artistry as illusion-making. It is in this context that I wish to reexamine the "roadside drama" theory. Since that concept of the *Tales* posits a consistent dramatic illusion, it provides a convenient measure of Chaucer's departures from his assumed practice.

Efforts to show how consistently "in character" are the actions, expostulations, and narrations of the pilgrims are based upon the assumption that Chaucer is projecting an illusion unified in fictionalized time and space. The fact that some of the pilgrims, notably the Pardoner and the Wife of Bath, talk a good deal about themselves and are therefore "characterized" by what they say adds support to the "dramatic" view. The logic of this concept has created an attractive image of the poem as "an organic whole, and that whole . . . essentially dramatic."[13] To the focal point of the Canterbury road on an April evening all persons and events are supposed to be referable; and, more important, incidents and speeches are supposed to characterize the pilgrims and thereby substantiate meaningful dramatic action. The General Prologue in many ways encourages these assumptions, but a close look at what goes on in some prominent passages, first in the General Prologue and then elsewhere, will indicate that Chaucer's sense of illusion is more flexible — not to say inconsistent — than the dramatic theory would allow.

The realistic illusion of the Canterbury road in April is supported by a passage near the end of the General Prologue in which Chaucer appears to be moving out of fiction altogether and into journalism:

> But first I pray yow, of youre curteisye,
> That ye n'arette it nat my vileynye,
> Thogh that I pleynly speke in this mateere,
> To telle yow hir wordes and hir cheere,
> Ne thogh I speke hir wordes proprely.
> For this ye knowen al so wel as I,
> Whoso shal telle a tale after a man,
> He moot reherce as ny as evere he kan
> Everich a word, if it be in his charge,
> Al speke he never so rudeliche and large,
> Or ellis he moot telle his tale untrewe,
> Or feyne thyng, or fynde wordes newe . . . (725-36)

It has been evident from the very beginning of the narrative that the role of objective witness is being assumed by the poet, and therefore, strictly speaking, the present passage is totally superfluous according to the requirements of illusion. Here Chaucer deliberately raises the issue of "truth" by insisting so strongly and so unnecessarily upon the authenticity of his report. The effect is, of course, calculated,

---

[13] J. L. Lowes, *Geoffrey Chaucer* (New York: Oxford University Press, 1934), p. 164.

and here as in innumerable other instances we recognize the presence of the poet behind the reporter. The humor of the passage arises from the play of these two viewpoints, since the excess of the reporter's earnestness in expounding the obvious is apparent only from the more knowing viewpoint of the poet, the latter, "superior" viewpoint being the one which governs the passage. The reader's imaginative experience is complicated and active, almost violent, for it consists not only of being absorbed in the immediate surface that is the reporter's perspective, but also an abrupt *dis*illusionment and ultimate transference of imaginative focus to the poet's perspective, that of better sense, finer discrimination, and fuller awareness of propriety. At places like this the poem in a sense divides. The effect is similar to what we have observed in *Troilus* and similarly can be explained in two ways, depending upon one's feelings about Chaucer's role as narrator in the poem. Donaldson has differentiated between the undramatized, "invisible" poet, standing outside the fiction, and the concrete pilgrim-reporter projected into it.[14] Then it becomes possible to describe a characteristic quality of Chaucer's fiction in terms of an observable shifting of focus, as the reader's attention is frequently shifted from illusion to actuality, from Chaucer the wide-eyed pilgrim-reporter to Chaucer the wise and witty poet. Bronson, on the other hand, chooses to effect an imaginative shift of the entire enterprise from a reading experience to a listening one.[15] We then imagine ourselves an audience of Chaucer's

[14] E. Talbot Donaldson, "Chaucer the Pilgrim," *PMLA*, 69:928-936 (1954). See also Ben Kimpel, "The Narrator of the *Canterbury Tales*," *ELH*, 20:77-86 (1953); and Ralph Baldwin, "The Unity," chap. 4, "The Poet and the Pilgrim."

[15] Bertrand H. Bronson, *In Search of Chaucer*, pp. 25-30, 66, 67. Donald R. Howard, "Chaucer the Man," *PMLA*, 80:337-343 (1965), emphasizes, with Bronson, the presence of the poet. Howard's article is further evidence that disagreement over the relationship of poet and "narrator" is less divisive than provocative of thoughtful and illuminating analysis. Howard recognizes that Chaucer often "masquerades" but argues that the man is always present in the stylization of his person and that this presence is dynamic, arising from the relationship between the bourgeois

contemporaries attending a court recitation by the poet. When Chaucer apologizes — in the name of authenticity — for certain forthcoming "rude" passages we perceive the twinkle in his eye and we smile because *we know* Geoffrey Chaucer and we know he is not a short-witted reporter but a shrewd and playful poet who has written many a lecherous lay. Though I believe, for reasons indicated earlier,[16] that the more fruitful critical approach is one that deals with the poem as a reading experience rather than as a listening one, I find the differences between Donaldson and Bronson of less than fundamental importance, for both critics perceive, each in his own manner of analysis, the doubleness of focus which plays one sense of the facts against another.

Such a perception is not available, however, from the standpoint of the roadside-drama interpretation, with its exclusive focus on the level of the pilgrim-reporter. The passage in question, when seen in the single focus of the drama theory, is deprived of its range of playfulness. It is explained thus: "The effect of this mock-apology is . . . a whetting of the reader's appetite for what is to follow."[17] But who is the reader whose appetite is whetted by this means? True enough, we are all irresistibly drawn to the account of the night's happenings, and the mock apology is one means of increasing its appeal. But this is only the direct and obvious appeal to a reader or listener like Harry Bailly, whose wit, like the speaker's, is short, and whose appetite for unusual and lurid truths — especially if they are firmly authenticated — is unlimited. Chaucer's deliberate

poet and his aristocratic audience. On the other hand, Morton W. Bloomfield, "Authenticating Realism and the Realism of Chaucer," *Thought,* 39:356 (1964), though maintaining that "the creator of these titles and comments [i.e., interruptions of the narrative] is not the pilgrim who is reporting the Canterbury pilgrimage," nevertheless recognizes that "he is related to him very closely," and that in these externalized passages Chaucer "is speaking to us from another part of his being."

[16] See above, pp. 67-70.

[17] R. M. Lumiansky, *Of Sundry Folk: The Dramatic Principle in the Canterbury Tales* (Austin, Tex.: University of Texas Press, 1955), p. 24.

The roadside drama theory

kept up
by the
idea that
the poems is
on the pilgrims

CHAUCER AND THE SHAPE OF CREATION

Chaucer's
high expectations
of audience

on the tales
written by
Chaucer the poet

cannot look
@ the Chaucer the
character as
Chaucer!

juggling with illusions makes it clear that he is reaching beyond the naïve to readers whose wit is long.

Chaucer would expect his reader — as he expected his own immediate audience — to recognize the deception and appreciate the artistry behind it. Chaucer is not simply disclaiming responsibility for the tales; he is disclaiming art. But even as he insists upon his fidelity to fact he has ensnared us in fiction. The pilgrim designated "Chaucer" is no more and no less "real" than those among whom he moves, who are designated Knight, Miller, Harry Bailly, etc. The poet whose art has lived gloriously for six centuries is not the maker of the Tale of Sir Thopas, but the maker of the maker of that tale. Though the distinction between the poet- and pilgrim-selves of Chaucer is rejected by some critics on the ground that it makes a factitious or overly subtle fragmentation of a normal, complex personality, such a distinction at least prevents the error of taking "Chaucer" as a real person walking among imagined figures. And it prevents the complementary misconception which the "roadside drama" theory has proliferated, namely, that the fictional characters are real persons consorting with the poet Chaucer. In such a view there is no fictional illusion at all, and the only limits to interpretation are the limits of the critic's understanding not of Chaucer's poetry but of "people" or life in general.

Rather than accept the pilgrim-Chaucer's protestations of truth at face value, the critic must make the effort to define Chaucer's sense of illusion and the distinctive assumptions it was based upon. It is instructive to see how far the roadside-drama theory has deterred us in this enterprise and carried us into psychological and historical speculation.

A severely compressed synopsis of the development of the drama theory must run somewhat as follows: The *locus classicus* is Kittredge's pronouncement that "the Canterbury Pilgrimage is . . . a Human Comedy, and . . . the stories are merely long speeches expressing, directly or indirectly, the characters of the several per-

122

THE CANTERBURY TALES

sons."[18] Eleven years after Kittredge, in 1926, Manly published *Some New Light on Chaucer*. Despite the author's frequent efforts to emphasize Chaucer's artistry and poetic skill, the effect of the book was to advance interest in the real persons upon whom Chaucer based his pilgrims. Thus, Bowden's *Commentary on the General Prologue to the Canterbury Tales* of 1948 could cite a large body of historical data which, as in the typical case of the Pardoner, "inclines us even more decidedly to the belief that the Pardoner must have been known to the poet and at least to some of his audience."[19] Clearly our subject has become people Chaucer knew, and in this dialectic the means for evaluating art has been usurped by the means for verifying chronicle. Finally, Lumiansky's *Of Sundry Folk* of 1955 establishes "The Dramatic Principle of the *Canterbury Tales*" and elucidates "the dramatic techniques by means of which the Pilgrims are kept as the center of focus throughout the *Tales*." Furthering our absorption in the "reality" of the roadside drama is this critic's manner of speaking of the tales as "performances" by actor-pilgrims. And finally we have Baldwin's appropriation of the dramatic principle, as described above.

The drama theory can illuminate only what goes on among the pilgrims, since it limits itself to the perspective of the "stage" as viewed by one of the participants, the pilgrim-reporter Chaucer. The dramatic critic can point out that the interplay between Host and Pilgrims "is characterized by interesting dramatic overtones that include a rather subtle play of human relationships . . ."[20] But he cannot include the subtle play of human relationships between ourselves and the lively-minded poet. Chaucer is indeed one of the

---

[18] G. L. Kittredge, *Chaucer and His Poetry* (Cambridge, Mass.: Harvard University Press, 1915), pp. 154-155.

[19] Muriel Bowden, *Commentary on the General Prologue to the Canterbury Tales* (New York: Macmillan Company, 1948), pp. 283-284. Chaucer's real people have been further pursued by George Williams, *A New View of Chaucer* (Durham, N.C., 1965).

[20] *Of Sundry Folk*, p. 25.

actors, but we are expected to see through this often gauche figure to the artful poet, who is delicately shaping illusion and inviting our appreciation of his skill. I do not suggest that this typically Chaucerian posturing is completely accounted for as an appeal to the reader's sophistication — there is more behind it, as I shall try to show presently — but it should be recognized that this dimension of the poem is inaccessible to the reader who is too deeply involved in the "drama."

To caution against imaginative surrender to a fictive scene may seem perverse, but not so, I think, when we understand that art can — and Chaucer's does — appeal to responses other than those isolated and identified by Coleridge. Chaucer induces us *un*willingly to suspend disbelief. His is an art of the conscious mind, and though much of the time we can't help responding instinctively, in the manner of Harry Bailly, Chaucer makes certain that we come out of it and recognize where we have been. Nor is this simply a quibble over the obvious. Of course we all know it is all fiction, but the *Canterbury Tales* is not to be read as though it really were drama, that is, as though the exclusive locus of involvement were the road to Canterbury and the ideal reader a Harry Bailly. Nor can the *Tales* be read as though it were a postromantic novel, which *is* dramatic to the extent that artistic success depends upon unmitigated immersion in the world of the fiction. With Faulkner we really are there, on the road to Jefferson. And with Conrad we really are confronting Marlow who really was there. But with Chaucer we are there, on the road to Canterbury, only some of the time, since Chaucer is there, in the role of reporter, only some of the time. The rest of the time, with his larger sensibility, he is standing back and remarking, virtually out loud, how wonderfully convincing fiction is. Such doubleness of attitude, if judged from a naturalistic point of view, would indicate one of two unfavorable verdicts: either Chaucer is too naïve and limited to be able to sustain an illusion, or he is too perverse and unromantic to be willing to accede to the

124

spell of his own fiction. But Chaucer has not been called naïve ("rude") or perverse since the prenaturalistic eighteenth century. And although the roadside drama has been read as a sustained illusion, this has been accomplished only at the cost of ignoring the many clear instances in which Chaucer consciously undermines his own achievement of illusion. Only recently has the question of illusion been seriously raised.[21]

Injudicious involvement in the drama has led to some bizarre interpretations of the poem, interpretations based upon a credulousness comparable to that of Harry Bailly lamenting the fate of the Physician's Virginia, or the Reeve taking up arms against an account of a carpenter cuckolded. The significant fact is, of course, that Chaucer has built this level of naïveté into the poem. A proper reading requires that this level of awareness itself be taken into critical account. But the larger perspective must be recognized, that in which we make contact with the poet and acknowledge, with him, the limits of the illusion. However convincing the scene is — and it is wonderfully convincing — Chaucer continually, and in varying ways, calls attention to the boundaries of the fiction. In Gothic fashion, he capitalizes the lineaments of construction, openly displaying his maker's art and achieving thereby a range of aesthetic effect not possible in organicist fiction. In Chaucerian fiction, in which illusion itself is often the subject and is *ipso facto* limited, it is inappropriate to exercise the kind of "creative" criticism that collaborates with the writer of naturalistic fiction in piecing together hints and symbols which explain the effects of an undepicted and obscure past upon the depicted, vivid present. Rather than approach

21 See Bloomfield, "Authenticating Realism," which clearly defines the problem by relating Chaucer's method of "authenticating" his fictions to the practices of other authors and to fictional technique in general. Bloomfield points out (pp. 355-358) that Chaucer "continually reminds us . . . that the poem is his creation and his world and that he is master of both," and he observes that Chaucer is showing us both the reality *and* the unreality of his *Canterbury Tales*. My ensuing comments on the subject of illusion follow closely my earlier study, "Chaucer's Sense of Illusion: Roadside Drama Reconsidered," *ELH*, 29:19-33 (1962).

CHAUCER AND THE SHAPE OF CREATION

Chaucer naturalistically, criticism ought to elaborate this very distinct difference: the limitations which Chaucer imposes upon illusion sharply curtail commerce with past time, whereas in later fiction the effect of unlimited illusion is to open the past to the reader's scrutiny. Critical reading of later fiction becomes in many respects an exercise of imaginative ingenuity comparable to the writer's creative effort. Chaucer's pilgrims have been subjected to "creative criticism" of this kind, and as a result many of them have moved outside their illusionary characters entirely.[22] They have assumed the infinite and unpredictable variety of "real life," including psychological life, and life determined or explained by a past assumed to be accessible to the critic.

The assumptions of the drama theory are that inconsistencies of characterization are due to natural causes, not to the limitations of a particular literary mode of representation. A good case in point is provided by explanations of the quarrel between the Miller and the Reeve. Following is one "dramatic" critic's approving paraphrase of another's findings: "It seems likely that the Miller-Reeve acquaintanceship must be of long standing, that the Miller worked years ago as servant boy in the Reeve's household at the time when the Reeve, then a carpenter, was made a cuckold by a cleric . . . the Reeve probably knows the content of the coming story and is therefore able to tell the Miller that he will be both sinful and foolish to ridicule or insult any man and to circulate such a rumor about a wife."[23] Clearly we have leapt over the boundaries of fiction as we pursue the "motivations" of this quarrel down the murky corridors of the past, the real historical past, be it noted, not a past that is part of Chaucer's illusion. And indeed this is no longer illusion at all. We have fallen into Chaucer's enticingly baited trap

22 Paull F. Baum's discussion of commentary on the Pardoner is a trenchant corrective of this kind of excess. *Chaucer: A Critical Appreciation* (Durham, N.C., 1958), pp. 44-59. See also Malone, *Chapters*, pp. 172, 163-235.

23 *Of Sundry Folk*, p. 51.

and taken game for earnest. A moment's further examination of the passage in question will make even clearer that the primary interest lies not in what takes place between Miller and Reeve but in what takes place between the double-visaged Chaucer and his audience.

There is no doubt about the outcome of this exchange: the Miller retains complete mastery; the Reeve makes a fool of himself. The measure of the Reeve's foolishness is his readiness to commit the primary error of perception, to confuse fiction with reality, game with earnest. The Miller has only to announce the subject of his tale — ". . . a legende and a lyf / Both of a carpenter and of his wyf, / How that a clerk hath set the wrightes cappe" — and the Reeve leaps to protest, not on the possibly legitimate grounds that ribaldry is offensive, but on the irrelevant and indefensible grounds that the unheard tale is not a tale at all. The Reeve's impulsive and violent protest against what he takes to be public charges of cuckoldry and adultery reveals his own churlish inability to distinguish between actual instance and fictional generalization. In this exchange the Miller gains superiority not through his knowledge of the Reeve's past experience of matrimony — as maintained by dramatically oriented criticism — but by the immediate demonstration of a higher quality of mind. It is the shrewd and urbane play of the Miller's logic that proves him the master of his blustering antagonist. Says the Miller, with a very delicate play of nuance:

> Leve brother Osewold,
> Who hath no wyf, he is no cokewold.
> But I say nat therfore that thou art oon. (3151-53)

The lines which follow, and conclude the Miller's Prologue, embody the pilgrim-reporter's second "apology," in which we are cautioned against attributing the Miller's ensuing "harlotrie" to the conscientious intermediary. Our reporter concludes, "Avyseth yow, and put me out of blame; / And eek men shal nat maken ernest of game." The humor emerges from the clash of two discernible points of view. Chaucer counts on the reader to distance himself sufficiently to perceive Chaucer the reporter trying to deny the identity of Chaucer the poet. Commenting in the single perspective of the drama theory, Lowes has seen here simply "Chaucer" warning squeamish readers to skip over the harlotry of the churls.[24] But squeamishness is not the *poet's* point — if it were he obviously could not have written the tales. The deluded reader is in a position exactly analogous to that of the Reeve. He, too, takes game for earnest, skips over the "indecent" tales, and remains the unaware victim of a superior wit. Of course, no actual reader is completely taken in — despite Lowes' fears to the contrary — but the drama theory posits this level of involvement as the ideal. Though this surrender to the "reality" of the journey is a large and essential part of the reading experience, it is not all of it. We should be equally responsive to the appearances of the illusion-making poet, however deceptive these appearances may be.

The scene we have been considering illustrates another weakness of the drama theory with respect to the very quality of urbanity we find displayed in the Miller. By all accounts the Miller is a man of no intellectual endowment, and in addition he is drunk. The narrator tells us three times how drunk he is; the Host says to him, "thy wit is overcome"; and the Miller himself says, ". . . first I make a protestacioun / That I am dronke, I knowe it by my soun." How, then, do we explain the Miller's cool, masterful toying with the Reeve? The customary explanation is "dramatic irony," as illustrated by this comment: "It may be that the Miller is . . . more sober than he pretends; under the guise of drunkenness he has enjoyed overriding the Host, and now he is having the fun of discomfiting the Reeve."[25] The difficulty with this interpretation is that it indiscriminately rejects not just some but all the evidence of the text. There is no reason to suppose the Miller sober if we are told by two

---

24 Lowes, *Chaucer*, p. 175.
25 *Of Sundry Folk*, p. 52.

observers and by himself that he is drunk. If we say that his treatment of the Reeve proves him to be sober, as many critics do, we are proceeding upon the untenable premise that the pilgrims are "real" people acting upon motives of their own which are inscrutable, even to Chaucer. The alternative is to acknowledge that the characterization of the Miller is inconsistent. On the one hand we have, in the present instance, explicit assertions, from three points of view, that the Miller is drunk; on the other hand we have his extremely adroit handling of the Reeve.

I think we move a long way toward understanding Chaucer's art when we acknowledge that disparities such as this one do occur, and quite frequently. To "interpret" Chaucer in such a way that consistency is achieved either by suppression or by negation of data is fruitless and leads to limitless proliferation of "versions." We must conclude, in the present instance, that both elements of the contradiction are valid. In one moment we see the Miller as a hopelessly drunken churl, and in the next moment we see the same person as a sober and sophisticated wit. Similar shifts of characterization abound in the *Canterbury Tales,* and they cannot be brushed away in the name of such subtle effects as might be attained in another mode of fiction through dramatic irony. The Miller is not an internally motivated, organically unified character; rather is he an externally shaped composite. That he is a vital, utterly compelling figure attests not only to Chaucer's artistry but also to the possibilities of inorganic form.

The "compositional" character of the Miller indicates the boundaries of Chaucer's narrative technique. Within this field he composes not only the pilgrim-characters but also the tales they tell and the characters and events within those tales. In the same composite fashion he brings together tales and tellers, on some occasions being more meticulous than on others in adjusting the details for consistency. Though this compositional method may appear limited and simplistic from the standpoint of organicism, it results — especially when practiced by a master like Chaucer — in a sparkling variety of formal structures, verbal styles, and moral perspectives. Sometimes the artifact, whether teller, tale, or character, seems peculiarly out of balance with itself, as in the case of the Miller, where the parts do not form a consistent whole. At other times a firmer consistency prevails, as in the case of the tale the Miller tells, though even here the unity is not of the kind which organicist criticism seeks in its own image. Within the framework of his inorganic technique, Chaucer's varieties of structural unity are many. But they follow the Gothic principle of juxtaposition. Gothic art is like a "panoramic survey, not a one-sided, unified interpretation dominated by a single point of view."[26] Characteristically, the total form is determined by the accumulation of individually complete elements. From this standpoint it can be said that in the *Canterbury Tales* the elements of a roadside drama are convincing in themselves; but it must also be said that the focal points they establish are constantly subject to displacement. We can say that the links of the framework at many points strain toward a naturalistic and dramatic ordonnance; however, the aesthetic character of the poem is determined by the dissonance between the dramatic and the static, not exclusively, or even mainly, by "drama."

Wölfflin's definition of two kinds of unity in painting clearly fits the situation confronting us in the *Canterbury Tales.* He distinguishes between "multiple unity" (*vielheitliche Einheit*) as in a head by Dürer, whose features are sharply individuated, and "unified unity" (*einheitliche Einheit*) as in a head by Rubens, whose features subordinate themselves to the total impression.[27] Following Wölfflin, Wylie Sypher has characterized the organizing principle of Gothic art as a multiple unity which brings together distinct

26 Arnold Hauser, quoted in Muscatine, *Chaucer and the French Tradition,* p. 167.

27 Heinrich Wölfflin, *Kunstgeschichtliche Grundbegriffe* (Munich: Hugo Bruckmann, 1915), pp. 167-210.

but incongruent perspectives. It is a commonplace observation about paintings of the late Middle Ages that naturalistic figures are juxtaposed against symbolic background; they are not organically fused with it. Thus Sypher, speaking of a fifteenth-century painting, can point out that the Gothic figures are secular but their world is not, and that "the proportions of the scene are alien to the men who inhabit it."[28]

What the art historian can remind the "dramatic" critic of Chaucer is that the background is larger than life, and also that it is part of the picture. In Chaucer's Gothic vision man's environment was not simply the English countryside but nature juxtaposed against supernature. The reality that exists beyond appearances was no less the concern of Chaucer than it was of Dante or Langland or the painters of Gothic miniatures. Chaucer's Canterbury pilgrimage, though exhibiting many of the lineaments of physical reality, was at the same time but the visible, severely limited representation of the spiritual pilgrimage of man.

My chapter on the Parson's Prologue and Tale will consider more fully the macrocosmic structure of the *Canterbury Tales* and its symbolic character. In the meantime we shall examine other individual tales in an effort to discern something of the variety of forms attainable within the Gothic mode of "multiple unity."

[28] Wylie Sypher, *Four Stages of Renaissance Style* (Garden City, N.Y.: Doubleday and Company, 1955), p. 54.

SIX   THE MERCHANT'S TALE: DRAMATIC DISUNITY AND INORGANIC UNITY

For several generations the predominant critical estimate of the Merchant's Tale has been that it is a tour de force of dramatic expression, an outburst of conjugal bitterness unified in the violent disillusionment of the Merchant. Critics thus driven by the imperatives of the drama theory achieved a remarkably uncontroversial consensus. Tatlock expressed the prevailing view in these often quoted words: "For unrelieved acidity the *Merchant's Tale* is approached nowhere in Chaucer's works . . . Without a trace of warm-hearted tolerance or genial humor, expansive realism or even broadly smiling animalism, it is ruled by concentrated intelligence and unpitying analysis."[1] A generation earlier Kittredge had called

---

[1] J. S. P. Tatlock, "Chaucer's *Merchant's Tale*," MP, 33:367 (1936).

the tale a "frenzy of contempt and hatred," and a generation later Hugh Holman brought together all the old terms, "savagely obscene, angrily embittered, pessimistic, and unsmiling," and contributed his own "dark cynicism."[2]

That there is humor in the tale had been admitted by Tatlock, but grudgingly and very guiltily: "One might feel half-ashamed of so greatly enjoying so merciless a tale . . ." More recently Bertrand Bronson has called for a less constrained approach to the comic quality of the tale.[3] Structural analysis will show, in support of Bronson's view, that the tale is not the unified characterization of a vicious and demented personality that it is conventionally assumed to be. On the contrary, it is a composite of quite discordant elements and therefore is not capable of generating the kind of intensity of concentration upon which the "dramatic" interpretation depends. The unity of the tale is loose and nominal, similar to the kind of unity which relates the Miller's Tale to the Miller. Once the pervasive influence of a supposedly full and rich psychological characterization of the Merchant-teller is revealed not to exist, we are able to respond in a more relaxed fashion to the humor of the tale, a humor that is sometimes subtle and ironic, sometimes exuberant and coarse. We should not be dismayed to find that Chaucer did not labor to integrate and polish these diverse elements according to modern prescriptions for unity.

The "savage" interpretation evolves from the very heavy emphasis which the prologue to the tale has been forced to bear. This outcry of conjugal grief — an explosive reaction to the tale of patient Griselda — indeed compels our attention. As an impulsive

---

[2] G. L. Kittredge, "Chaucer's Discussion of Marriage," *MP*, 9:435-467 (1912); C. Hugh Holman, "Courtly Love in the Merchant's and the Franklin's Tales," *ELH*, 18:241-252 (1951). The same view is expressed by G. G. Sedgewick, "The Structure of the *Merchant's Tale*," *UTQ*, 17:337-345 (1948); and Germaine Dempster, *Dramatic Irony in Chaucer* (New York, 1959), pp. 46-58.

[3] B. H. Bronson, "Afterthoughts on the Merchant's Tale," *SP*, 58:583-596 (1961). The only other comic interpretation is John C. McGalliard, "Chaucerian Comedy: The Merchant's Tale, Jonson, and Molière," *PQ*, 25:343-370 (1946).

and direct expression of bitter personal disillusionment it both shocks and engrosses us. But it is a failure of discretion to read the broad-ranging and unusually diffuse Merchant's Tale in the narrow light of this moment of anguish. We shall see that the disparate and often elaborately developed parts of the tale are often totally dissonant with the attitude of bitter despair expressed in the Prologue. And yet the prevailing interpretation has uncompromisingly imposed a prism of bitterness over the tale and read everything through it.[4] What does not at once *seem* savage has been too easily corrected by appeals to irony, and thus this most puzzling and inconsistent of all the Canterbury Tales has been simply and surely "unified."

Speaking in his Prologue, the Merchant does indeed express disillusionment and despair: "Wepyng and waylyng, care and oother sorwe I knowe ynogh, on even and a-morwe . . . and so doon other mo that wedded been." But to what extent this outcry dominates the tale that follows is open, I believe, to considerable debate. The insistent tone of one critic, enjoining us that "we must always remember that he is uncontrolledly angry, and therefore that the tale must always be read as sharpened into his own mood"[5] suggests that the critic is aware of how much forcing is necessary to effect such a reading. Severe distortion and frequent invocations of "irony" have resulted from the concerted effort to compress the diverse elements of this tale into so simple a formula. Rather than insist that the Merchant's Prologue reaches backward and forward in time — backward into the pre-pilgrimage personal experience of the Merchant and forward into the narration of the tale of January and May — it would seem prudent to settle for what Chaucer has given us. He has dramatized a response to the Clerk's Tale of patient Griselda — and in this sense "dramatic" is the appropriate term.

---

[4] The imprudence of this procedure is pointed out by Bronson, who reminds us that "in approximately half of the more complete MSS of the Canterbury Tales, there is no Merchant's Prologue." "Afterthoughts," p. 584.

[5] Sedgewick, "The Structure," p. 340.

THE MERCHANT'S TALE

Typically Chaucer invests this situation with a subtly human mixture of nuances and attitudes. The Clerk's ironically comic envoi provides the occasion. Indeed, the last line of the envoi, advising wives that they "Be ay of chiere as light as leef on lynde, / And lat hym care, and wepe, and wrynge, and waille," provides the cue and even the wording for the Merchant's outburst. In the Merchant's response Chaucer has embodied a compelling and very personal expression of powerful feeling. But even here, in the midst of so much pain, the tinge of comedy is present. We sense it at once in the sudden contrast between the Merchant's and the Clerk's usages of the same Biblical phrasing. The Clerk's jocularly ironic "And lat hym care, and wepe, and wrynge, and waille" is followed immediately by the Merchant's serious and personal "Wepyng and waylyng, care and oother sorwe I knowe ynogh . . ." By abruptly juxtaposing these two very different intonations of the same language Chaucer produces a type of comic situation of which he was very fond: the spectacle of one who unknowingly makes earnest of game. This is an instance similar to Chaucer's mock apologies at the end of the General Prologue and in the Miller's Prologue, though here the humor, subtle at best, is further muted by the force and genuineness of the Merchant's grief. But for Chaucer the spectacle of one whose personal feelings disable his sense of what is going on is the stuff of comedy, not of pathos. This impression is furthered by the overstatement of the Merchant's case against wedlock, an overstatement which adds to the humor because it is more evident to us (and to the poet) than to the Merchant. Neither is the humor lessened by the traditional antifeminist language of the charge:

> I have a wyf, the worste that may be;
> For thogh the feend to hire ycoupled were,
> She wolde hym overmacche, I dar wel swere. (1218-20)

How seriously can we take a man who because he has a cavity thinks the whole world has the toothache? Here is the Merchant:

> Were I unbounden, also moote I thee!
> I wolde nevere eft comen in the snare.
> We wedded men lyven in sorwe and care. (1226-28)

The qualification offered three lines later — "As for the moore part, I sey nat alle" — comes too late to alter our assessment of the man. The extent of his foolishness becomes clear when he reveals that his knowledge of wedlock is the fruit of two months' experience.

In addition to the comic elements of the Merchant's Prologue there are other reasons to believe that Chaucer did not conceive of an organic unity-in-passion fusing the Prologue with the tale. An obvious reason, pointed out by Bronson, is that in many of the better manuscripts the Prologue does not appear. Therefore we may conclude that Chaucer composed it independently and inserted it arbitrarily between the Clerk's envoi and the tale of January and May. The rationale for such placement is an externally perceptible one: the Prologue offers an amusing contrast with the spirit of the Clerk's words, and it is nominally appropriate to the following tale; that is, it is about marriage and, further, it is about a man having difficulties with a new wife.

The absence of interior connectivity is further indicated by the relationship between the Merchant's Prologue and the portrait of the Merchant in the General Prologue. The latter offers no hint of any kind — either by explicit description or by implication — that there is any connection between this figure and the subject of marriage. He is simply and exclusively a Merchant, shrewd, acquisitive, and very possibly dishonest. Likewise his personal qualities offer no suggestion of the Merchant of the later scene. He is a pompous man, vain and self-satisfied, and the face he exposes to the world is dignified and aloof:

> This worthy man ful wel his wit bisette:
> Ther wiste no wight that he was in dette,
> So estatly was he of his governaunce . . . (GP, 279-81)

THE MERCHANT'S TALE

That the self-possession of such a man should break down under severe emotional strain is an attractive hypothesis, but all that Chaucer offers to sustain it is the name Merchant applied in two instances which display very different kinds of person. Again we have an arbitrary collocation of elements, each complete enough in itself but neither being necessarily an organic counterpart of the other.

Such a reading may seem unimaginative and uncompromisingly literal, but only, I think, if we regard critical imagination as the capacity to supply what isn't there. If the elements that make up our sense of the Merchant do not form a homogeneous compound, the most we can say about Chaucer's art in this respect is that he worked with independent parts and with separated moments, not with dependent parts in a continuum of organic relationship.

The Merchant's tale itself is as independent and as self-contained as the two versions of the Merchant, and it relates to those in the same nominal fashion, though less to the vain and pompous Merchant than to the embittered one. The tale is plainly about marriage. It falls into four more or less clearly defined sections: the rhetorical debate on marriage (almost half the tale, to line 1699), the courtly romance centering in the garden, the mythical fantasy of Pluto and Proserpina, and the raucous fabliau episode of the conclusion. To maintain that these structurally distinct and stylistically dissonant parts of the tale are governed by "concentrated intelligence and unpitying analysis," as Tatlock has expressed it, seems to me a serious distortion. Analysis will reveal that the governing intelligence is not concentrated but diffuse, and that the psyche of the embittered Merchant-husband is not a satisfactory focal point for defining a dramatic and organic unity. If we do not find an organic unity based in the character of the Merchant we need not be disappointed; there are other kinds of unity, and other kinds of satisfaction, as a fresh look at the tale will reveal.

The long encomium on marriage at the beginning of the tale

137

has attracted much notice. Like most Chaucerian problems, it has been solved through irony. Kittredge calls it "one of the most amazing instances of sustained irony in all literature," and he sees no reason to wonder at it. The ironic overpraise of wedlock is for him a "perfect expression of the Merchant's frenzy of contempt and hatred." But when we attend carefully to this long section of the tale we find, I believe, that it does not sustain the effect of dramatic irony.[6] Try as we might to maintain a sense of an embittered husband *pretending* to praise matrimony — and we must envision a remarkably poised and subtle raconteur — the illusion disintegrates after twenty or thirty lines, about one-fifth of the way through the encomium. We are indeed enmeshed in a web of irony as the speaker asks (line 1288), "Who is so trewe, and eek so ententyf / To kepe hym, syk and hool, as is his make?" But the Merchant of the Prologue has no part in the irony. The speaker before us at this point — however inconsistent with dramatic propriety — is actually the familiar Chaucerian innocent, here undertaking the glorification of marriage. Our amusement arises from his notable lack of success. His approach is academic, as indicated by the extended paraphrase of Theophrastus (lines 1295-1310). He could not, of course, have chosen a less likely instrument for the advancement of his stated purpose than the notorious anti-feminist Theophrastus. And the only opposition he brings to bear against the long and eloquent denunciation of women and wedlock is the single petulant question, "What force though Theofraste liste lye?" We are entertained by the spectacle of so solemn and pedantic an orator unwittingly demolishing his own position. This is high comedy, not savagery.

The panegyric on marriage continues with the exempla of gentle, loving women. Among the good wives cited are Rebecca,

---

[6] Kittredge, "Chaucer's Discussion," pp. 451-452. John M. Manly, pursuing the question of suitability of tale to teller, registered a dissent similar to mine in his note to this passage in his edition, *Chaucer's Canterbury Tales* (New York, 1928), p. 596.

who betrayed her husband (though the circumstances were mitigating), and Judith, who wrought violent death upon Holofernes. The whole long passage is a crazy quilt of assertions and examples which do not quite coincide with the sentiment they purport to advance. The humorous imbalance is sustained by the closing remarks of the eulogizer of matrimony:

> Housbonde and wyf, what so men jape or pleye,
> Of worldly folk holden the siker weye;
> They been so knyt ther may noon harm bityde,
> And namely upon the wyves syde. (1389-92)

There is no savage Merchant here. The irony is purely of a local kind. It is integrally concerned with the humor of the passage and does not extend beyond the immediate situation.

The encomium is an independent, self-contained chapter in the endless book against women. Its humor derives from a technique frequently practiced by Chaucer. Words and meaning stand slightly awry; appearance and truth are rendered askew. The imagination is baffled by the effort to retain through this long and complex discourse on women and wedlock the sense of an embittered husband speaking in a "frenzy of contempt and hatred." Such a reading can be produced only by an inordinate effort of the intellect and the will.

There is, of course, a relevance between the emergent point of the mock encomium and the feelings of the Merchant. Both are against women. But the relevance is loose and nominal, not organically dependent upon a thoroughgoing characterization of the Merchant. The mock encomium is an independently worked out satire on women which has its own lineage in the academic antifeminist tradition. It fits into the Merchant's Tale only because the subject — women and wedlock — is relevant, not because it sustains or develops the illusion of an embittered, darkly cynical husband. The delicate play of viewpoints, the amusing self-defeat of the solemn

139

moralist — these are the marks of the poet Chaucer, not of the stolid, cynical Merchant-husband he has sketched in the Prologue. Chaucer has freely displaced one speaker, viewpoint, and mood by another — the bitter bourgeois husband by the foolish academic debater. He has done this with total disregard for consistency of characterization and organic unity of structure and style.

Unity disintegrates at other points in the tale as well. Once the possibility of inconsistency of illusion is admitted one need only take a broad glance at the tale as a whole to see what a pastiche it is. The first half, as I have indicated, consists almost exclusively of rhetoric — long speeches, elaborately developed, whose burden is lore, the ancient and much distilled wisdom of classical and patristic commentators on women and wedlock. Prancing around and occasionally through these disquisitions is the old goat January, serving the minimum requirements of narrative continuity. But the first half of the tale, unlike the second, is almost entirely talk, with very little action or movement of any kind. The essence is rhetoric and its ironic manipulation. The second half is a courtly romance, suitably distorted and debased to accord with the antifeminist and antiromantic bias of the story. The important point is that although the second half is related to the first in plot and subject, the two parts are independent literary entities so far as style, tone, attitude, and general feeling are concerned. The speaker who describes the garden in the second half of the tale is a sophisticated literary man, one who is steeped in the courtly tradition:

> He [January] made a gardyn, walled al with stoon;
> So fair a gardyn woot I nowher noon.
> For, out of doute, I verraily suppose
> That he that wroot the Romance of the Rose
> Ne koude of it the beautee wel devyse;
> Ne Priapus ne myghte nat suffise,
> Though he be god of gardyns, for to telle
> The beautee of the gardyn and the welle,
> That stood under a laurer alwey grene. (2029-37)

THE MERCHANT'S TALE

I think no plea of sustained dramatic irony can persuade the imagination that this speaker is identical to the foolish encomiast of the beginning of the tale, *or* to the embittered husband of the Merchant's Prologue, *or* to the single-minded businessman of the General Prologue, whose "resons" were always "sownynge . . . th'encrees of his wynnyng."

To define the attitude of the tale toward the characters is another difficulty which is not satisfactorily resolved in terms of the life and temperament of the Merchant. It is generally agreed that January is the surrogate for the Merchant and the central figure of the tale. I have been urging that the correlation between the Merchant and the tale as a whole is much less consistent and thoroughgoing than has been supposed, and I would like to point out here that January is much less central to the first half of the tale than to the second. While in the latter he at least takes a prominent part in the events, in the rhetorical half of the tale January, though the instigator of the discussion, remains little more than a name put to a stock viewpoint which forms a part of the long and diffuse debate on wedlock. The imbalance between the kinds of role January plays in the two parts of the tale adds to the general disunity of the tale.

Traditionally January has been taken very seriously as a character. Even in the comic interpretation offered by J. C. McGalliard the "full and rich psychological characterization" of January is found to be the foundation and shaping purpose of the entire tale.[7] All of the elements of the tale, even the rhetorical roles of Placebo and Justinus, are taken to be integral to the characterization of January. When January is taken so seriously as a moral agent (however immoral) it becomes very difficult to see the tale as a comedy. There is no disagreement, of course, over the kind of person January is, only about the degree to which he controls the total effect of the tale.

---

[7] "Chaucerian Comedy," p. 354.

CHAUCER AND THE SHAPE OF CREATION

It is difficult to find the kind of characterization which McGalliard describes as that of "whole men" who "act and move and live in society . . . as husbands, fathers, brothers, citizens, heads of a household." Those who would see the Merchant's Tale as this kind of rich and unified dramatization of a "whole man" must disregard to an alarming extent the discontinuities and irrelevancies characteristic of Chaucer's narrative method. For example, the narrator's encomium on wedlock, though touched off by some rash remarks of January's, cannot easily be seen as part of a "full and rich psychological characterization" of January. Rather is it a lavish disquisition, superimposed upon the meager words and actions of January, serving to elucidate the antifeminist theme of the tale. The encomium exemplifies a distinct narrative method — that of giving voice to a viewpoint extrinsic to the action — which invalidates at once any structural comparison with drama. Chaucer's method does not allow for the organic development of character through action.

Primarily Chaucer's narrative method serves to distance us from the characters. Insofar as the Merchant's Tale is seriously concerned with January at all, it displays him as a spectacle which we witness from a safe distance. Clearly he is a gross and foolish old man, but to measure our response to him in terms of either revulsion or pity is to assume a kind of intimacy which the structure of the narrative does not in fact allow. Bronson has said that in the case of January and May in the denouement sentiment is irrelevant.[8] I would add that in the tale as a whole Chaucer's techniques of distancing support, even necessitate, such a judgment and preclude charges of callousness or cynicism. In this tale we are involved not with a person but with a personification. Our attention is engaged with consequences and moral generalizations, not with personality. In contrast to January is a character like Othello, whose situation in many ways resembles January's. Othello is more a

---

8 "Afterthoughts," p. 593.

person and less a personification, and we are not so decisively removed from him. Engrossed with Othello we indeed experience deeply personal and disturbing feelings. Observing January we experience reassurances about the nature of things. We are gratified and pleased to see that such pride and such lechery go before precisely such a fall.

The ways in which Chaucer deploys a narrating voice define a basic difference between narrative and drama. The many instances of the narrator's outspoken comment upon the characters and events continually interfere with the progress of the action, and they effectively shape our responses to the tale. Here again we shall find that charges of a "cold intelligence" narrating with "unrelieved acidity" simply do not fit the narrative situation. On the contrary, the narrator's many and always arresting comments show an astonishing diversity in attitude and tone. Rather than being "unrelieved" or "cold," the mind controlling the narration is remarkably inconsistent, so much so that it cannot be compressed into a unified characterization, such as that of an embittered Merchant-husband, without misrepresenting the nature of the narrative.

I have spoken of the disparity between the elegant literary tone of the garden section and the dry academic tone of the debate section. I would like to suggest further that the tale as a whole is an extremely varied and discordant mixture of many of the voices which Chaucer habitually uses. Much of the difficulty of the tale is caused by this clashing of styles, no single one of which dominates the narration.

The voice of epic apostrophe, for example, is often heard, as at the moment when January is struck blind. The narrator addresses Fortune in this way:

> O sodeyn hap! o thou Fortune unstable!
> Lyk to the scorpion so deceyvable,
> That flaterest with thyn heed whan thou wold stynge;
> Thy tayl is deeth, thurgh thyn envenymynge.

143

CHAUCER AND THE SHAPE OF CREATION

O brotil joye! o sweete venym queynte!
O monstre, that so subtilly kanst peynte
Thy yiftes under hewe of stidefastnesse . . . (2057-64)

This is the voice which in a more leisurely narrative, such as the
Man of Law's Tale or the Knight's Tale, has the scope to establish
its controlling character, although even in those tales the consistency
is not as firm as some commentators would wish. There is, of course,
irony behind this impassioned address to Fortune, but it does not
originate in the savagery of a disillusioned Merchant-husband.[9]
The positioning of this eloquent outcry, amid the affairs of a silly
old man and his inconsequential young wife, is a masterful piece of
ironic inappropriateness. This perfectly tempered and timed overstatement reveals not the Merchant in an uncontrolled frenzy but
the poet Chaucer expressing his incomparable sense of the ridiculous.
The compassionate voice, with its moralistic overtones and elevated
style, is the appropriate instrument for elaborating the figure of
unstable Fortune. The point of this passage is not the sympathy
expressed for January but the absurdity of expressing it in this
elevated manner. The humor depends upon our awareness that in
contrast to this situation there are appropriate moments for such
impassioned outcries against the order of things. The effect, once
more, is comic. The overstated concern emphasizes the true triviality
of January. The center of our interest is not January, nor is it the
embittered Merchant ironically pretending lamentation. Our interest
centers on the very act of elocution in which Chaucer is engaged as
he launches a beautifully eloquent — and in the context perfectly
specious — version of the conventional lamentation. Though January is inconsequential as a person and his imminent betrayal compels
neither pity nor fear, one cannot take the extreme position that

---

9 The same voice is heard in the Nun's Priest's Tale (3226): "O false mordrour,
lurkynge in thy den! O newe Scariot, newe Genylon . . ." The passage is as ironic
and humorous as that cited from the Merchant's Tale and equally irrelevant to the
pilgrim-character presumably being dramatized.

THE MERCHANT'S TALE

January's downfall carries no moral significance whatever. The question is not whether or not such significance exists, but how seriously it is to be taken. Very seriously indeed, commentators have almost unanimously replied. And the moral ramifications of January's blindness have been diligently pursued and earnestly expounded, with the result that delight has been vanquished by instruction and Chaucer has been read as though he were Spenser, or even Bunyan.

In contrast to the overblown apostrophe to Fortune is this delightfully understated expression of sympathy for May as she awaits January's pleasure:

> He was al coltissh, ful of ragerye,
> And ful of jargon as a flekked pye.
> The slakke skyn aboute his nekke shaketh,
> Whil that he sang, so chaunteth he and craketh.
> But God woot what that May thoughte in hir herte,
> Whan she hym saugh up sittynge in his sherte,
> In his nyght-cappe, and with his nekke lene;
> She preyseth nat his pleyying worth a bene. (1847-54)

Again the governing viewpoint is characteristically Chaucerian in its combination of detachment and compassion. (Neither quality, of course, is appropriate to the Merchant.) The humor of this passage, like that of the other, comes from the zest for detail and the unerring sense of contrast and timing. Here, however, our laughter comes suddenly, with the deft, playful, and masterfully abbreviated allusion to May's point of view. Our amusement is increased by the inadequacy of her response: the paraphrase of her reaction, "She preyseth nat his pleyying worth a bene," bespeaks a young lady of little sensibility and less sense, hardly a person deserving of very deep sympathy. The view that she is a "deep one," whose depths Chaucer purposely leaves to our imaginations, seems to me as unsupportable as the "psychological" interpretation of January. It originates similarly in a confusion between the critic's understanding of people and his understanding of art.

These two passages — one expressing sympathy for May, the other expressing sympathy for January — point to the crux of the critical problem. In order to achieve a consistent case for a bitter antifeminist speaker, critics have had to undertake an extensive program of resolving contradictions. Thus the sympathetic attitude toward January is supposed to indicate the Merchant's empathy with the hero of his tale, while the derisive attitude toward January is supposed to indicate either the Merchant's disgust with himself or his blindness to the similarity to his own case. All of these are arbitrary lines of interpretation, and all are pursued on the assumption that there *is* a consistency which must be revealed. The case of May-interpretation is the same: the critic feels compelled to shape contradictions into a unitary hypothesis. Multiple appeals to irony result in an enlargement of the Merchant's sensibilities far beyond the meager indications provided by the text. Ultimately the critic following such roads can say only that the tale expresses the infinite possibilities of the human psyche. When we reach this point criticism is lost and art is robbed of all meaning. It is much more fruitful to examine the work dispassionately and without preconceptions, with an aim to define its unique character.

In a different approach to the tale C. A. Owen, Jr., has enlarged upon the dramatic interpretation and found that "the controlling images in the poem . . . are the linked ones of the garden, the blindness, and the tree."[10] For Owen the tale is a unified matrix of images. Thus one "crucial passage" early in the tale, which begins "Mariage is a ful greet sacrament," is found to send "echoes and reverberations through the two consultations and the marriage to a crowning climax in the garden scene at the end." The first difficulty with this approach is that one passage is no more crucial

10 "The Crucial Passages in Five of *The Canterbury Tales:* A Study in Irony and Symbol," *JEGP,* 52:299 (1953).

than any other. One can drop his finger at random anywhere in the text and find something about marriage, and any of the foolishness in the tale (of which there is much) can be interpreted as "blindness." The debatable question is the mode and character of the relationship in which such passages exist. Owen reads the tale as the unified symbolic enlargement of an idea present in January's mind from the beginning. In doing so he disregards both the irregular structure of the narrative and the humor. He maintains that "the story does not stop with a single literal fulfillment. Through Proserpina's vow it suggests repetition through the ages. And it creates in the literal world the symbolic fulfillment of the idea." Reverberating symbolism of this kind may be characteristic of *Moby Dick* or *Heart of Darkness,* but such a reading seems to me quite out of phase with the discontinuities and the humor of the Merchant's Tale. The ingenious unification belongs more to the critic than to the tale. It culminates in an enforcement of the moral lesson, along the lines of the traditional interpretation of the tale: "The Merchant participates in the blindness of his creature January in not realizing the extent to which he is talking of his own sore in the tale." Malvolio's virtue once more triumphs over Chaucer's cakes and ale.

The difficulties I have been considering have led some critics to suggest that the tale was not originally intended for the Merchant. A. C. Baugh, for example, cited textual evidence, such as the line "As doon thise fooles that been seculeer," to argue assignment to an ecclesiastic, and the Friar seemed the most likely.[11] Retaliation was quick, in the name of intensity, coherence, and irony, all qualities that depend upon preserving the character of a bitter Merchant-narrator.[12] Contrary to both views, structural and stylistic evidence

[11] "The Original Teller of the Merchant's Tale," *MP,* 35:16-26 (1937). Manly (ed. *Canterbury Tales,* p. 624) suggests the Monk.

[12] Germaine Dempster, "The Original Teller of the *Merchant's Tale,*" *MP,* 36: 1-8 (1938).

indicates that it makes no difference which pilgrim one wishes to assign to the tale. None will fit, for the tale does not "characterize" a single, unified pilgrim-personality. The basis of Chaucer's art is not the so-called dramatic principle, but rather an aesthetic principle whose roots lie deep in the traditional concept of structure as aggregative order.

The fairy section is more damaging to a unitary hypothesis than any of the elements so far considered. This episode illustrates very well what Charles Muscatine has pointed out as the Gothic tendency of Chaucer's art to follow the principle of juxtaposition of parts, as distinguished from continuous development of one part into an organic whole.[13] The squabble between Pluto and Proserpina is a self-contained episode (lines 2219 to 2319) of delightfully humorous character. Its presence in the tale is justified by the relevance of its subject matter; but while we can say that it fits into the tale, we cannot say that it develops the characterization of the Merchant. In fact, it bears a very strong negative relation to our sense of either an embittered husband or a purposeful businessman. The tone and style are highly cultivated:

> Bright was the day, and blew the firmament . . .
>
> .   .   .   .   .   .
>
> And so bifel, that brighte morwe-tyde,
> That in that gardyn, in the ferther syde,
> Pluto, that is kyng of Fayerye,
> And many a lady in his compaignye,
> Folwynge his wyf, the queene Proserpyna,
> Which that he ravysshed out of Ethna
> Whil that she gadered floures in the mede —
> In Claudyan ye may the stories rede,
> How in his grisely carte he hire fette —
> This kyng of Fairye thanne adoun hym sette
> Upon a bench of turves, fressh and grene . . . (2219; 2225-35)

---

13 *Chaucer and the French Tradition*, pp. 167-173.

THE MERCHANT'S TALE

Like the earlier debate carried on by January and his advisers, the contest between Pluto and his wife derives its materials from the antifeminist tradition. A minimal relevance to the tale as a whole is thereby assured, despite the structural imbalance and stylistic incongruity. The dramatic vitality of the scene, reminiscent of the Nun's Priest's Tale, readily engages our interest at the same time that it must dismay the reader intent upon continuity and consistency. Despite the fact that Proserpina has the last word, the eternal wiliness of the female has been fully displayed in the process. The emergent viewpoint of the episode is masculine, and this is what makes the rendering of Proserpina's victory so amusing — even for a female reader, I should think. But as in the earlier marriage debate there is no justification for identifying the general antifeminist viewpoint with the specific cynicism of the Merchant. The fairy episode is another self-contained element which fulfills its own character before it contributes to the structure of the tale as a whole.

The lively finale of the tale offers further difficulties for those who would insist upon consistency, and further entertainment for the less demanding. The act of betrayal in the pear tree is narrated in a manner quite outside the character of a merciless Merchant; January stoops down,

> and on his bak she stood,
> And caughte hire by a twiste, and up she gooth —
> Ladyes, I prey yow that ye be nat wrooth;
> I kan nat glose, I am a rude man —
> And sodeynly anon this Damyan
> Gan pullen up the smok, and in he throng. (2348-53)

We can be sure that by shattering the fictional illusion at such an untimely moment the speaker would exasperate listeners like Harry Bailly, but as for listeners like Geoffrey Chaucer and ourselves — we are delighted. The "real" presence that intrudes at this critical juncture in the fictive action is not one which repels us by a "frenzied expression of contempt and hatred." Far from savage, the speaker is gauche and obsequious. The posture is familiar. It is that adopted by Chaucer in the General Prologue as he apologizes that his wit is short, and in the Miller's Prologue as he dissociates himself from the churl's tale, and in many other instances in the *Tales* and elsewhere. The affectation of helplessness in the face of facts is part of the repertoire of the Chaucerian narrator.[14] It has nothing to do with characterization of individual pilgrims, and it is just as entertaining in the Merchant's Tale as elsewhere. The humor increases as this "rude man" a few moments later narrates the action attendant upon January's recovery of his sight:

> . . . on his wyf his thoght was everemo.
> Up to the tree he caste his eyen two,
> And saugh that Damyan his wyf had dressed
> In swich manere it may nat been expressed,
> But if I wolde speke uncurteisly . . . (2359-63)

The delicacy and solicitousness of the speaker is so obviously an affectation, in the light of the rude forthrightness he has just apologized for, that it becomes impossible for us to look with solemnity upon the events he is narrating. Such breaks in the narration provide a level of entertainment outside the events of the tale. The ending, taking into account these posturings of the speaker — which, after all, *are* part of Chaucer's art — is magnificently funny, especially if we can release ourselves from the need to read it as part of a large-scale characterization of a darkly cynical Merchant-narrator.

Structural and stylistic evidence seems to indicate conclusively that there is no single viewpoint governing the narrative. The tale is less a unified presentation than a composite of several narrating attitudes and positions, often mutually contradictory. Each is assumed by the poet in accordance with the demands of the particular situation. I think it is a mistake to decry or to obscure the dis-

---

14 Curtius cites "affected modesty" as one of the established *topoi* of antique rhetoric sustained through the Middle Ages. *European Literature*, pp. 83-85.

continuities that result. If there is no "organic unity" in terms of the character of the Merchant, we should be satisfied with the "inorganic unity" which could compose so many comic attitudes toward lust and marriage into so diverting a tale. Admittedly the total design lacks the balance and carefully adjusted intricacy of the Knight's Tale. And it also lacks the dynamism and economy of the Miller's Tale. But for variety of comic approaches to folly it is matchless. Chaucer has allowed himself an unusual amount of freedom to improvise around the thin but firm and fertile plot of the *senex amans*. However diffuse the tale becomes and however out of balance its parts are with one another, a loose, composite form of unity is maintained. Although the narrative viewpoint is altogether inconsistent, the moral viewpoint remains firm. It is completely unobtrusive, however, and it functions aesthetically rather than didactically; that is, it serves as the poet's silent measure of the comic possibilities inherent in impropriety and incongruity.

SEVEN   THE KNIGHT'S TALE: NOBILITY IN THESEUS' WORLD AND CHAUCER'S ART

Among the Canterbury Tales, the Merchant's Tale represents an extreme of discordant unity. Only the Monk's Tale exceeds it in structural discontinuity, to the extent, indeed, that the Monk's Tale is not really an aggregate of parts at all, but an aggregate of tales. In contrast to these the Knight's Tale displays a high degree of structural consistency. Yet the structure of the tale is still governed by the conventions of Gothic practice, and the achieved unity is a "multiple unity" — an aggregate of individual unities — rather than an organic or "unified" unity.

Following upon the studies of Charles Muscatine and William Frost, we are in little danger of mistaking the essential character of the Knight's Tale.[1] Neither characterization nor plot is its defini-

---

[1] Charles Muscatine, "Form, Texture, and Meaning in Chaucer's *Knight's Tale,*"

tive element. Rather, the tale offers a magnificent representation, primarily in visual and architectonic terms, of a profound and humane philosophical concept. "Order, which characterizes the structure of the poem, is also the heart of its meaning. The society depicted is one in which form is full of significance . . . in which life's pattern is itself a reflection, or better, a reproduction of the order of the universe."[2] Muscatine emphasizes the pervasiveness of symmetrical patterning in the tale, a patterning which dominates not only the characters and events of the fiction but also the rhetorical elements of the narration, which constitute an unusually generous array of descriptions, set speeches, and lyric plaints. The distinction between scene and rhetoric — that is, between content and form — is especially interesting to pursue in the case of the Knight's Tale, for symmetry and formality govern both, and the interplay of the two modes of formalized expression produces a harmony quite unlike the structural anarchy of the Merchant's Tale.

Both in what it says and in how it says it, the Knight's Tale celebrates rationality as the sustaining and shaping force in the lives of individual men, in the social order, and in the cosmic order. Within the fictional world of Athens form defines the chivalric way of life. External to the world of the fiction, formality and deliberate balancing of structural components characterize the mode of narrative presentation.

PMLA, 65:911-929 (1950), adapted for *Chaucer and the French Tradition*, pp. 175-190; William Frost, "An Interpretation of Chaucer's Knight's Tale," *RES*, 25: 289-304 (1949). See, however, Richard Neuse, "The Knight: The First Mover in Chaucer's Human Comedy," *UTQ*, 31:306 (1962): "The geometric design of the *Knight's Tale* functions more as a comic *mechanism* than as a means of expressing a concept of order."

2 Muscatine, *Chaucer and the French*, p. 181. In addition to the order of society and the order of the cosmos, John Halverson has discerned in the tale a third order, that of folk culture: "There are . . . clear echoes in the *Knight's Tale* of ancient ritual and folk customs which insist on and promote the continuity of life and life-giving forces of nature." "Aspects of Order in the Knight's Tale," *SP*, 57:611 (1960).

CHAUCER AND THE SHAPE OF CREATION

Content and Theme: Theseus' Noble World

Though the significance of form in Theseus' world is most brilliantly evident in the lavish ceremoniousness of the tourney, the display of formality is the essence of lesser occasions throughout the tale as well, so much so, indeed, that the idea of form itself becomes a major theme. As an example we shall consider the initial encounter between Palamon and Arcite in the grove, which introduces a sequence of incidents illustrating the efficacy of form in man's confrontation of passion and contingency. This passage also illustrates the depth to which the idea of form permeates the depicted world of the tale.

Having overheard the disguised Arcite's love plaint, and having recognized him as his "mortal foo," Palamon, though enraged, does not leap to pummel Arcite out of hand. Rather, he leaps to address him with an articulate and detailed statement of charges, a statement which, though hurled in passion, manages before delivering the demand for satisfaction to survey all the circumstances behind the encounter and define their moral significance:

> "Arcite, false traytour wikke,
> Now artow hent, that lovest my lady so,
> For whom that I have al this peyne and wo,
> And art my blood, and to my conseil sworn,
> As I ful ofte have told thee heerbiforn,
> And hast byjaped heere duc Theseus,
> And falsly chaunged hast thy name thus!
> I wol be deed, or elles thou shalt dye.
> Thou shalt nat love my lady Emelye,
> But I wol love hire oonly and namo;
> For I am Palamon, thy mortal foo.
> And though that I no wepene have in this place,
> But out of prison am astert by grace,
> I drede noght that outher thow shalt dye,
> Or thow ne shalt nat loven Emelye.
> Chees which thou wolt, for thou shalt nat asterte!" (1580-95)

THE KNIGHT'S TALE

Arcite in his turn is similarly impassioned and similarly restrained. Fiercely he seizes his sword, but not until he has heard Palamon out: "This Arcite, with ful despitous herte, / Whan he hym knew, and hadde his tale herde, / As fiers as leon pulled out his swerd . . ." Arcite, a worthy knight, recognizes the worthiness of his foe, who would do battle for his lady, and therefore offers to forego his own immediate advantage of arms and provide the means for a fair duel to the death on the morrow.

> "Have heer my trouthe, tomorwe I wol nat faille
> Withoute wityng of any oother wight,
> That heere I wol be founden as a knyght,
> And bryngen harneys right ynough for thee;
> And ches the beste, and leef the worste for me.
> And mete and drynke this nyght wol I brynge
> Ynough for thee, and clothes for thy beddynge.
> And if so be that thou my lady wynne,
> And sle me in this wode ther I am inne,
> Thow mayst wel have thy lady as for me." (1610-19)

On both sides, in stately balance, the quality of this confrontation enforces the thematic idea that victory without ceremony would be meaningless. And ceremony means structuring the impulses of passion. Even in the explicit ethic of the tale, love is acknowledged to be exempt from the conventional restraints — "who shal yeve a lovere any lawe?" — and therefore the containment of such awesome forces represents a triumph all the more impressive. The chivalric mode of life is a tense equilibrium between the consciously imposed forms of noble action and the potentially explosive demands of personal passion.

The same quality of stateliness and violence combined characterizes the ensuing single combat:

> Ther nas no good day, ne no saluyng,
> But streight, withouten word or rehersyng,
> Everich of hem heelp for to armen oother

155

As freendly as he were his owene brother;
And after that, with sharpe speres stronge
They foynen ech at oother wonder longe.
Thou myghtest wene that this Palamon
In his fightyng were a wood leon,
And as a crueel tigre was Arcite;
As wilde bores gonne they to smyte,
That frothen whit as foom for ire wood.
Up to the ancle foghte they in hir blood. (1649-60)

Being worthy knights, Palamon and Arcite submit their personal feelings to the controlling forms of chivalric combat. Fighting for a lady, they pursue the highest ideal, and therefore they exhibit, in the forms of ceremony, the noblest restraint.

When Theseus interferes in the bloody combat and transfers the action to a public arena, the result is enhancement of the ceremonial aspects of the conflict and reduction of the drama of personal passions. Also, the emphasis shifts from Palamon and Arcite to Theseus, for the tourney is very much the Duke's spectacle. The shift of emphasis reaffirms the decisive role of Theseus in the tale, the role of agent of the foresight of God and supreme arbiter of the life of Athens. As the apex of authority and the maker of order in his world, Theseus constitutes a majestic public affirmation of the ideals enacted by Palamon and Arcite, both in their loving and in their warring. By elevating the conflict between the knights from a personal death struggle to a public spectacle, with blunted weapons, Theseus generalizes the noble ideal of formality. The energy and enthusiasm of spectators and participants alike and the exuberant atmosphere of the event — embodied in some of Chaucer's most stunning descriptive verse — render the tourney a grandly impressive celebration of the idea of order. All of the details of the year-long preparations contribute to this theme. The arena itself, being circular, is symbolic of perfect order, and its perfection — it is described as the most "noble theatre" in the

THE KNIGHT'S TALE

world — is not only ideal but practical, as the ordinary tourney-goer would soon discover, for "whan a man was set on o degree, / He letted nat his felawe for to see" (1891). The three chapels are decorated in equal degrees of richness, those of Mars and Venus appropriately flanking that of Diana at equal distances. And by Theseus' decree the opposing armies consist of the perfectly rounded number of one hundred knights each.

The chance death of Arcite after his victory threatens to reduce the entire noble spectacle to a mockery, but instead it provides the occasion for the tale's most profound exploration of the idea of order. In recognizing the deadly potency of chance in even the most nobly and scrupulously structured of human affairs, Theseus' "Firste Moevere" speech shows the way to ultimate resolution of the irrationalities of this world. It is fitting, of course, that the agent of cosmic vision should be Theseus. As he orders the noble life of his world, so does he order his world's relationship with the higher, enveloping order of the cosmos. Theseus expounds the classical story of creation and locates man's proper life in submission to the perfect harmony of the universe.

In Theseus' disquisition, as in the *Timaeus* and its long medieval tradition, the deepest meanings for human beings are derived metaphorically from contemplation of the rational structure of the cosmos. The "Firste Moevere" is the limitless dispenser of limitation, who, "with that faire cheyne of love . . . bond / The fyr, the eyr, the water, and the lond / In certeyn boundes, that they may nat flee." Not only the harmony that stabilizes all the elements, but also time, the measure of all movement, is dispensed from eternity by "that same Prince and that Moevere," who

> "Hath stablisshed in this wrecched world adoun
> Certeyne dayes and duracioun
> To al that is engendred in this place,
> Over the whiche day they may nat pace . . ." (2995-98)

CHAUCER AND THE SHAPE OF CREATION

Theseus expresses in traditional Platonic terms the doctrine that these elements, delimited both in substance and in time, are divisions of the wholeness of creation:

> Thanne may men by this ordre wel discerne
> That thilke Moevere stable is and eterne.
> Wel may men knowe, but it be a fool,
> That every part dirryveth from his hool;
> For nature hath nat taken his bigynnyng
> Of no partie or cantel of a thyng,
> But of a thyng that parfit is and stable,
> Descendynge so til it be corrumpable.
> And therfore, of his wise purveiaunce,
> He hath so wel biset his ordinaunce,
> That speces of thynges and progressiouns
> Shullen enduren by successiouns,
> And nat eterne, withouten any lye. (3003-15)

The completeness and perfection of the order of creation enforces inescapably the lesson that "whoso gruccheth ought, he dooth folye, / And rebel is to hym that al may gye."

To observe that Theseus' oration culminates the thematic development of the tale and translates nobility of life into the highest terms of absolute, universal order is to agree essentially with almost all recent interpretations of the poem. Dale Underwood, for example, has ably expounded the Boethian character of the final, hierarchical vision of universal order. He points out that at the "divine level of order" the tale transcends both Theseus and its putative teller the Knight: "The poem is finally, then, the poet's theatre, world, and tale, in which he images the form and principle not only of Fortune and of man but, encompassing and transcending these, the universe of divine order."[3] Though I believe in the validity of this statement, I cannot agree that Underwood's discussion

[3] Dale Underwood, "The First of *The Canterbury Tales*," *ELH*, 26 (1959); reprinted in and here cited from *Discussions of the Canterbury Tales*, ed. C. A. Owen, Jr. (Boston: D. C. Heath and Co., 1961), p. 43.

demonstrates that validity, since this statement concerns the formal structure of the poem, as composed by Chaucer, and Underwood's entire discussion concerns the content of the poem, that is, the form of life in Theseus' world. I stress this matter because it offers an opportunity to clarify a widespread confusion in Chaucer criticism, a confusion both verbal and substantive. When Underwood speaks of the order and the form of the poem he really means the content, for he illustrates by summarizing the order of events. The "principle of order in the form and movement of the poem" is one of "incessant fluctuation," such as the fluctuation between the glory of Theseus' homecoming and the lamentation of the suppliant ladies he encounters, and that between the "joye" and "honour" of the conqueror and the "angwissh" and "wo" of Palamon and Arcite in the conqueror's prison.[4] Chaucer is, of course, responsible for "ups and downs" of this kind in the narrative, but the formal principle of fluctuation observed here defines the imagined world within the fiction, as the precarious order of that world was distinguished for us by Frost and Muscatine. In order to demonstrate how Chaucer the maker encompasses and transcends the form and principle of Fortune and of man — as Underwood asserts he does — we must examine the structure external to the fluctuations of the world depicted. Muscatine showed the way here — though evidently he has been misunderstood — when he spoke of the "tension between the poem's symmetrically ordered structure and the violent ups and downs of the surface narrative."[5] What I wish to do is demonstrate to a fuller extent than Muscatine attempted[6] the ways in which

---

[4] *Discussions of the Canterbury Tales*, p. 38.

[5] *Chaucer and the French*, p. 187. See also Paul G. Ruggiers' sensitive and sound interpretation, *The Art of the Canterbury Tales*, p. 152: "In spite of the readily apparent parallelism and symmetry, the *Knight's Tale* presents a number of stumbling blocks to the new reader, principally in the free admixture of styles, the presence of comic stringencies within passages of considerable solemnity, the adducing of personal attitudes, not found in Boccaccio, which from time to time ruffle the surface tone."

[6] *Chaucer and the French*, pp. 178-183.

CHAUCER AND THE SHAPE OF CREATION

Chaucer's construction of the narrative relates to the ideas of nobility and formality depicted within the world of the tale.

Structure: Chaucer's Noble Art

As we have seen to be the case in other of his narratives, Chaucer here also works as a composer of parts, and the structure of the tale is clearly discernible as a collocation of independently fashioned and purposefully juxtaposed elements.

Pervaded as it is by a serious and seriously treated thematic idea, the Knight's Tale displays little trace of the clashing contrasts and inconsistencies found in the Merchant's Tale. While the latter treats its subject, marriage, in a variety of ways and from a variety of viewpoints, in the Knight's Tale subject, style, and viewpoint reinforce one another at almost all times. Though the narrator occasionally lapses into rustic idiom — even in his most serious efforts Chaucer cannot sustain a perfectly straight face — the tale is a display of chivalric values, seen from a viewpoint which is sympathetic and, for Chaucer, remarkably consistent. Because the parts of the tale partake of an almost unbroken thematic and attitudinal texture, their outlines are less plainly evident than they would otherwise be. But Chaucer makes no effort to conceal the structural seams of the tale.

The four parts into which the tale is divided by Latin rubrics bring into dynamic equipoise the two major elements of chivalric life, love and combat. The first two parts elaborate the experience of noble love for a lady; the second two parts, centering on the tourney, display the noble enterprise of fighting for her. Though in the tale as a whole action is minimal and the narrative character tends toward the static and spectacular rather than the sequential and developmental, there is nevertheless a difference in emphasis between the two halves of the tale in this respect. The second half, though more clamorous and colorful than the first, actually contains

160

less narrative movement since the action is concentrated in the single setting of the arena. And even there we find much more spectacle than action, the contest itself comprising a bare fifty-two lines (2100-51). Being virtually devoid of movement in time and space, the second half of the tale assumes a planimetric character. Around the still center of the tourney descriptive passages are aligned in direct reflection of the balanced forces of the two armies and their accoutrements. In contrast to this richly textured emblem, the first two parts of the tale contain considerable movement among spatially separated protagonists — Palamon, Arcite, Emily, and Theseus. Examination of representative sections from the earlier and later parts of the tale will reveal how Gothic principles of structure impart a common quality of conscious, deliberate stateliness to both the dynamic and the static elements of the tale.

The tale deliberately and meticulously exploits the symmetry inherent in the love triangle. Once the sight of Emily ignites the fire of love in the hearts of Palamon and Arcite, Chaucer devotes almost exactly equal attention to each. This balance is attained at the sacrifice of continuing forward movement of the narrative — a sacrifice which caused Chaucer no apparent pain. The mode of the narration is always to treat the present moment exhaustively and exclusively, without reference to the past or to other focal points in the present. Consequently the narrative moves abruptly from one side to the other, as indicated by the frequently used formula, ". . . lete I now Arcite, / And speke I wol of Palamon a lite" (1449-50). The result is a succession of formalized pairings, in which each step forward is accompanied by one to each side.

At the beginning Chaucer establishes the role and character of Theseus and the atmosphere of victory and melody that surrounds him. Out of the rubble of one of the Duke's chivalric deeds, a deed compounded of power and compassion, Chaucer brings the two young knights to imprisonment, and then he sets the scene for love. The images and the idiom are conventional and lend themselves

161

perfectly to the formalized staging of the decisive amorous event. We are conducted to the event, so to speak, by two separate narrative roads. The first centers on the garden and Emily. It is followed by one which centers on the prison tower and the two knights. First the garden:

> . . . it fil ones, in a morwe of May,
> That Emelye, that fairer was to sene
> Than is the lylie upon his stalke grene,
> And fressher than the May with floures newe . . . (1034-37)
> Er it were day, as was hir wone to do,
> She was arisen and al redy dight;
> For May wole have no slogardie a-nyght. (1040-42)

The lovely Emily, whose coloring competes with the flowers and whose voice competes with the angels, has entered the garden "To doon honour to May," and there we leave her. This jewel-like passage is very clearly delineated, from the opening formula "it fil ones" (1034) to the brief mediating passage (1056-61) which ends it and points us in the direction of the prison tower, the scene of the next section of narrative:

> And as an aungel hevenysshly she soong.
> The grete tour, that was so thikke and stroong,
> Which of the castel was the chief dongeoun,
> (Ther as the knyghtes weren in prisoun
> Of which I tolde yow and tellen shal)
> Was evene joynant to the gardyn wal
> Ther as this Emelye hadde hir pleyynge. (1055-61)

By modern, organicist standards the transition from garden to prison (1055 to 1056) is abrupt and graceless, but measured against Chaucer's general practice the movement here is unusually smooth. The parenthetical reminder — a kind of solicitous afterthought — that this dungeon is the one in which the knights are imprisoned is an unusual effort toward inner continuity.

The next line repeats what has already been made clear, that it is a bright spring morning. Thus, ignoring what has gone before, this formula produces the effect of a new beginning and imparts a formally structured quality to the ensuing account of events in the tower:

> Bright was the sonne and cleer that morwenynge,
> And Palamoun, this woful prisoner,
> As was his wone, by leve of his gayler,
> Was risen and romed in a chambre an heigh . . . (1062-65)

Gradually this scene moves toward contact with the one previously presented: we are told that from the tower Palamon could see the noble city, "and eek the gardyn, full of braunches grene, / Ther as this fresshe Emelye the shene / Was in hire walk . . ." Complete congruence of focus occurs nine lines later when Palamon, having carelessly glanced out the window and cast his eye upon Emily, "bleynte and cride, 'A!'" (1078) This convergence is "prepared" a few lines earlier by an opening formula that imparts to the occurrence a rhetorical setting and formalized status, thus signalizing a new stage in the narration:

> And so bifel, by aventure or cas,
> That thurgh a wyndow, thikke of many a barre
> Of iren greet and square as any sparre,
> He cast his eye upon Emelya,
> And therwithal he bleynte and cried, "A!" (1074-78)

The coming together of knight and lady is not simply an emotional occasion within the fiction, which we experience vicariously and empathetically. It is also an aesthetic occasion entailing a structural impact, which we experience directly. The mode of presentation, in which the converging scenes — the garden and the tower — are rendered independently, produces this twofold release of energy, emerging from the structure as well as the substance of the narrative. Content and form thus work concurrently toward the same end — to represent dramatically and also by structural impact

163

the power of chance in human affairs. Thus the implications of the phrase "by aventure or cas," which ramify the rich philosophical implications of the tale, are generated in the tale's fundamental structural materials.

The *demande d'amour* which concludes Part One is not formulated before the contretemps has been not only dramatized in the fiction but structured in the narrative presentation. As I have said, once the fires of love are ignited, Palamon and Arcite diverge, and to enhance our sense of their moral conflict the narrative structure places them in a series of formally balanced oppositions, culminating eventually in the tourney. The first of these occurs after Arcite has been released from prison and banished. The narrative then presents in sequence two depictions of grieving lovers, equivalent in substance and almost exactly equal in form and extent, though one lover grieves as a prisoner in Athens and the other as a free man in Thebes.

The first begins "How greet a sorwe suffreth now Arcite" (1219) and extends for fifty-five lines. It includes Arcite's bitter gesture to his rival — "O deere cosyn Palamon . . . Thyn is the victorie of this aventure" (1234-35) — and a long lamentation on the vanity of human wishes and the inscrutability "of God or of Fortune."

The second is deliberately poised counter to the first:

> Upon that oother syde Palamon,
> Whan that he wiste Arcite was agon,
> Swich sorwe he maketh that the grete tour
> Resouneth of his youlyng and clamour. (1275-78)

Equally long (fifty-eight lines as against fifty-five), this passage includes a countergesture of ironic capitulation — "Arcita, cosyn myn, / Of al oure strif, God woot, the fruyt is thyn" (1281-82) — and an equivalent oration on the whimsicality of the gods and the injustice and dreadfulness of his own position: "What governance is

164

in this prescience, / That giltelees tormenteth innocence?" This unit of the presentation is terminated unequivocally by the narrator:

> Now wol I stynte of Palamon a lite
> And lete hym in his prisoun stille dwelle,
> And of Arcita forth I wol yow telle. (1334-36)

The fact that he does not tell us forth of Arcite underscores the fact that these formulas are important not for what they say but for what they do, that is, articulate the divisions of the narrative. The narrator simply proceeds at this point to summarize the contretemps and cast it in the playful rhetoric of the *demande d'amour:*[7]

> Yow loveres axe I now this questioun:
> Who hath the worse, Arcite or Palamoun?
> That oon may seen his lady day by day,
> But in prison he moot dwelle alway;
> That oother wher hym list may ride or go,
> But seen his lady shal he nevere mo. (1347-52)

Recent commentary has not failed to appreciate and stress the importance of Theseus as the center of all forces in the world of the tale. It is much less clearly apparent, I believe, how Chaucer's inorganic mode of composition supports this emphasis. Once the love triangle is defined and the rival protagonists separated in space — Arcite banished and Palamon left in the Tower — the lines of the narrative diverge more widely than was the case in Part One, and yet their inevitable course is to converge upon Theseus. The segments of narration are so disposed that this movement toward Theseus occurs in discernibly articulated stages.

Though prefigured in Part One, the cumulative convergence

---

[7] This is an example of the Chaucerian narrator failing to observe the imperatives of his own narration. The resulting humor, emerging from the narrator's failure to distinguish earnest from game, is incongruent with the prevailing viewpoint, which is close to and sympathetic toward the depicted chivalric action. Such clashes of perspective are relatively rare in the Knight's Tale. Both their importance and the importance of their infrequency in this tale will become more fully apparent in the following chapters.

of structural forces upon Theseus begins in Part Two. The prelimi-
nary stage is the chance confrontation of Palamon and Arcite in the
grove. The outcome of this encounter is the appearance of Theseus,
whose path, also by chance, intersects theirs. From the point of view
of narrative composition — that is, from the maker's viewpoint —
these "chance encounters" are, of course, predetermined junctures in
a complex total pattern. Examination of the structural patterns
eventuating in Theseus in Part Two will provide us with an insight
into the total configuration of the tale.

The turn toward Theseus is signaled by the narrator, who steps
forth, early in Part Two, to effect an abrupt shift in the direction of
the narrative. Having recounted Arcite's adventures and his return,
incognito, to Athens, and having faced around to balance against
that an account of Palamon — ". . . lete I now Arcite, / And
speke I wole of Palamon a lite" (1449) — the narrator turns from
his story to himself, and in advertising his inadequacies produces a
typically Chaucerian expedient of structural articulation:[8]

> Who koude ryme in Englyssh proprely
> His martirdom? for sothe it am nat I;
> Therfore I passe as lightly as I may. (1459-61)

The new segment begins with a typical narrative *incipit* and, couch-
ing the account in allusions to the forces of destiny, proceeds to
relate the facts of Palamon's escape from prison:

> It fel that in the seventhe yer, of May
> The thridde nyght, (as olde bookes seyn,
> That al this storie tellen moore pleyn)
> Were it by aventure or destynee —
> As, whan a thyng is shapen, it shal be —
> That soone after the mydnyght Palamoun,

8 It is of incidental interest to note that this self-conscious apology is characteristic of the Chaucerian narrator, as we have observed that figure in *Troilus*, the
Canterbury framework, the Merchant's Tale, and elsewhere, and that it contributes
nothing toward dramatization of a particular Knight-pilgrim-teller.

THE KNIGHT'S TALE

> By helpyng of a freend, brak his prisoun
> And fleeth the citee faste as he may go . . . (1462-69)

The account of Palamon's escape and flight to the forest is contained in a clearly delineated twenty-six-line unit of narration (1462-87). Upon its completion the narrator articulates the transition to Arcite, again in very explicit fashion:

> Now wol I turne to Arcite ageyn,
> That litel wiste how ny that was his care,
> Til that Fortune had broght him in the snare. (1488-90)

Though the ensuing Arcite-segment is some fifty lines longer than the Palamon-segment, the effect is of balance and formalized disposition. The beginning is unmistakably a beginning and imparts to the passage a quality of structural self-sufficiency:

> The bisy larke, messager of day,
> Salueth in hir song the morwe gray,
> And firy Phebus riseth up so bright
> That al the orient laugheth of the light . . . (1491-94)
> And Arcita, that in the court roial
> With Theseus is squier principal,
> Is risen and looketh on the myrie day. (1497-99)

The ensuing narrative brings Arcite — "by aventure or cas" — to the very spot where Palamon lies concealed in the grove. The emphasis upon chance and coincidence of course stresses an important thematic concern of the poem, but we should observe that this emphasis is not simply the result of contrivance of plot and verbal reference to "aventure." It emerges unmistakably from the mode of narrative presentation. As we have noted, the actions of the protagonists are recounted in two separate lines of narrative. Because the two lines of action are so firmly separated, their "chance" convergence at this point in the forest at this particular time produces a powerful impact. The kinetic effect of this structural conjunction

167

lends persuasive support to the important thematic idea that the forces of destiny are potent and inscrutable.

Between the moment of convergence and the actual duel, which culminates this episode, occurs the chivalric challenge and response. Having seen earlier how this passage illustrates the ethical values of Theseus' world, we may note in the present context that it also displays the formal values of Chaucer's art. In keeping with the narrative mode, the verbal confrontation of the two knights is presented as a formalized, balanced collocation of rhetorical units, Palamon's challenge (1574-95) being counterbalanced by Arcite's response of virtually equal length (1596-1619).

The ensuing duel is prefaced by an outburst from the narrator in the form of an apostrophe to Cupid which, in addition to intensifying the emotional atmosphere preparatory to the coming struggle and emphasizing the thematic implications of such a battle for love, also serves to articulate the structural division between two distinct elements of the narrative. The duel is to take place "on the morwe, er it were dayes light" (1629). After suitable preparations by the antagonists and delivery of an epic simile by the narrator, the clash occurs. We have observed earlier that the ceremonial nature of the encounter is of thematic importance. Complementing the deliberation and formality observed by the protagonists, the narrative structure assumes a balanced stateliness which is delicately pictorial, despite the violence of the scene portrayed. Although with respect to plot the important action of Part Two is the convergence of the two knights at this juncture in the narrative, even at this peak of intensity action is subordinate to spectacle, that is, the spectacle of a confrontation in mortal combat. Of the nine lines devoted to the actual combat (1653-61) — even this total is remarkably meager in comparison to the descriptive and figurative rhetoric which precedes it — only two depict action: ". . . they foynen ech at oother wonder longe" (1654) and "Up to the ancle foghte they in hir blood" (1660). The rest is description, scrupulously balanced in reflection

168

of the balance of forces within the fiction. One antagonist is a lion, the other a tiger, and both together are wild boars:

> Thou myghtest wene that this Palamon
> In his fightyng were a wood leon,
> And as a crueel tigre was Arcite;
> As wilde bores gonne they to smyte,
> That frothen whit as foom for ire wood. (1655-59)

The distancing achieved by the phrasing "Thou myghtest wene" enhances the sense of stabilized spectacle and concomitantly diminishes the sense of violent, uncontrolled action. The effect is therefore one of gratification rather than horror, despite the fact that the scene is drenched in blood. We may justly say that the carnage is beautiful, for the scene produces the satisfaction of aesthetic inevitability. It is the result of a convergence of equally strong and equally noble forces, a convergence accomplished through appropriately formal organization of the narrative.

The appearance of Theseus on this scene produces the climax of the first half of the tale in respect to every important poetic element — structure, action, and theme. Structurally it forms the convergence of a third and ultimate line of action upon this crucial spot in the wood, and it is narrated, like the other two, as a separate, parallel event. Intersecting the point where the lines of Palamon and Arcite have already met, it forms a structural nexus which is a high point of complication in the deliberate aesthetic organization of the tale. Yet from the interior viewpoint within the fictional world, the chance appearance of Theseus at this time and place serves a thematic purpose by signaling the ubiquity and inscrutability of destinal forces in the affairs of men.

The narrator accomplishes the transition to Theseus by his customary expedient, viz., simply halting in midstride and announcing the new subject:

> Up to the ancle foghte they in hir blood.
> And in this wise I lete hem fightyng dwelle,
> And forth I wole of Theseus yow telle. (1660-62)

CHAUCER AND THE SHAPE OF CREATION

The importance of the advent of Theseus is emphasized by the formalized structuring of the narrative at this point, for his actual appearance is preceded by a prologue which describes and affirms the power of "the destinee, ministre general, / That executeth in the world over al / The purveiaunce that God hath seyn biforn . . ." (1663-65). Following this ten-line passage on the incapacity of man to comprehend these powers, the thematic relevance is secured, unsubtly, by the narrator's forthright if somewhat ambiguous assertion, "This mene I now by myghty Theseus." Though this line may refer to what follows, namely the account of the Duke's customary manner of doing observance to May, the effect is to link Theseus with destiny, if only by collocation of the two passages. The narrator's earlier stated intention to tell us of Theseus also serves to link the Duke with destiny, the two direct allusions to Theseus thus occurring as prelude and postlude to the disquisition on destiny.

The new segment of action begins as did the other two, with an opening formula of its own, "Cleer was the day" (1683), which is followed by an unusual parenthetical allusion to the earlier narrations, "as I have toold er this." But despite the expressed awareness of an earlier rendering, the opening formula nevertheless appears, launching an independent narration safely on its new course. The Duke is going hunting, and as he is unaware of anything in the wood other than the hart he pursues, so is the narration of his ride unencumbered by any allusion to Palamon and Arcite:

> Cleer was the day, as I have toold er this,
> And Theseus with alle joye and blis,
> With his Ypolita, the faire queene,
> And Emelye, clothed al in grene,
> On huntyng be they riden roially.
> And to the grove that stood ful faste by,
> In which ther was an hert, as men hym tolde,
> Duc Theseus the streighte wey hath holde. (1683-90)

THE KNIGHT'S TALE

The procession of this festive royal company thus proceeds in ironic independence of the parallel scene of fierce single combat. The mode of narration parallels these two scenes and then brings them together in a startling yet satisfying convergence, startling because of the sharp contrast between regal festivity and ferocious battle, satisfying because the lines of action come together with such an inevitable rightness.

Thus for the second time by chance the path of Theseus has crossed that of Palamon and Arcite:

> And whan this duc was come unto the launde,
> Under the sonne he looketh, and anon
> He was war of Arcite and Palamon,
> That foughten breme, as it were bores two. (1696-99)

This encounter is more intense and complicated than the first, following the sack of Thebes, because it is the culmination of three distinct lines of action converging in turn upon a single point. The tripartite structuring of the narration achieves here an elevation of intensity which supports the thematic development of the poem, for the power and majesty of Theseus are now to be fully displayed.

The intervention of Theseus culminates the first half of the tale. In establishing the conditions for the tourney Theseus raises the action to the high plateau of spectacle which constitutes Parts Three and Four of the tale. Here attention is concentrated almost without variation on the single focal point of the arena. Consequently the kind of abrupt movement between spatially separated segments of action is not a conspicuous element of the second half of the tale. This is not to say, however, that the structural mode of the tale changes. Like Dante's "multifoliate rose," the tourney is a comprehensive figure which contains within itself the distinctly structured elements that constitute its wholeness. Balance is the prevailing aesthetic principle, and it is achieved through the deliberate collocation of independently wrought units of description. The elements of structure are as sharply individuated as in the first half of the poem, but spatial compression within the fictional scene results in a more static quality of narrative. The rich overtones of chivalric spectacle radiate from the central point of the tourney and make of the second half of the tale a predominantly visual exposition of the grandeur of love and war. In fact, so richly variegated is the texture of visual and auditory imagery that it almost completely submerges the action. If the interplay of Palamon, Arcite, and Theseus forms only a minimal framework of plot in the first half of the tale, it becomes patently a mere excuse for something else in the second half.

The reader impatient to learn who wins Emily will riffle through to the final lines and will, of course, miss entirely both the substance and the point of the tale. For in its second half the narrative outgrows its protagonists and very nearly outgrows its theme. That is, it moves not only beyond action but also beyond descriptive spectacle to express itself in the abstract terms of pure structure.

Though we can understand the idea of a tourney as an elevation of the action, it is difficult to justify the elaborate description of the arena (which constitutes most of Part Three) as a contribution integral to the enlargement of the action. The difficulty is quite obvious. There is no clear reason why Palamon should be the Knight of Venus and Arcite the Knight of Mars rather than vice versa. And why Emily should pray to Diana is equally obscure, for the action does not depict her as an unwilling (nor for that matter as a willing) object of the amorous contention. It may perhaps be argued that Arcite, having disguised himself and sneaked hypocritically into the service of Theseus, is therefore Martian, but if he is a warrior-lover Palamon is a lover-warrior, and between the two there is little to choose, especially since, as we have seen, all the elements of the narrative — plot, characterization, description — tend to balance the claims of the two upon our judgment.[9]

Parts Three and Four comply with the demands of public spectacle, and therefore the second half of the tale displays an indifference to many of the concerns of the first half. Since the public spectacle is a translation — commanded by Theseus — of the private confrontation of the knights there is a clear enough relationship between the two halves of the tale, but it is a relationship more of congruence than of integration. The distinction is important, I think, because it enables us to see that the two major divisions of the poem quite independently serve the same expressive purpose — to exalt man's capacity for noble action. Palamon and Arcite are lovers who find the noblest form for the expression of their personal passion. In the second half of the tale the Duke, always imminent, emerges from the background and assumes overt control of the realm. He too loves, but impersonally, on a level which is associated with public life and ultimately with the order of the cosmos. Parts Three and Four capitalize the role of Theseus. The tourney and its aftermath display his orderly disposition of the things of his world — physical and moral — and his noble public acquiescence to the things of the world beyond him. The form of the narrative, adhering closely to the form of Theseus' world, is deliberately and grandly structured. The controlling aesthetic pattern emerges, of course, not as classical Athenian but as Chaucerian Gothic.

The arena is a structural marvel, and the description of it is cast in appropriate expository form. The opening lines of Part Three (1881-1917) present a general view of this "noble theatre"

[9] On the vexed matter of the "equalization" of the two knights I concur with Ruggiers, *The Art,* pp. 157-158, and Robert A. Pratt, "Chaucer's Use of the *Teseida*," *PMLA,* 62:598-621 (1947), the latter maintaining (p. 615) that although "Palamon's complete submission to love and Venus perhaps makes him a little more attractive than the more practical and aggressive Arcite . . . Chaucer wisely does not overdo the differentiation between these two . . ." An opposing view is expressed by P. V. D. Shelly, *The Living Chaucer* (Philadelphia, 1940), pp. 135ff.

173

constructed by Theseus — its dimensions, its circular shape, the placement of the chapels of Venus, Mars, and Diana at the eastern and western gates and on the north wall respectively. Then, in thoroughgoing scholastic fashion, the general proposition is analyzed part by part (1918-2088): a forty-eight-line description of the chapel of Venus, followed by eighty-three lines on the chapel of Mars, and then thirty-seven lines on that of Diana. Though irregular in size, these passages are similar in shape, and they are individually delineated through the agency of the narrator, who in typically unsubtle fashion serves this structural purpose. Openly reminding himself of his charge, he at the same time directs us from part to part:

> But yet hadde I foryeten to devyse
> The noble kervyng and the portreitures,
> The shap, the contenaunce, and the figures,
> That weren in thise oratories thre. (1914-17)

The description of the temple of Venus, which comes first, is in two parts. The first and longer part enumerates in figurative terms and personified abstractions the elements of love as they are pictured on the walls:

> The broken slepes, and the sikes colde,
> The sacred teeris, and the waymentynge,
> The firy strokes of the desirynge
> That loves servantz in this lyf enduren;
> The othes that hir covenantz assuren;
> Plesaunce and Hope, Desir, Foolhardynesse,
> Beautee and Youthe, Bauderie, Richesse,
> Charmes and Force, Lesynges, Flaterye,
> Despense, Bisynesse, and Jalousye . . . (1920-28)
> Festes, instrumentz, caroles, daunces,
> Lust and array, and alle the circumstances
> Of love, which that I rekned and rekne shal,
> By ordre weren peynted on the wal . . . (1931-34)

THE KNIGHT'S TALE

Also depicted on the walls are the legends of universally representative lovers, such as Narcissus, Solomon, and Medea, all of whom, regardless of station, were subject to the will of Venus.

The second part of the description turns from the walls of the temple to the statue of the deity, the transition being articulated by the narrator, who concludes the preceding enumeration of legendary lovers with the summary remark, "Suffiseth heere ensamples oon or two, / And though I koude rekene a thousand mo." The statue of Venus is conventionally symbolic of courtly attributes and richly colorful, "glorious for to se." Before her (though she is "fletynge in the large see") stands her son, blind Cupid.

Abruptly the narrator articulates his next presentation, the temple of Mars:

> Why sholde I noght as wel eek telle yow al
> The portreiture that was upon the wal
> Withinne the temple of myghty Mars the rede? (1967-69)

Why should he not, indeed. Not, certainly, because the plot demands it. What does demand the intricately detailed and full-bodied description of the temple of Mars is the aesthetic principle of structural balance. As an independently wrought rhetorical unit this description is justifiable partly on philosophical and moral grounds, war being the obverse of love in the human condition. But its more decisive justification is architectonic and aesthetic. It fulfills, "in measure and number and weight," the implications of the temple of Venus. Being only tangentially relevant to the "plot" of the tale, the two temples together constitute a tribute both to the idea of order and to the human capacity to construct. This is true not only within Theseus' world, where the glory of the edifices is exuberantly declared, but also outside the fiction. In constructing these examples of rhetorical *effictio* Chaucer displays his own powers of composition. If his rhetorical constructs lack the mathematical precision of the elements of a Gothic wall section, they

175

nevertheless adhere to the general features of Gothic structure as we have defined them earlier: clarity of articulation, totality of enumeration, and structural reiteration or homology of parts.

If the description of the Martian temple is longer than that of the temple of Venus (eighty-three lines compared to forty-eight), it nevertheless observes the same form. It is independently structured between limits clearly articulated by the narrator (lines 1967 and 2051); it is similarly divided into two parts — the temple walls (1970-2040) and the statue of the god (2041-2050); and it enumerates exhaustively the constituent elements of the subject. Chaucer's presentation of the dark atmosphere of violence is as complete and as completely right as is his treatment of its antithesis, the bright woe of the Venerian life:

> First on the wal was peynted a forest,
> In which there dwelleth neither man ne best,
> With knotty, knarry, bareyne trees olde,
> Of stubbes sharpe and hidouse to biholde,
> In which ther ran a rumbel in a swough,
> As though a storm sholde bresten every bough.
> And dounward from an hille, under a bente,
> Ther stood the temple of Mars armypotente,
> Wroght al of burned steel, of which the entree
> Was long and streit, and gastly for to see.
> And therout came a rage and swich a veze
> That it made al the gate for to rese.
> The northren lyght in at the dores shoon,
> For wyndowe on the wal ne was ther noon,
> Thurgh which men myghten any light discerne . . . (1975-89)

The figures which inhabit this dark world are visualized with memorable élan, personified abstractions mingling with concrete types:

> Ther saugh I first the derke ymaginyng
> Of Felonye, and al the compassyng;
> The crueel Ire, reed as any gleede;

THE KNIGHT'S TALE

The pykepurs, and eek the pale Drede;
The smylere with the knyf under the cloke;
The shepne brennynge with the blake smoke;
The tresoun of the mordrynge in the bedde;
The open werre, with woundes al bibledde;
Contek, with blody knyf and sharp manace . . . (1995-2003)

Thus, with encyclopedic comprehensiveness Chaucer anatomizes the idea of violence, as he had earlier done with the idea of love.

The temple of Diana triangulates the other two. Its value too is primarily architectonic and only secondarily thematic. In the latter sense it bears a relationship of iconographic correspondence (not of organic integration) with the virtue and purity represented by Emily, in the same way that the temples of Mars and Venus relate to the chivalric contention of Palamon and Arcite. But primarily the effect achieved by the temple of Diana is aesthetic and structural, not "literary." That is, mode and form count more than content or verbal meaning. Again, what matters most is the architectonics of "measure and number and weight." Diana's temple, representing the still point of neutrality, is centered between the contending forces of Mars and Venus and stabilizes the total configuration. The three temples taken together constitute a visual, tangible image. Its elements represent values relevant to the tale, and they are justifiable in terms of the plot. But the image outgrows the requirements of theme and plot and thrusts its own structural and aesthetic values into the center of our consciousness. The satisfaction of Theseus, "that at his grete cost arrayed thus / The temples and the theatre every deel . . ." is an overt expression of what Chaucer must have felt himself over his own feat of rhetorical construction — ". . . Whan it was doon, hym lyked wonder weel" (2090-92). Chaucer's three-part *effictio* is obviously and openly a putting-together, a construction, which capitalizes the structural possibilities of poetic language and places relatively less emphasis upon semantic and metaphorical expression. This configuration displays the Gothic

177

attributes of a rationally ordered, cumulative structure of finite parts. Chaucer's elementary particles are the sharply defined concretizations of abstract qualities — the personifications and concrete universals, such as "the smylere with the knyf under the cloke" — which he composes, in all their individuated perfection, into the aggregative totalities of the three descriptions. These follow one another in narrative succession; each is explicitly articulated and delimited, and each consists of two major divisions (one the walls, one the statue). The three descriptions, because they are analogously structured and contiguous, form a coherent configuration, which we apprehend primarily as an aggregate of visible, tangible elements, sharply individuated and richly diversified, yet ordered according to a discernible pattern of balance. The form of the narrative is very closely allied to that of the projected image. Precise equivalence is of course impossible, a poem not being an arena. And it is not simply the sequentiality of language which inhibits composition according to the structural principles of measure and number and weight. A poet need not concern himself with gravity as an architect must, and unless the poet is as rigorously conscious of quantitative proportions as was Dante — which Chaucer certainly was not — he will be likely to indulge his impulses to a greater extent than three-dimensional construction would permit. But even though some of the elements of Chaucer's configuration are larger, or "weightier," than others, I think analysis makes clear that the Knight's Tale is in a very literal sense a construction, a deliberately composed collocation of finite parts. A unique aspect of the Knight's Tale among other examples of Chaucer's inorganic art is that much of it is *about* construction as well as being itself exemplary of it.

Throughout the Knight's Tale the attitude which governs the presentation is relatively consistent, especially if we consider in comparison a tale like the Merchant's. Even though the two halves

THE KNIGHT'S TALE

of the Knight's Tale are different in so many ways, as we have seen — one part following the feelings and actions of individuals in widely varying spatial relations with one another, the other presenting a public spectacle concentrated in a single focal area — the tonality does not disintegrate as it does in the Merchant's Tale. The Knight's Tale emerges as a sustained exposition of chivalric values, despite occasional Chaucerian lapses from enthusiasm. Among the secular tales the Knight's is one of the least ironic and one of the most consistently sympathetic — even eulogistic — toward the attitudes it portrays. Both major divisions of the tale, despite their generic differences, project the presuppositions of chivalry, in which power and tenderness are complementary, not contradictory, and in which dignity and splendor are essential to both. I think we should recognize further that in addition to the depiction of such values in the world of the fiction, the Knight's Tale asserts in the example of its own structure a celebration of *homo faber,* a tribute to man's capacity to build — to build a social order, ethical conventions, splendid buildings, noble poems — and to endow these works with dignity and grandeur.

For Chaucer, however, the vision of human nobility had its limits. He could no more excise from his consciousness his sense of mortality and fallibility than he could have left *Troilus* without its ending. The Knight's Tale is not univocal in its celebration of human nobility. Chaucer tempers his pride with humility and his enthusiasm with skepticism. His reservations are evident not only in his development of the philosophical implications of the action but also in the occasional inconsistencies in the narrative point of view. These take the form of lapses in the generally serious and sympathetic presentation of the action. Despite the extreme stylization of the action — as in the two knights' love-longing, the single combat, the tourney — the tone rarely departs from the depicted attitude sufficiently to mock it. But there are occasions when the tone lapses toward irony, and in a tale so richly and steadily elaborative of the ideals of noble life I think the importance of these occasions needs to be appraised.

Charles Muscatine, in his primarily stylistic analysis of the tale, has noted that on numerous occasions "the leavening, balancing element of common sense is signalized . . . by a lapse of the high style and the introduction of colloquialism."[10] Thus a speech of Theseus (1785-1825), a eulogy of love, delivered in the high style, is leavened by such humorous lapses into low style as, "She woot namoore of al this hoote fare, / By God, than woot a cokkow or an hare!" Muscatine is careful to point out that the effect of this passage is not to satirize or undermine the elevated sentiment of the speech. Neither, I think, does it undermine our sense of the elevated character of Duke Theseus. The reason is that the character never does "come alive" sufficiently to emerge from the matrix of characteristically Chaucerian language. The "meaning" of Theseus is conveyed in the constructed, inorganic quality of the character, which is a vehicle for actions and statements expressive of chivalric idealism. Consequently Theseus' language is Chaucer's language, in contrast to the language of an organically conceived character in modern fiction, whose existence depends upon the illusion that he is alive and therefore independent of the mind and language of the author. Stylistic inconsistencies and "lapses" of this kind are characteristic of Chaucer in varying degrees in all the tales. It is the language of his art, differentiated only from the language of his religion, as we have seen in the ending of *Troilus,* where stylistic mixtures and virtuoso variations of tonality are subsumed in the language of piety. Thus even into the most aristocratic tale of the Canterbury group, Chaucerian lapses find their way.

Though the narrator is generally very close in sentiment and style to the nobility and excellence he portrays in Theseus' world, he

10 *Chaucer and the French,* p. 185.

too reveals the Chaucerian mixture of the high and the low. The leavening which Muscatine observes to be part of the balance of attitudes in this very balanced tale is really part of the Chaucerian outlook, which is present even in tales that are not thematically and structurally concerned with order and balance to the extent that the Knight's Tale is. But even in this prolonged celebration of ceremony in love, war, and art Chaucer cannot entirely forego equivocation, and this not only in the language of the characters but also in that of the narrator. It is evident in those moments when the narrator loses touch with his matter, which he does relatively infrequently in this tale. But always the effect, arising from the incongruous intrusion of rusticity upon nobility, is humorous. For example, after describing sympathetically Arcite's love rites in the grove, the narrator reaches into the barnyard for a meaningful metaphor:

> Whan that Arcite hadde romed al his fille,
> And songen al the roundel lustily,
> Into a studie he fil sodeynly,
> As doon thise loveres in hir queynte geres,
> Now in the crope, now doun in the breres,
> Now up, now doun, as boket in a welle. (1528-33)

Chaucer's indifference to consistency of tonality in the presentation of this serious tale of splendor and mortality has nothing to do with characterization of a particular Knight-teller. This is the voice of Chaucer the pilgrim of the Canterbury frame, Chaucer the narrator of *Troilus,* Chaucer the dreamer of the vision poems. In the context of the Knight's Tale this voice does not assume comparable prominence, since departures from the style and sentiment of chivalry are rare.

The most conspicuous of these departures occurs near the end of the tale, in a context so incongruous that the effect is unusually bizarre, even for so inveterate a mixer of styles and outlooks as Chaucer. I mean the description of Arcite's funeral pyre, a fifty-three-line comedy of rhetorical manners set between the two most

solemn events of this ceremonious tale, the death of Arcite and
Theseus' closing oration.

Arcite's funeral is the final ceremony of the poem, and Theseus
produces it with fitting grandeur:

> Duc Theseus, with al his bisy cure,
> Caste now wher that the sepulture
> Of goode Arcite may best ymaked be,
> And eek moost honurable in his degree. (2853-56)

The colors, like the atmosphere, have darkened for this last solemn
ritual. The procession of mourners is scrupulously described in a
passage of sustained solemnity (2882-2912), which begins, "Tho
cam this woful Theban Palamoun," includes Emily, "The rewe-
fulleste of al the compaignye," and the bearers of the bier: "The
nobleste of the Grekes that ther were / Upon hir shuldres caryeden
the beere, / With slakke paas, and eyen rede and wete . . ."

In keeping with the event depicted, the narrator maintains this
solemn tone as he proceeds to describe the magnificent funeral pyre.
But in the fifth line of this description, italicized here, the comedy
begins:

> Heigh labour and ful greet apparaillynge
> Was at the service and the fyr-makynge,
> That with his grene top the hevene raughte;
> And twenty fadme of brede the armes straughte —
> *This is to seyn, the bowes weren so brode.* (2913-17)

The labor of style is apparently too demanding. The narrator descends abruptly from the height of his eloquence to explain his
metaphor in plain English. This line, clashing with the prevailing
mood of noble solemnity, signals a shift of focus from the funeral
scene of the fiction to the incongruously comic scene of the presentation, in which the narrator is struggling at cross-purposes with himself both to condense his description and to tell us what he is leaving
out:

But how the fyr was maked upon highte,
Ne eek the names that the trees highte,
As ook, firre, birch, aspe, alder, holm, popler,
Wylugh, elm, plane, assh, box, chasteyn, lynde, laurer,
Mapul, thorn, bech, hasel, ew, whippeltree, —
How they weren feld, shal nat be toold for me;
Ne hou the goddes ronnen up and doun,
Disherited of hire habitacioun,
In which they woneden in reste and pees,
Nymphes, fawnes and amadrides;
Ne hou the beestes and the briddes . . . (2919-29)
Ne how the ground . . . (2931)
Ne how the fyr . . . (2933)

Chaucer has here entered upon a tour de force of rhetorical play. The fifty-three-line description of the pyre is a veritable symphony of "ne how," in which the negative formula appears sixteen times, each time introducing the positive enumeration it purports to obviate. The joke is not on Chaucer but on his art; more directly it is on his narrator, whose perceptions are not quite acute enough to recognize the discrepancy between intention and act. The humor of the passage, together with the tonal discontinuity between the narrator's situation and that of the fictional characters, secures the Chaucerian viewpoint, from which we now look *at* the narrator rather than with him. This kind of focal shift is familiar in Chaucer. As in *Troilus,* it assures the essential clarity of vertical articulation, which complements the equally clear articulation of narrative sequence. In the present instance, as elsewhere, centering our attention on the narrator serves to emphasize the procedures of construction at the expense of fictional illusion. That Chaucer could so freely indulge his sense of structure suggests that for him the comedy of limitation is at least as profound as the seriousness of unlimited fictional illusion. Even when the fiction celebrates the noblest human achievements, as in the Knight's Tale, Chaucer cannot forbear to recognize its limitations. Such disengagements, especially when they are as discordant as the depiction of the funeral pyre, serve to remind us that Chaucer is not "expressing" or "rendering" experience in the fashion of modern fiction. Rather he is describing or expounding. The difference is distance. Chaucer insists upon the option to withdraw at any time to the actuality from which he shapes his fictional creation.

In the present instance the return to the fiction provides the occasion for a discourse on one of the most serious of Chaucerian themes, the order of Creation. Everything about Theseus' oration on the First Mover attests to the high value Chaucer places upon it — the fact that it is given to Theseus, the maker of order in his world, the length of the speech and its placement as the culmination of the action, the unmitigated seriousness. But despite its effectiveness, this celebrated disquisition on first and last things is less convincing as a testimony to the possibilities and limitations of mortality than is Chaucer's own practice as a maker and breaker of illusion in the Knight's Tale.

EIGHT   THE MILLER'S TALE:
LOW THEME AND HIGH ART

Chaucer has often been praised for his encyclopedic command of both literary genres and social types. What has often been said in moral extenuation of his impartial depiction of the broad spectrum of mankind applies also to his accomplishment in diverse genres: each is excellent of its kind. The bourgeoisie and its appropriate literary genres are no less dear to Chaucer than the nobility and its attendant forms of expression. Chaucer's literary professionalism, in conjunction with his wide social perspective, allows him easy entry into both the noble world of romance and the coarse world of fabliau. He can represent with impeccable propriety the manners and morals of each. But in praising Chaucer's "negative capability" and in recognizing the range of his spectrum we should observe certain critical precautions. The posture which Chaucer assumes in

185

relation to the "Human Comedy" is fundamentally different from that of Balzac or John Livingston Lowes. Writing within a mimetic tradition that posits a distinct gap — and hence a margin for artifice — between artist and subject, Chaucer is not a detached sensibility vibrating freely to the diverse impulses of life all around him. What is more important, he does not pretend to be — except where it suits his purpose so to pretend. We have examined some of these pretenses, as in the Prologue to the Miller's Tale, where Chaucer would have us believe that he is simply reporting, unedited, the churlish tale of the churlish Miller as that worthy expressed himself on the Canterbury road. The comedy is effective because it appeals to a basic assumption of mimetic tradition, namely, that between art and life a separation exists. The reader who is duped into forgetting this and into seeing distinction as fusion, game as earnest, is a fit subject for ridicule. When the mimetic assumption loses its hold — as in modern literature and much modern criticism — it must be imaginatively reinstituted by the critical reader if mimetic art is to be understood on its own terms and not on those of another art.

In observing how brilliantly the Miller's Tale contrasts with the Knight's and how sympathetically and without prejudice Chaucer depicts the undignified and ignoble world of the Miller we should remain aware that in both cases Chaucer is producing an illusion. He is doing this as an artist, not as an interviewer of varieties of citizen. As the stylistic studies of Muscatine and others have emphasized, the language of Chaucer's fabliaux is not the language of the barnyard; it is the "low style" in a long tradition of cultivated rhetoric. The fabliau as Chaucer shapes it bears the quality of his artistry as clearly as does the romance. Chaucer absorbs the popular tale into the aesthetic tradition in which he as an artist participates, and thus we find the Miller's Tale to be as different from the tale of Heile of Bersele[1] as the Knight's Tale is from *Sir Degaré*. And we find that

---

[1] See *Sources and Analogues of Chaucer's Canterbury Tales,* ed. W. F. Bryan and Germaine Dempster (New York, 1953), p. 112.

THE MILLER'S TALE

it implies an audience as alert to literary sophistication as is the audience implied by the Knight's Tale. To push the comparison with popular tale and popular romance a bit further, we may note that the measure of the artistic triviality of works such as *Sir Degaré* or even *Havelok the Dane* is their casualness, their indifference to all but the simplest elements of literary substance. The point is that high genre does not certify art and low genre does not preclude it. In approaching the Miller's Tale I think we can pass beyond comparative evaluation of romance and fabliau, nobility and bourgeoisie, to considerations of the aesthetic character of the tale.

In structural and architectonic terms the Miller's Tale is not so different from the Knight's Tale as considerations of genre, imagery, and theme would lead us to believe. Whereas the setting and characters of the Knight's Tale provide the basis for eulogistic display of an aristocratic ethic and searching commentary on its philosophical limitations, the elements of the Miller's Tale are peculiarly neutral. They do not advance the vision of a way of life, either noble or corrupt, and the moral commentary of the closing lines — "Thus swyved was this carpenteris wyf," etc. — does not pretend to take its subject seriously.[2] Whereas the Knight's Tale is based on a serious idealism, the Miller's Tale is based on a couple of old jokes. Thematically barren and morally neutral, the Miller's Tale is an example of inorganic narrative in a relatively "pure" form. What matters is not the ethical value of a resplendent setting, not the moral value of perseverance through painful, extended deprivation, not the intellectual and spiritual value of a rationale of life and death — what matters is simply the art, the exultation in a master's making. This is not to imply that action is all. The action of the Miller's Tale is embellished by deft and masterful character-

[2] D. W. Robertson, Jr., *A Preface to Chaucer,* pp. 385-386, differs sharply, maintaining that these lines represent a "purification" effected by the false flood in the tale, just as the original flood purified the world. Though Robertson acknowledges the humor of the tale, his emphasis here as elsewhere is upon serious theological implications, as he sees them.

izations, by the Chaucerian zest for sensory perception, by artful handling of conversational idiom, by a refined, playful sense of irony, both verbal and situational. The action itself, however, is central, and its prominence is enhanced by the compression which a nonthematic narrative makes possible. Moreover, the action is superbly artful in itself and in this respect is far removed from the simple sequentiality and the crude rough-and-tumble narration of the typical fabliau or popular tale.

A generation ago E. M. W. Tillyard tucked into his general critical study *Poetry Direct and Oblique* a just and illuminating appraisal of the Miller's Tale. At the time it did not make a noticeable impact upon scholars particularly interested in Chaucer, perhaps because it did not come to their notice but more likely, I believe, because it did not accord with the prevailing view among Chaucerians that Chaucer's particular virtues were dramatic and psychological. A recent reprinting of Tillyard's commentary in a setting more readily accessible to students of Chaucer[3] bodes well for a renewed understanding of the fundamentals of Chaucer's narrative art.

Tillyard emphasizes the capability of plot to convey abstract, aesthetic meaning. Though he does not deny the contributory importance of characterization in making the plot substantial, Tillyard separates the two in a manner that may strike the organically oriented critic as overly simple. But medieval tradition, as I have tried to show, supports such an inorganic interpretation. When action is seen to be separable from theme, language, and character — as form in inorganic art is separable from content — the value and meaning of plot must be sought in nonrepresentational and nonmetaphorical terms. Thus Tillyard points out that the abstract qualities of the plot — its shape, rhythm, motion — carry the tale beyond the normative implications of comedy: ". . . the plot of *The Miller's Tale* acquires an abstract significance analogous to that

---

[3] *Discussions of the Canterbury Tales*, ed. Charles A. Owen, Jr.

THE MILLER'S TALE

of good music or of the best Byzantine mosaics. And when Chaucer delivers his master-stroke, bringing back the carpenter into the story through Nicholas's yelling for water, he gets beyond the social bounds of comedy and impels the reader's mind to exult and to expand as it does in enjoying the very greatest art."[4] Seen in this light the action of the tale can be appraised on aesthetic rather than on moral or psychological grounds.

The sudden re-entry of the axe-wielding carpenter upon the scene of action is the climactic moment in the narrative. I think Tillyard's appraisal of the reader's experience of mental exultation at this moment is not an exaggeration, and the musical analogy is just. The tale is comparable to a fugue in that the entry of the carpenter, securing the climax, is like the entry of the fugue subject at the high point of complication: we know almost unconsciously that it is hovering there throughout the development, just beyond the edges of our awareness, yet its bold entry is both a surprise and a satisfaction. The art lies in timing and proportion.

If in *Troilus* and the Knight's Tale the imperatives of romance and moral truth eventuate in prolixity, display, and leisurely exposition, Chaucer proves in the Miller's Tale that he is a master of compressed narration and controlled explosion. An unerring sense of timing and proportion assures the success of the climax and therefore of the tale as a whole. Virtues of this kind are best measured in quantitative terms, for the impact of the Miller's Tale comes from the movement of weighted materials through time and space. The climax thrills us because it has been delayed in time until all the conditions are right for it; and its agent, the carpenter, has been removed in space from the area of our attention so that his re-entry conveys the energy of movement and palpable impact.

In concentrating on the quantitative elements of the tale I do not wish to imply that qualitative considerations are irrelevant, but

[4] *Discussions of the Canterbury Tales,* p. 48.

only that they subserve the action and are limited to that function. For all its similarities to counterpoint the tale is not music. Its elements are characters, and the quality of these characters contributes enormously to the effect of the tale. Indeed we must begin with the characters, as the tale itself does.

The tale divides readily into sections which are signalled either by the familiar formulas of transition or by abrupt change of scene. But before the action begins the characters — all except Absolon — are introduced. Their presentation constitutes a distinctly structured preamble to the action. Nicholas, John, and Alison appear as a sequence of portraits, each superbly definitive. The quality of each figure is of course totally germane to the action; in fact, the nature of the action is readily inferred from the portraits: "Hende" Nicholas, this clerk both "sweet" and learned, who knows of "deerne love . . . and of solas"; the old carpenter, rude of wit, newly married to a young wife; and Alison, incomparable in her natural freshness and animal vigor. Plainly the action will be to rearrange the presented sequence — clerk–husband–wife — so that the mean is lifted out and the extremes come together. But this remains an implication, however patent, and the mode of the narration is simply to present three characters prior to setting them into temporal and spatial relations. The presentation of characters entails the first eighty-three lines of the tale. Immediately following upon the description of Alison, the transition from preamble to action is abrupt and complete:

> Now sire, and eft, sire, so bifel the cas,
> That on a day this hende Nicholas
> Fil with this yonge wyf to rage and pleye,
> Whil that hir housbonde was at Oseneye . . . (3271-74)

The mode of relationship between preamble and action exemplifies the coordinateness which is characteristic of inorganic art in general but is particularly important in the Miller's Tale. These

THE MILLER'S TALE

two sections of the narrative are juxtaposed as coordinate elements, each separate and possessed of structural integrity, just as in the preamble the three portraits stand as separate, coordinate entities. When, somewhat later, Absolon is introduced, it is in similar fashion. The narrative which had followed Alison to church is suspended in favor of a self-contained, twenty-six-line portrait of this witless, cavorting dandy (3312-38). The stop-and-go mode of narration assures that action and descriptive characterization maintain independent, coordinate status. In passing it should be noted too that the introduction of Absolon effects an abrupt shift in the mode of narration from sequential to dilatory; the mixture of course modifies the headlong quality characteristic of fabliau and popular narrative in general and brings the tale more in line with the expository technique we have found to be characteristic of Chaucer's art. The sharp delineation between action and description is plainly evidenced in the rhetorical outlines of Absolon's portrait, which begins with the initiatory lines "Now was ther of that chirche a parissh clerk, / The which that was ycleped Absolon" and ends with the conclusive couplet "But sooth to seyn, he was somdeel squaymous / Of fartyng, and of speech daungerous." With the succeeding line the action abruptly resumes, now containing Absolon and proceeding to bring him into contact with Alison:

> This Absolon, that jolif was and gay,
> Gooth with a sencer on the haliday,
> Sensynge the wyves of the parisshe faste;
> And many a lovely look on hem he caste,
> And namely on this carpenteris wyf. (3339-43)

This is the way contacts are made in inorganic narrative. As we noted in the Knight's Tale and elsewhere, lines of action are independently developed and then guided, by an exterior logic, into convergence. Absolon's entry into the tale produces a second three-part combination — Absolon–Nicholas–Alison — which dances an

191

independent counterpoint to that of Nicholas–John–Alison. Here, too, the effort is to eliminate the mean and thus allow the extremes to come together, but where Nicholas succeeds in removing the carpenter Absolon fails to remove Nicholas.

The interplay of these two triangles constitutes much of the art of the tale. We see that Nicholas succeeds — at least in his immediate aim — because he is clever and patient while Absolon is neither. Nicholas, in fact, is an artist, an architect of intrigue. The contrast between the extravagant architectonics of his strategy and the easy availability and meager value of his goal is very amusing. We are never completely unaware of this comic incongruity as we follow Chaucer's detailed and serious attentiveness to the working out of Nicholas' elaborate plan. As the three climb into their tubs we find ourselves on the brink of comic release. But the long process is not to be peremptorily resolved. This line of action, along with the carpenter, is left hanging as the narrative turns away to follow Alison and Nicholas back down the ladder and to tell of their "bisyness of myrthe and of solas," which lasted through the night.

Against this two-part segment of the action — the carpenter snoring in the rafters, Nicholas and Alison playing in the bed — the narrative of Absolon is abruptly and paratactically juxtaposed, without so much as a "meanwhile." There is an overlap in time, for the narrative of Absolon begins on the morning of the day which on the other track is already over. But this retrogression is not conducted in the form of a controlled flashback; rather it is a separate rendering, in a different spatial setting, of time already accounted for. Again the new line of action begins abruptly, punctuated by the initiatory demonstrative:

> This parissh clerk, this amorous Absolon,
> That is for love alwey so wo bigon,
> Upon the Monday was at Oseneye
> With compaignye, hym to disporte and pleye . . . (3657-60)

THE MILLER'S TALE

The intersection of the two triangles of lovers occurs with a delightful jolt, which Chaucer delicately and vividly attenuates. In the scene at the window, the impact of the two lines of action is developed and nurtured until by artistic fission it ignites the dormant third line of action and sets off the ultimate explosion.

The scene at Alison's window displays the narrative mode of the whole tale in compressed, microcosmic form. It consists of a sequence of coordinate rhetorical units. The loci of the action they convey shift continually between outside the window, inside the bedroom, and away from the house altogether (as Absolon deals with the blacksmith), and therefore the movement of the narrative is spasmodic and clangorous rather than smooth and continuous. One moment does not prepare for the next and flow smoothly into it. Abruptness and discontinuity of action are the essential qualities of the narration in this scene, as in the tale as a whole. For example, the effectiveness of that marvelous moment when Alison slams the window shut results from the abruptness with which the line occurs in relation to what precedes. Up to that point we have been made very much aware of the window as a firm demarcation between Absolon on the outside, pleading to his "lemman," and Alison and Nicholas on the inside. The narrative mode has supported the comedy by abruptly juxtaposing, without comment, the honeyed tonality of Absolon's fey and artificial love speech and Alison's "Go fro the wyndow, Jakke fool" (3708). And it has further coordinated and opposed the inside and the outside by a series of quick exchanges as Alison speaks independently first with Absolon and then with Nicholas. Immediately preceding the slam and giggle the narrative settles on Absolon, outside. Here Chaucer abruptly slows down the pace by pausing to clarify the visual and tactile details of the scene, even to the point of a scene-setting double metaphor for the darkness of the night. The impression conveyed is of an independent narration, centering on Absolon, from whose point of view we see and feel the action. The startling effect of the last two lines in the excerpt below results from the abrupt and total switch from the established setting and point of view:

> This Absolon gan wype his mouth ful drie.
> Derk was the nyght as pich, or as the cole,
> And at the wyndow out she putte hir hole,
> And Absolon, hym fil no bet ne wers,
> But with his mouth he kiste hir naked ers
> Ful savourly, er he were war of this.
> Abak he stirte, and thoughte it was amys,
> For wel he wiste a womman hath no berd.
> He felte a thyng al rough and long yherd,
> And seyde, "Fy! allas! what have I do?"
>   "Tehee!" quod she, and clapte the wyndow to,
> And Absolon gooth forth a sory pas. (3730-41)

Suddenly — with "Tehee!" — we are on the other side of the window. The absence of syntactical connectives between the two opposing passages produces the sense of a leap rather than a flow. The movement would be less violent — and less effective — if our attention had not been so totally absorbed and stabilized in the Absolon-section.

As the tale approaches its climax the tempo and number of such shifts of focus increase rapidly. On three closely consecutive occasions leading up to the cry of "Water!" Chaucer exploits the possibilities of coordinate collocation to dazzling effect. So complete is his control that on each occasion he compresses powerful opposing forces to the explosive pinprick of a single rhyme-word. The first of these occurs as Absolon, hot poker in hand, purrs outside the window:

>   . . . "God woot, my sweete leef,
> I am thyn Absolon, my deerelyng.
> Of gold," quod he, "I have thee broght a ryng.
> My mooder yaf it me, so God me save;

THE MILLER'S TALE

> Ful fyn it is, and therto wel ygrave.
> This wol I yeve thee, if thou me kisse."
>   This Nicholas was risen for to pisse,
> And thoughte he wolde amenden al the jape. (3792-99)

The electrifying effect of this rhyme is due not simply to the extreme semantic antipathy between the two words but to the suddenness with which this antipathy is invoked and the total contextual contrast borne by the two words. This stark collocation is possible within the mode of Chaucer's art. Abruptly we find ourselves on the other side of the window with the unsubordinated, initiatory phrase "This Nicholas was risen . . ." and as we complete the line the rhyme hurls us back into comic awareness of the scene we have left. The placement of the rhyme makes a difference too, for if it occurred at the end of one narrative unit rather than between two the effect would have been simply to conclude. As it is, two distinct units are bound together by rhyme sound and propelled violently apart by semantics and narrative structure.

The second instance occurs a few lines later, as Absolon, in the darkness, seeks bearings for the accurate thrust of his poker:

> "Spek, sweet bryd, I noot nat where thou art."
>   This Nicholas anon leet fle a fart . . . (3805-06)

Again completeness of structural separation of the two narrative focal points assures the effect, and its comic character is immeasurably enhanced by the nature and the placement of the rhyme.

The third instance follows rapidly. It culminates in Nicholas's cry for water, which precipitates the climax. The rhyme of herte / sterte in the passage quoted below is semantically not so startling as kisse/pisse and art/fart, but it carries such a tremendous load of structural weight that the impact is overwhelming, for it brings the long gone and almost forgotten carpenter back upon the scene and with him the large segment of the narrative that had been

peremptorily suspended and left dangling. The climactic effect of
the husband's return depends upon our prior and complete involvement in the narrative of the scalded Nicholas:

> Of gooth the skyn an hande-brede aboute,
> The hoote kultour brende so his toute,
> And for the smert he wende for to dye.
> As he were wood, for wo he gan to crye,
> "Help! water! water! help, for Goddes herte!"
> This carpenter out of his slomber sterte,
> And herde oon crien "water" as he were wood,
> And thoughte, "Allas, now comth Nowelis flood!" (3811-18)

The structural separation of the Nicholas unit and the carpenter
unit is reinforced by the sudden and complete shift of tone, which
is itself an attribute of the complete shift of viewpoint. The quiet,
bland tonality of "This carpenter out of his slomber sterte," though
it comes as a sudden contrast, is perfectly appropriate in the context
it introduces. One moment we are with the wildly prancing
Nicholas, the next with the slumbering John. But adding to the
effect of the shift and contrast is the sudden, vivid renewal of our
awareness of John's suspended presence.

The rhyme on "sterte" yokes the two opposing units together,
but even more powerfully propels them apart and drives the narrative forward. We hear the cry of "water!" from John's point of view,
through the veils of slumber. The sudden, syntactically unprepared
shift culminates the progressively increasing turbulence of the narrative up to this point. The movement from Nicholas to John —
from downstairs to upstairs now, rather than from outside to
inside — is the final shift of viewpoint because the disparate parts
of the narrative now fall marvelously together, converging with
the plummeting carpenter at the feet of Alison and Nicholas. The
rest is noise.

A kind of miracle has been accomplished, but it is primarily
an aesthetic achievement, not a moral one, and given the terms of

the tale, animadversions on the justness of the outcome are relevant only to the degree that the jingling moralization implies, and it implies very little:

> Thus swyved was this carpenteris wyf,
> For al his kepyng and his jalousye;
> And Absolon hath kist hir nether ye;
> And Nicholas is scalded in the towte.
> This tale is doon, and God save al the rowte! (3850-54)

NINE THE CLERK'S TALE: THE LIMITS OF DISCONTINUITY

In the Clerk's Tale Chaucer founders dangerously on one of the besetting problems of inorganic narrative — the maintenance of continuity and of a minimum degree of integration among individuated structural elements. The Clerk's Tale does not display the kind of continuous discontinuity found in the Merchant's Tale, but it attempts to negotiate some treacherous leaps and turns, and not always with success. Thinly textured and relatively unequivocal as it is, the Clerk's Tale plainly displays its broken back; the break occurs between Parts II and III, when the realistic premises of the tale are suddenly rescinded and the tale turns into something not simply surprising but completely inconsistent with its own established framework.

Despite a brave and colorful effort, I think James Sledd has failed to unify the Clerk's Tale, though he did succeed in releasing it from the grip of the drama theory, thereby restoring its status as a literary entity rather than an accessory to a thesis about marriage.[1] Though the earlier critics were carried away by Kittredge's zeal for dramatic linkage with the "marriage group," their awareness of a fundamental discontinuity in the tale was sound. Sledd is right in challenging Lounsbury's reasons for being morally revolted by monstrous Walter and mousy Griselda, but he is wrong in presuming that because realistic assumptions — either modern *or* medieval — are inappropriate the tale is therefore unified according to its own literary assumptions. The fact is that the tale rests upon two contradictory sets of assumptions, realistic *and* symbolic. The transformation of Walter from a "real" man to a "monster" is total — and hence incredible. (The fact that the same transformation occurs in the folk sources and in Petrarch as well as in Chaucer is interesting but not relevant to the critical problem.) Sledd denies that a total transformation occurs: ". . . the first two parts of the *Clerk's Tale* present the characters of Walter and Griselda and relate them one to the other in such a way that when later the element of the marvelous is introduced, we are receptive to it."[2] Sledd offers very little textual support for this assertion and for the opinion that "God's grace, our knowledge of Walter's secret pity and repentance, and the narrator's broad hints that all may yet be well, combine to take the edge off Griselda's sufferings and to assure us that Walter is not so ruthless as she might believe . . ."[3] If anything, our knowledge of Walter's "secret pity and repentance" — which is very meager knowledge at that — only adds to our sense of the monstrousness of his deed, that is, to submit his wife to twelve years of grief even though he is penitent all the while. Nor does it relieve

[1] James Sledd, *"The Clerk's Tale:* The Monsters and the Critics," *MP*, 51: 73-82 (1953), reprinted in and cited from *Chaucer: Modern Essays in Criticism*, ed. E. Wagenknecht (New York: Oxford University Press, 1959).

[2] Sledd, p. 235.

[3] Sledd, p. 237.

the monstrosity in this love that the scene in which Griselda's son is taken from her "is deliberately left undeveloped." That we are promptly told on this occasion that "al fil for the beste" does not affect the fictional situation at all.

The adventures of Griselda are recounted with the simplicity of a saint's life, and their substance is the cruelty wrought upon her and the suffering she endures. To try to reduce the depth of her suffering seems perverse, and the only reason some critics are tempted to do so is that such an interpretation offers the only way to reconcile Walter's cruelty with his compassion. The first one-third of the tale unequivocally presents Walter as a virtuous, compassionate, rational, likable young nobleman; if the rest of the tale is to be read in accordance with these premises it must be "interpreted" to mean other than what it says, for it says that Walter is a monster. Such a willful "interpretation" immediately suggests the alternative of reading the latter portions as they are and "reinterpreting" Parts I and II to mean that Walter is not *really* a virtuous, compassionate young man. Such arbitrary procedures lead to critical chaos. The only viable alternative is to read both sections as they are, whether we approve of discontinuities or not, and try to reach an understanding of the aesthetic facts. The Man of Law's Tale or the typical saint's life presents no such difficulty, for in them evil is never presented as good unless some form of hypocrisy — i.e., evil — is plainly intended. For Sledd the need to show that Walter is not so ruthless as we and Griselda might believe arises from the *a priori* thesis that the tale has structural unity, that signs of Walter's goodness and penitence are visible in the long process of his cruelty, that signs of an eventual happy ending dilute the effect of Griselda's suffering, that, in sum, "we really cannot worry too much about the children, or Griselda, or the Pope himself." It is quite true that we cannot worry too much about Griselda, but for reasons that have nothing to do with structural unity, reasons which in fact spring from the demonstrable disunity of the tale. For the most part we do not feel deeply for Griselda as a suffering woman; we behold Griselda as a symbol of virtue under torment. We do not know her well enough or deeply enough to "worry" about her or her children. She is a one-dimensional figure whose purpose is to display heroic endurance in the face of undeserved and irrational cruelty. But the agent of her torment is not God or Fortune or any nonrational force. It is the Marquis Walter, the good man, whom we *do* know well because he has been presented in a realistic social context; he is defined as the center of a society's real concern about its ruler and his succession, and he participates in reasoned dialogue concerning the delimited human problem of marriage.

B. H. Bronson has said, in a discussion which I have found very enlightening, that Walter's too too solid flesh is the rock which splits the effort to turn the story into a religious parable.[4] The truth of this observation emphasizes the fact that at its center the Clerk's Tale is a discordant mixture of a man and a symbol, each bearing its own context of literary and aesthetic premises and each making its own kind of demands upon imaginative credibility. We are faced with a situation similar to that in the Merchant's Tale. As in that tale, each context is fully realized in itself and admits none of the compromises which a principle of subordination would effect. We have seen that in the Knight's Tale and the Miller's such collocations cause a minimum of disturbance because the co-ordinated elements are of similar content and texture. But in the Clerk's Tale, as in the Merchant's, the clash is noticeable indeed, exploding into pathos in one and humor in the other.

The fact that Walter proves after all *not* to be the hero of the tale (in either sense of the word) produces both narrative discontinuity and moral discontinuity. But even when we have adjusted our responses — in Part III — to accommodate a new central character, a new morality in the original central character, and a new kind

---

[4] Bertrand H. Bronson, *In Search of Chaucer*, p. 108.

of tale, we are still left to cope with an unusual inconsistency in the role of Griselda. Although she is plainly enough a domestic saint and hence more a personification than a person, the lapses in the symbolic surface of the character are too numerous and too poignant to be overlooked or subsumed under a loose definition of symbol. It is the glimpses of an anguished human being which intensify our responses to the tale and produce the kind of pathos not characteristic of symbolic spectacle. Whereas Walter changes once and changes totally, Griselda seems constantly to be straining against the symbolic bonds of her role. Bronson has cited some of the instances in which Griselda's maternal and personal feelings burst out and claim our deep sympathy — the passage, for example, in which by reflexive action the swooning mother clutches her children to her with such a force that only "with greet sleighte and greet difficultee / The children from hire arm they gonne arace" (1102-03) ; and the passage in which Griselda, suffering the ultimate outrage of expulsion from Walter's house, for the first time allows words disrespectful of her husband to escape her lips: "O goode God! how gentil and how kynde / Ye semed by youre speche and youre visage / The day that maked was oure mariage!" (852-54)

These poignant scenes are what we most cherish in the tale, and their poignancy arises directly from the tensions which Bronson has so acutely delineated for us, tensions between the personification and the person of Griselda. Those first and last words of complaint are forced and squeezed out of Griselda by the sheer enormity of the weight she has borne for so long in willing silence. The superhuman personification, in other words, is the background and source for the very human person: "The pure symbol of meek and trusting submission has put on corruption, become a human figure . . ."[5] As a domestic saint Griselda can expand into the human dimension

---

[5] Bronson, p. 107. On this quality of Griselda as both single-dimensioned symbol and deeply feeling human being, see also Raymond Preston, *Chaucer* (London and New York, 1952), p. 252.

and carry our sympathy with her in a way that a saint of God could not. The submissiveness of the Christian martyr is absolute, but the very phrase "domestic saint," which fits Griselda so well, contains the human possibility. As we view Job's outburst, in a comparable situation, we are not so much sympathetic as awed and fearful, for crying out against God is unlike crying out against a man, however unnatural that man may be. But when Griselda, at the extremity of an ordeal which we have been shown and told to be unjust, lets fall a rebuke upon her tormentor we inwardly exult. Indeed, Part V of the Clerk's Tale, especially Griselda's speech to Walter (814-89), is one of the great moments of Chaucerian poetry; the rhetoric, tone, and imagery are perfectly attuned to the pathos and exaltation of the action. I think we do not reflect on the reasons for Walter's cruelty or, for that matter, on the disparity between his virtuous character and his monstrous character. This is Griselda's story — once we are past Part II, that is — and our interest centers on the ordeal of "this flour of wyfly pacience."

At the very end the vestiges of Walter's story are reclaimed and he is restored to the condition of a beneficent ruler and loving husband. Having proceeded a step beyond the ultimate of depravity by recalling his expelled wife to wait upon her successor, Walter is finally convinced of Griselda's goodness: " 'This is ynogh, Grisilde myn,' quod he." Henceforth he is the virtuous nobleman we knew in Parts I and II, and his own explanation of his conduct suffices:

> ". . . I have doon this deede
> For no malice, ne for no crueltee,
> But for t'assaye in thee thy wommanheede,
> And nat to sleen my children — God forbeede! —
> But for to kepe hem pryvely and stille,
> Til I thy purpos knewe and al thy wille." (1073-78)

For her part Griselda is amazed and overcome, but significantly all of her emotion is directed toward God and toward her children. She has not a word to say to Walter, neither in censure *nor* in forgiveness. Even in this highly emotional scene of reconciliation the two principal characters of the tale remain separate entities. They do not relate to one another in any personal or organic way. All that we see of man and wife together is a brief glimpse from a distant vantage point:

> Walter hire dooth so feithfully plesaunce
> That it was deyntee for to seen the cheere
> Bitwixe hem two, now they been met yfeere. (1111-13)

The reconciliation then is nominal rather than organic. No effort is made to probe the mind of Griselda or to account for the mind of Walter. The two are brought together by no inner propulsion or irresistible attraction but simply by the external demands of narrative structure. Aside from the brief assertion that "Walter hire gladeth" we have no sense of any emotional connection between the two, but only the assertion that "Ful many a yeer in heigh prosperitee / Lyven thise two in concord and in reste" (1128). Nor could the situation be otherwise, given the fundamentally bifurcated structure of the narrative.

The tale is told — as the moral makes clear — not for its own sake, but to demonstrate a truth. (The tale to which the moral refers is not the entire Clerk's Tale but only those parts which concern Griselda — Parts III-VI — and depict Walter as a monster.) The governing intelligence of the maker asserts itself to make certain we have not been misled by the realistic touches into thinking this merely a story about wives and husbands:

> This storie is seyd, nat for that wyves sholde
> Folwen Grisilde as in humylitee,
> For it were inportable, though they wolde;
> But for that every wight, in his degree,
> Sholde be constant in adversitee
> As was Grisilde . . . (1142-47)

THE CLERK'S TALE

In this warning against too deep an involvement in the literal, realistic surface of the tale we detect a trace of Chaucerian irony, but nothing like the broad display of worldly wit which is to follow in the envoi. In stating the moral Chaucer expresses a serious concern that the fiction may have appeared too real; such a concern, given the ingredients of this tale, is clearly understandable. Chaucer goes on to conclude the tale of Griselda in high moral seriousness, in three earnest stanzas extolling the Boethian doctrine of "vertuous suffraunce" which Griselda exemplifies so well.

Then in a stroke of audacity Chaucer converts the entire solemn enterprise to the uses of wit and satire, and at the same time, in a dazzling feat of rhetorical ingenuity, he fastens the tale securely to the Canterbury framework. This larger dimension, which has exerted no influence upon the narration of the tale, is suddenly invoked, after the moralized conclusion of the tale, by the line, "But o word, lordynges, herkneth er I go" (1163). At once we are back on the road. The narrator, whose voice in the tale — as Bronson has observed — is indistinguishable from the poet's, now separates from the poet to become the Clerk of the pilgrimage, and concomitantly Chaucer withdraws himself and us to a point of broader vantage.

Typically, the substance of the ensuing comedy is misunderstanding, the deliberate distortion of perception. In the envoi the Clerk seizes upon the chaff of the tale (Griselda's wifeliness) and playfully raps Alice of Bath about the ears with it. We may assume that the earthy Alice senses only approbation of her own modern attitude in the Clerk's reminder that Griselda is dead and with her her patience. And she would also respond without urging to his call to wives to "Folweth Ekko, that holdeth no silence, / But evere answereth at the countretaille." Perception of the verbal irony requires the kind of intellectual detachment which Alice conspicuously lacks. That other inveterate literalist, Harry Bailly, in the stanza which evidently served to conclude the Clerk's contribution

205

before Chaucer composed the envoi,[6] draws a characteristically personal and off-center interpretation: "By Goddes bones, / Me were levere than a barel ale / My wyf at hoom herd this legende ones!"

We may conjecture that Chaucer developed the idea of the envoi from the germ contained in this account of Harry Bailly's reaction to the tale. The incursion of the Clerk and his reference to the Wife of Bath serve the same linking purpose served by the incursion of the Host, and the comic substance of the envoi is an enlarged variation on the Host's belligerently literal and personal misinterpretation of the tale. In both cases the conclusion is a structural device, deliberately appended to the completed tale, whose purpose is to connect the tale with the preexisting Canterbury framework. It is no disservice to Chaucer to notice the manipulative nature of this procedure. If, as we have repeatedly observed, Chaucer characteristically conceived of his art in terms of concrete structural elements, it was necessary to devise means of connecting one unit to another. In the present instance Chaucer developed the envoi beyond the simple structural purpose of linkage in order to exploit the possibilities of comic irony. The transition from solemnity to comedy is abrupt, as transitions are in inorganic art, and here the change is unusually jolting because it is not only a structural change but a total shift of mood. It succeeds nevertheless, primarily because it is consistent with Chaucer's narrative practice, both in general and in the context of the Clerk's Tale. Also, inorganic structure can accommodate so abrupt a change of mood because the change is not retroactive; it does not blur the outlines of the tale, which is a finished entity before the shift occurs. As we have seen elsewhere, inorganic art depends on collocation rather than sub-

---

[6] Baugh maintains — I think rightly — that Chaucer intended finally that the envoi should replace, not complement, the stanza containing "the murye wordes of the Hoost." *Chaucer's Major Poetry*, p. 440. The last words of the envoi are then echoed directly in the opening line of the Merchant's Prologue, "Wepyng and waylyng, care and oother sorwe . . ."

ordination, and here, too, the link does not modify the elements it connects.

Chaucerian pathos, as exemplified in the tale of Griselda, elicits a deeply sympathetic response. It is part of the richness of Chaucer's art that it can engage our feelings so fully. In the Clerk's Tale these moments stand out as high points of poetic excellence, even though the narrative elements from which they emerge do not form a consistent matrix. The Clerk's Tale remains for us the tale of Griselda and her "vertuous suffraunce." We do not — and need not — lament the lack of organic integration between the first one-third and the last two-thirds of the tale. Despite the loss of Chaucer's heart and ours to Griselda, Chaucer cannot forbear in the end to indulge in the kind of conscious illusionism which disengages the heart and gratifies the mind. The Clerk's envoi forms a concentric ring of wit around the tale. But of course it is only provisionally the end, for the framework of pilgrimage, as we have noted earlier, finally delivers us into the world beyond the mortal limits of rational discernment.

TEN THE WIFE OF BATH'S PROLOGUE: THE STRUCTURE OF AUTOBIOGRAPHY

Of all the Canterbury pilgrims, the Wife of Bath has achieved the most lasting and loving fame. The name is so well known and so firmly attached to a concept of woman that it becomes difficult to distinguish between the Wife of Bath as we know her — a great and vital original — and "The Wife of Bath's Prologue," a work of literary art composed by Geoffrey Chaucer. So artfully does Chaucer project the illusion of autobiography that our awareness is captured and dominated by the woman herself, a woman infinitely various yet all the more consistently "human" for the frailties and inconsistencies she displays.

To attempt to relate such a figure to an inorganic mode of literary art may seem an unrewarding effort. But if the argument of this book has been at all persuasive, it should be apparent that

THE WIFE OF BATH'S PROLOGUE

inorganic structure is in no way inimical to vital and exciting artistic achievement. The vitality, however, resides with the poet and emanates from the way he projects his materials. The Wife, in view of the length and the contentiousness of her Prologue, is, of course, one of the most "dramatic" of the pilgrims. But I think that if we set out to investigate the literary genesis of the character, that is, its origins in a literary composition, we can at once make some illuminating distinctions between the lady and the text.

The importance of such distinctions is illustrated by default in a recent study of "The Development of the Wife of Bath" by R. A. Pratt.[1] In attempting to account for this development Pratt applies a thorough knowledge of Chaucer's sources to a study of Chaucer's text as we have it. The result is a convincing demonstration of the irregular, much revised, pastiche-like quality of the materials concerned with the Wife. One might on the face of it expect such an analysis to yield support for an inorganic interpretation, but on the contrary, Pratt maintains that the irregular, fragmented character of the materials adds to the humanity of the Wife. He argues that Chaucer's additions and revisions and re-orderings over a period of time successively increased the complexity of the Wife: Chaucer's original conception, as reflected in the portrait in the General Prologue and in her presumed original tale, now assigned to the Shipman,[2] lacks the autobiographical detail and the antimatrimonial doctrine, and Chaucer's subsequent additions and shifts built the Wife into "a personality that is rich, deep, and convincing."[3] While it is true that Chaucer added many

---

[1] Robert A. Pratt, "The Development of the Wife of Bath," in *Studies in Medieval Literature in Honor of A. C. Baugh,* ed. MacEdward Leach (Philadelphia: University of Pennsylvania Press, 1961), pp. 45-77.

[2] Pratt summarizes the evidence and the chain of assumptions leading to the conclusion that "the Man of Law originally told the story of *Melibee;* that his epilogue originally introduced the Wife of Bath; and that she originally told the tale of adultery now assigned to the Shipman" (pp. 46-48). See also Chaucer, *Complete Works,* ed. F. N. Robinson, p. 732.

[3] Pratt, "The Development," p. 76.

individualizing details to the Wife, including her astrological affinities to Mars and Venus and allusions to temporal and spatial dimensions beyond the immediate scene, it is difficult to follow Pratt to the depth to which he probes her personality: "The essential mystery of the Wife deepens as we are made aware of the cosmic background of the planets. When she tells her tale, successive shadowy egos loom behind her in deepening perspective: old Alice on the Canterbury road, the young Alice in her memory and 'in the feeldes,' the 'olde wyf' of the tale, the heroine transformed to be young and fair, and the 'elf-queene' who 'daunced ful ofte in many a grene mede.' "[4]

The extent of personal autonomy here attributed to the character rivals and indeed overshadows the autonomy of the poet's controlling viewpoint. Hence we lose the ironic perspective, and the Wife finally emerges for Pratt as a spokesman for a cause of her own rather than a creature of her creator: "In addition to these dimensions, Chaucer has given the Wife yet another by portraying her against the intellectual and emotional background of anti-matrimonialism, a tradition . . . strong in the leading university of fourteenth-century England . . . thus Alice becomes significant not merely for her magnificent individuality, but also as a representative of a point of view — often labelled modern and Protestant by latter-day Chaucerians — equally momentous in our day and in hers."[5]

The conclusions ultimately to be drawn about the paradoxes and contradictions of the character draw us outward beyond the character to the poet, in a direction opposite to the inward turn taken by Pratt after his analysis of the diverse materials of the text. The many sources which Chaucer drew upon and variously shuffled and juxtaposed to form the Wife and her prologue and tale — Theophrastus, St. Jerome, Eustache Deschamps, Walter Map, Jean

[4] "The Development," p. 77.
[5] "The Development," p. 77.

210

de Meun — all have in common, or are thus interpretable, one
pervasive attitude: opposition to women and wedlock. These
authorities constitute the classical antifeminist tradition. Chaucer
culled this literature as he composed the Wife of Bath. It seems to
me at least debatable whether or not dramatic characterization
sweeps doctrinal theme and satiric intent before it, as Pratt so
strongly implies. Inducement to read the Wife that way is persuasive. Nowhere else does Chaucer activate a character to such an
extent outside the context of a narrative. But I think the absence of
a "story" context does not in itself contribute to a decisive difference
between, say, the Wife and January, who also has a lot to say about
women and wedlock. As we saw in the Merchant's Tale, the emphasis which decisively counters characterization is not narrative
action but doctrine; and the literary purpose, at least so far as the
treatment of January is concerned, is the satiric deployment of that
doctrine. In a similar way though to a lesser extent, the composition
of the Wife suggests that Chaucer's motivation was primarily
thematic, that he was concerned with making an entertaining and
artful presentation of the traditional, authoritative, pronouncements
on antifeminism, to which end the cumulative individualization of
the Wife becomes a means. An impressive argument along these
lines was presented by Wayne Shumaker some years ago,[6] though
apparently Pratt for one was not persuaded.

Shumaker discerned in the Wife a mixture of conventionality
and originality, his contention being that, contrary to traditional
opinion, conventional elements were not only present but even, if
truth be told, predominant: ". . . if some necessity were put upon us
to impoverish our reading of her Prologue by denying one set of her
qualities, I believe Chaucer would prefer us to relinquish her
individuality."[7] Such a judgment, based upon acknowledgment of

[6] Wayne Shumaker, "Alisoun in Wander-Land: A Study in Chaucer's Mind and
Literary Method," *ELH*, 18:77-89 (1951).
[7] Shumaker, p. 89.

211

the many unique details of her life and appearance and an awareness that she is "less remote, less ideal, less abstract" than Blanche
or even Dorigen, nevertheless reflects a sound appraisal of the
importance of the conventional generalizations, the established
attitudes of the "authorities," in the makeup of Chaucer's most
"original" character. Shumaker's point is that although the Wife
represents an advanced stage of Chaucerian "realism" she does not
move beyond the limits of Chaucer's "realism," which always, in
traditional medieval fashion, subserves rationally apprehensible
general ideas. In her transmission of long-fixed attitudes toward
virginity and marriage the Wife demonstrates that Chaucer's
"strongest interest is in the general — in what is not (as it would
have seemed to him) self-limiting and therefore trivial. He is not
a patient searcher of men's hearts, but a docile scholar who imposes
upon his perceptions . . . a framework of systematized notions."[8]

D. W. Robertson, Jr., maintains, in a similar vein, that "those
who grow sentimental over her 'human' qualities are, from a fourteenth-century point of view, simply being misled."[9] While Robertson's exegesis of the Wife as "an elaborate iconographic figure
designed to show the manifold implications of an attitude" opens
up to us a rich matrix of Christian doctrine and Scriptural symbolism, and instructs us in the polysemous interpretation of marriage
under the New Law, we must, I think, question the extent to which
Robertson subordinates art to doctrine. It is essentially a matter of
extent rather than direction, for while Robertson is sensitive to
Chaucer's hand in the shaping of the Wife, and even acknowledges
the humor of this "example of carnal understanding and its consequences," under his scrutiny the Wife of Bath's Prologue emerges
as a work of spiritual admonition fully as pious in intent as the
Parson's Tale, but more subtle. Thus Robertson builds from the
concrete situation of the Wife's narrative a multileveled series of

8 Shumaker, p. 88.
9 D. W. Robertson, Jr., *A Preface to Chaucer*, p. 331.

THE WIFE OF BATH'S PROLOGUE

analogies ending in Christ: the Wife "does her best to subvert the traditional hierarchy of husband over wife as it reflects the hierarchy of Christ over the Church and parallels the hierarchy of the spirit over the flesh, or the 'newness of the spirit' over 'the oldness of the letter' . . . He who allows his wife to dominate him will be served as the wife of Bath seeks to serve her husbands; he who allows the flesh to dominate the spirit will find it a tyrant like the wife; and, finally, he who disregards the spirit of the Scriptures in favor of experience will find himself enslaved to the Old Law, unredeemed by the 'freedom wherewith Christ hath made us free.' "[10] It is possible, of course, that "these ideas and their corollaries must have been what Chaucer had in mind when he wrote the first 162 lines of the wife's prologue." But it is questionable that the text itself can bear such a heavy load of doctrinal freight.[11]

No doubt, as the more conventional commentary has emphasized, Alice of Bath is unusual among the pilgrim characters. To a degree unmatched except perhaps by the Pardoner, Chaucer has endowed her, as Pratt has observed, with extension in space and extension in time. But it is important to recognize, as I think Shumaker did, that her spatial and temporal experience comes in the form of externally applied characteristics. The coordinates of her being do not activate a past in the modern, existential manner; rather they vivify an extraordinary portrait in the splendid diversity of a Gothic composition. But there is more to the Wife of Bath's Prologue than the woman herself. The essential condition for discovery of what lies beyond is the recognition that there are limits

[10] *A Preface,* p. 330.

[11] In his review of Robertson's *A Preface,* Robert E. Kaske, expressing on this point reservations similar to my own, urges a "distinctly less rigorous judgment on the Wife of Bath than that which results from Professor Robertson's interpretation" and suggests that "Chaucer's emphasis in these first 162 lines of her Prologue falls less on an outright denunciation of her than on the subtler comedy — none the less 'human' for being theologically uncompromising — of her accepting enthusiastically and totally the concessions granted to a physical existence only rather grudgingly by Paul and Jerome." "Chaucer and Medieval Allegory," *ELH,* 30:184 (1963).

to the dramatic autonomy of the Wife. What exists beyond the depicted life of the character is not only — and not initially — the stages of Christian understanding that loom so large in Robertson's exegesis. What lies immediately behind the life of the character is the art of the poet, which in the deepest sense is Chaucer's life, his personality, his way of seeing things. I think we must attend to this largely neglected middle area, between the dramatic critic's lusty Alice of Bath and the exegetical critic's Christian verities, if we are to arrive at a just estimate of Chaucer's achievement.

The "dramatic" view of the Wife stresses her right to a habitation and a name in that land of our imagination peopled by the great characters of great fiction. Without wishing to challenge that right, I would like to draw attention to the inorganic ways in which the poet, through his manner of structuring the Wife's Prologue, conveys meanings and perspectives that counterpoint and often invert our sense of the lady who looms up in our imagination. There is a disparity between what the Wife says and what the Wife of Bath's Prologue says, and this disparity forms the comic essence of Chaucer's achievement. Too much insistence upon the Wife's "dramatic" autonomy causes us to miss this larger dimension of the Prologue, and results, as in Kittredge's interpretation, in seeing the essence of the Wife's discourse to be a "rude personal assault" upon the Clerk.[12]

I should like to examine some of the ways in which Chaucer superimposes his authority upon the Wife's experience. The opening lines do indeed present a virtually full-blown dramatization of the Wife as a woman of more than common experience, but they also suggest, though much less explicitly, the prism through which Chaucer intends for us to view her:

> Experience, though noon auctoritee
> Were in this world, is right ynogh for me

12 G. L. Kittredge, "Chaucer's Discussion of Marriage," *MP*, 9 (1911-12); reprinted in *Chaucer, Modern Essays in Criticism*, ed. E. Wagenknecht, p. 194.

THE WIFE OF BATH'S PROLOGUE

> To speke of wo that is in mariage;
> For, lordynges, sith I twelve yeer was of age,
> Thonked be God that is eterne on lyve,
> Housbondes at chirche dore I have had fyve, —
> If I so ofte myghte have ywedded bee, —
> And alle were worthy men in hir degree. (1-8)

This speaker is the very embodiment of marital experience, as she plainly and engagingly states. But the extravagance of her experience implies its own judgment and qualification, and here, I think, Chaucer signals his own interest in the ensuing discourse: he is interested in the subject of marriage, and for him the Wife is at least as much an instrument for *his* comment on that subject as she is the embodiment and mouthpiece of her own. Despite the vitality which the Wife assumes in the reader's imagination, what she says — and she only *says* — is controlled by Chaucer, and within the Wife of Bath's Prologue the framework of Chaucer's thinking on the subject of women and marriage is literary, that is, shaped and defined by the major documents of the antifeminist tradition. Chaucer portrays Alice of Bath as a woman at bay in the clerks' arena. Out of the generosity and warmth of his own spirit he endows her with certain irresistibly attractive qualities, such as candor and fidelity to her own nature. But this is only to say that Chaucer dilutes the ancient vitriol, for the controlling viewpoint, however subtly conveyed, is unmistakably antifeminist.

Enlarging upon an observation made some years ago by R. F. Jones,[13] Pratt has discerned three sections in the Wife's Prologue which differ distinctly from one another in tone, purpose, and source. The first, ending at line 192, is the Wife's sermon on multiple marriage and virginity, which is "combative and argumentative" in tone. The second (193-452) is her account of her experience with her first three ("good") husbands, and the style

[13] Richard F. Jones, "A Conjecture on the Wife of Bath's Prologue," *JEGP*, 24:512-547 (1925).

here is "expository and descriptive." The third section (453-828), on her experience with her fourth and fifth ("badde") husbands, is "narrative and dramatic."[14] Though I disagree with Pratt's conclusions, I find his analysis of the compositional pattern of the Prologue to be a firm base for my own discussion.

The opening section, the Wife's "argumentative and combative" sermon on marriage and virginity, presents a woman in unusual circumstances: she has been married not twice, or even thrice, but five times. When we remind ourselves that Chaucer *chose* to utilize this large a number, we realize that the conditions thus chosen for depiction preclude our regarding the Wife as a disinterested party; that is, she is set up very early as the unknowing victim of comic satire.[15] The conditions do not, for all that, preclude sympathy for the lady, and perhaps even a sense of the pathos of her situation. Such, I think, is the feeling Chaucer evokes for the Wife in her opening lines as she attemps to defend herself against the accumulated power of an ascetic, male-oriented exegetical tradition. But Chaucer soon introduces the element which will counteract and eventually dispel our empathy with a woman wronged: speaking of Solomon, whom she cites as one of many Scriptural examples of multiple marriage, she can't help but exclaim,

14 Pratt, "The Development," p. 50.

15 Robertson also sees her as a negative exemplar, but for him the satire is no laughing matter. He uses the Wife's Scriptural allusion to the Samaritan woman as a bridge to a discussion of the sacramental aspects of Christian marriage, the argument being that the Wife's disdain for the New Law of the spirit and grace and her adherence to the Old Law of the senses and the flesh brings her into disagreement not simply with St. Jerome but with Christ (*A Preface*, pp. 319-322). Robertson marshals a number of medieval commentaries on the sanctity of marriage because of its sacramental relationship to the marriage of Christ and the Church, and he urges that "There is no reason why Chaucer's audience should not have remembered these things." The problem for us, I think, is not how well schooled Chaucer's audience was in the mysteries, but with what force the mysteries would have impinged upon that audience's response to a secular poet's depiction of a secular woman's humorously illogical harangue about marriage. It is a question of balancing exegetical knowledge against literary judgment, and I think Chaucer would have expected the latter from his contemporary audience as well as from us who come after.

216

THE WIFE OF BATH'S PROLOGUE

> As wolde God it were leveful unto me
> To be refresshed half so ofte as he! (37-38)

This is the kind of candid self-revelation which so endears the Wife
to us, but at the same time it is the germ of her womanish disease
(as St. Jerome would diagnose it), the disease of concupiscence.
While we might not "in real life" hold with the clerical argument
against women, neither can we in the literary situation of the Prologue hold with the Wife. Despite the sometimes persuasive arguments of her sermon to the effect that "In swich estaat as God hath
cleped us I wol persevere," she reveals herself to be every bit as
abandoned to carnality as St. Jerome might have expected.

Chaucer highlights the polarity between what the Wife says
and what she is by both rhetorical and dramatic means. While the
course of the Wife's sermon is moving from polygamy to virginity
to marriage and procreation to the "debt" a husband owes a wife,
her unconscious self-revelation is moving its independent way from
vitality to concupiscence to the brink of sadism, which is reached
in the closing exchange with the Pardoner about the whip of
tribulation which she has wielded in marriage. This kind of interplay is itself the essence of comic satire, but even within the sermon,
as distinct from its antithetical undertone, Chaucer is able to make
clear to us that the Wife's aim is not truth but self-justification. Her
defensiveness is at once evident in her lengthy insistence that Scripture is ambiguous and inconclusive on the number of marriages one
may successively enter into. Following upon this largely gratuitous
defense of her quantitative position, the Wife's argument for
marriage as against virginity is plainly an additional effort of self-
service. Here again Scripture serves her well, and she can quote
St. Paul without distortion (as distinct from her later handling of
him) to the effect that "it is better to marry than to burn" and that
"every man has his proper gift of God, one after this manner and
another after that" (I Cor. 7, 9). The humor of these passages

217

arises mainly from our sense of the Wife's failure to evaluate her opposition with any accuracy and her consequent failure to appraise herself. If she were as responsive to experience as she so loudly claims to be, she would of course have realized that the war against marriage had been long since lost, and that the limitations of the case for virginity no longer required elucidation. Neither man's bodily nature nor God's procreative intent required the expository and argumentative services of the Wife of Bath. As her sense of perspective fails her, she moves away from us and becomes a comic spectacle. She takes antifeminism to be a realistic argument rather than the rationalistic, self-gratifying rhetoric of the clerks. In taking game (however offensive) for earnest she suffers the well-known Chaucerian fate of the overly credulous. The Wife presents the spectacle of a woman who occupies a position of strength and is fighting desperately against a force which is impotent to dislodge her. Having thus presented her as a gratuitously aggressive female, Chaucer has seen to it that the beneficiary of her zeal is antifeminism.

Her stature as a champion of the feminine position further diminishes as she proceeds to define her concept of marriage. Her text is "God bad us for to wexe and multiplye," and she effects a facile linkage between marriage and procreation. As she sees it, her role is pious executor of God's naturalistic will. But Chaucer sees it differently. He softens the ground beneath her with a damaging piece of negative evidence: he offers no indication that any of her five marriages was blessed with issue. In such a context her cry of "Welcome the sixte" is distinctly qualified. Though she is at great pains to argue that the generative members were made for "ese of engendrure" as well as for "office," it is apparent to us that for her "ese of engendrure" means "ese," and this is the motive that underlies all of her display of learned argumentation.

Then Chaucer goes beyond negative evidence in making clear what the welcome sixth can look forward to. The Wife's distortion

218

of I Corinthians 7 and her promise to bring tribulation upon the
flesh of her husband carries her beyond sensuality to a sadistic
extreme. The Pauline dispensation of mutuality in marriage is
transformed in her reading. Paul's balanced phrasing, "Let the
husband render unto the wife her due, and likewise the wife unto
the husband," becomes in the Wife's paraphrase, ". . . man shal
yelde to his wyf hire dette" (130). On this score she becomes
increasingly strident:

> In wyfhod I wol use myn instrument
> As frely as my Makere hath it sent.
> If I be daungerous, God yeve me sorwe!
> Myn housbonde shal it have bothe eve and morwe,
> Whan that hym list come forth and paye his dette.
> An housbonde wol I have, I wol nat lette,
> Which shal be both my dettour and my thral,
> And have his tribulacion withal
> Upon his flessh, whil that I am his wyf.
> I have the power durynge al my lyf
> Upon his propre body, and noght he. (149-59)

Hovering behind the shrill pronouncements of these last lines are
the quiet words of the Apostle, "The wife hath not the power over
her own body, but the husband; and likewise the husband hath not
the power over his own body, but the wife." The more the Wife
declaims, the more evident to all but herself does her enormity
become. Though the situation is a variant of the Chaucerian comedy
of perspectives, it here verges close to the grotesque. But Chaucer
redeems it for comedy when in the person of the Pardoner he
dramatizes a response which moves outside the Wife's terms altogether. The Pardoner does not argue the point of the Wife's
Scriptural interpretation, nor does he attack the vulnerable feminism
of the Wife herself. His response is oblique, humorous, and, for
the Pardoner — considering the depraved egomania generally attributed to him — remarkably self-effacing:

> "Now, dame," quod he, "by God and by seint John!
> Ye been a noble prechour in this cas.
> I was aboute to wedde a wyf; allas!
> What sholde I bye it on my flessh so deere?
> Yet hadde I levere wedde no wyf to-yeere!" (164-68)

It is inevitable that this passage should be interpreted in the context of the Pardoner's Prologue and Tale and the portrait in the General Prologue, and Chaucer was no doubt quite aware of the intricate play of ironies he was here setting in motion. Nevertheless, however intriguing these reverberations are, it would be imprudent to regard the Pardoner's morality, physiognomy, and premarital problems as any more than muted background to the very demanding and sharply defined present context. At this high point of the Wife's impassioned and verbose declamation Chaucer has introduced the most effective kind of satire — the brief, telling thrust of wit. As is usual in such a situation — both in life and elsewhere in the *Canterbury Tales* — the self-absorbed victim misses the nuance and mistakes the meaning, while the satirist and his audience collaborate against him. The Pardoner here embodies the antifeminist viewpoint which dominates the Wife of Bath's Prologue. He does not attack the Wife, nor does he dispute her concept of wedlock. He is humility, rationality, and courtesy combined; he is the antifeminist's man, and as such he simply opts against marriage. Against his reasonable and understated response the Wife looms all the more monstrous as a marital partner. Marvelous though she is as a spectacle, it would take an intrepid man indeed, and a foolish one, to approach any closer. Although her very being depends upon the viability of her wifeliness, her response to the Pardoner fully substantiates his judgment, and her arrogance reveals her to be incapable of serving her own vital interest:

> "Abyde!" quod she, "my tale is nat bigonne.
> Nay, thou shalt drynken of another tonne,
> Er that I go, shal savoure wors than ale.

THE WIFE OF BATH'S PROLOGUE

> And whan that I have toold thee forth my tale
> Of tribulacion in mariage,
> Of which I am expert in al myn age,
> This is to seyn, myself have been the whippe, —
> Than maystow chese wheither thou wolt sippe
> Of thilke tonne that I shal abroche." (169-77)

Once more, following this least ingratiating of all the Wife's outbursts, the Pardoner's courteous, conciliatory language — "Dame, I wolde praye yow, if youre wyl it were . . ." — articulates more effectively than argument the lineaments of the arch shrew.

In the second section of the Prologue (193-450), in which the Wife describes her treatment of her three "good" husbands, Chaucer utilizes a different means to satirize the feminist position. Pratt's designation "expository and descriptive" recognizes a distinction between this and the "combative and argumentative" first section of the Prologue. It may very well be — as Pratt conjectures — that originally this section followed directly after line 6 ("Housbondes at chirche dore I have had fyve"). I am less concerned here with reconstructing the order in which Chaucer composed and arranged these sections than with making clear that they are separable, distinct not only in content but also in structure and style. Although according to Pratt's version of the "drama" theory the disparities in structure and style contribute to the "humanity" of the Wife, I think it becomes apparent when we try to reconcile the Wife of section two with the Wife of section one that characterization is inadequate as a unifying concept. The Wife of the opening section is an actively rationalizing but thinly disguised sensualist, to whom marriage is a means of satisfying her powerful, at times sadistic, bodily appetites. The ruling passion of the Wife of section two is sovereignty. So powerful is the drive to mastery that her body, like her veracity, is sacrificed to it, not in the sense that she offers herself but, quite to the contrary, that she withholds herself:

> Namely abedde hadden they meschaunce:
> Ther wolde I chide, and do hem no plesaunce;

221

> I wolde no lenger in the bed abyde,
> If that I felte his arm over my syde,
> Til he had maad his raunson unto me;
> Thanne wolde I suffre hym do his nycetee. (407-12)

The appetite for sensual gratification which is so dominant in section one is nowhere evident here; lechery has been displaced by avarice:

> For wynnyng wolde I al his lust endure,
> And make me a feyned appetit. (416-17)

Though the definition of the Wife as a hearty, lustful creature has wide currency, it seems to accord only with the first section of her Prologue.

As Pratt has pointed out, section two is "expository and descriptive," but we should observe at once the comic disparity between the Wife's exposition and Chaucer's. The Wife is talking to and for women, while her maker is managing her talk so that it works to debase women and gain sympathy for men. Of course Chaucer has the advantage over his own creation, but the point is that he exploits it.

Section two is a rhetorical tour de force in which the militant feminist herself expounds a veritable encyclopedia of woman's defects. The signposts of progress in this exposition are the nineteen repetitions of the phrase "Thou seyst" which occur in her 144-line display of how she customarily addresses her husbands (235-378). The result of this emphasis is cumulative damnation of the lady by her own tongue. Her strident tone and her predatory intentions strike a marvelously comic contrast against the accumulating, un-stated case for her victims. The humor, of course, is all Chaucer's, and it develops in direct proportion to the Wife's growing bellicosity and self-absorption.

This two-edged discourse begins as the Wife presents the first of a long sequence of quotations, her intention being to show how

222

THE WIFE OF BATH'S PROLOGUE

she devastates the speakers and Chaucer's being simply to present
a long sequence of quotations. The tenor is established by the first
three, which occur in succession without a break:

> Thou seist to me it is a greet meschief
> To wedde a povre womman, for costage;
> And if that she be riche, of heigh parage,
> Thanne seistow that it is a tormentrie
> To soffre hire pride and hire malencolie.
> And if that she be fair, thou verray knave,
> Thou seyst that every holour wol hire have;
> She may no while in chastitee abyde,
> That is assailled upon ech a syde. (248-56)

Here are three clearly articulated charges against wives, occupying
eight and a half lines of the nine-line passage. The remaining half-
line is a crude epithet — "thou verray knave" — uttered vigorously,
but in the context ineffectually, against the husband's argument.
This 18-to-1 ratio is an accurate index of the weighting of the Wife's
discourse. There are sixteen more of these savory old chestnuts
drawn from the storehouse of Theophrastus, Deschamps, and Jean
de Meun, varying somewhat in length and rhetorical complexity
but adding up to a massive indictment of woman. Scattered among
these are about six expressions of the feminist viewpoint, the
longest of these being a single two-line outburst, "With wilde
thonder-dynt and firy levene / Moote thy welked nekke be to-
broke!" (276-77) Not only are these outbursts ineffectual against
the accumulated antifeminist rhetoric, but their shrewish tone is
additionally self-defeating. The discourse builds up to a climactic
ending as the Wife enumerates three more denouncements of
woman:

> Thou liknest eek wommenes love to helle,
> To bareyne lond, ther water may nat dwelle.
> Thou liknest it also to wilde fyr;
> The moor it brenneth, the moore it hath desir

> To consume every thyng that brent wole be.
> Thou seyest, right as wormes shende a tree,
> Right so a wyf destroyeth hire housbonde;
> This knowe they that been to wyves bonde. (371-78)

This conclusion is followed immediately by Chaucer's comic master-stroke: the Wife boasts that thus she *deceived* her husbands, "al was fals"; they had never really said such things in their drunkenness at all. And so, following the Wife's wonderfully self-annihilating presentation of her husbands' sentiments, we witness the irony of ironies, the comic *coup de grace*: she made it all up herself!

The final section of the Prologue is more "dramatic" than the other two in the sense that it is more autobiographical and less rhetorical. In a good part of it the Wife appears more human and also more humane as she recounts the specific circumstances and events of her last two marriages. Her account of how, lovesick at forty, she gave herself — heart, "quoniam," money, and property — to young Jankyn presents her in touching contrast to the venal shrew of the preceding section. To see this contrast as evidence of the Wife's capacious personality is to see not quite enough, I think, for the center of gravity, here as elsewhere in the Prologue, is not the Wife's character but Chaucer's theme. Although the Wife's account of her courtship of Jankyn is disarming for its candor and its touch of pathos, its principal effect is to display the wiliness of a woman in love:

> I bar hym on honde he hadde enchanted me, —
> My dame taughte me that soutiltee.
> And eek I seyde I mette of hym al nyght,
> He wolde han slayn me as I lay upright,
> And al my bed was ful of verray blood;
> But yet I hope that he shal do me good,
> For blood bitokeneth gold, as me was taught.
> And al was fals; I dremed of it right naught . . . (575-82)

and her concupiscence as well:

THE WIFE OF BATH'S PROLOGUE

> As help me God! whan that I saugh hym go
> After the beere, me thoughte he hadde a paire
> Of legges and of feet so clene and faire
> That al myn herte I yaf unto his hoold . . . (596-99)
> I ne loved nevere by no discrecioun,
> But evere folwede myn appetit . . . (622-23)

But this autobiographical narrative, tinged as it is with antifeminist sentiment, is merely a framework for the principal business, which is not the Wife's confessional narrative but Chaucer's satirical exposition. Jankyn's book is the source of a seemingly limitless succession of proverbs, anecdotes, and tales, all in support of the antifeminist theme and all diverting enough in their own right; but that we should hear them from the mouth of the arch-wife herself is Chaucer's ultimate comic turn. Chaucer's method here is similar to that which he employed in section two, where the Wife quotes her husbands' sentiments at such great length. But while Chaucer allowed her an occasional expletive in that long sequence, the present anthology of antifeminist tales comes pure and unspoiled from her lips. In her transmittal of the tale of suffering Socrates, for example, Chaucer allows her no editorial comment at all, not even innuendo:

> No thyng forgat he the care and the wo
> That Socrates hadde with his wyves two;
> How Xantippa caste pisse upon his heed.
> He wiped his heed, namoore dorste he seyn,
> But "Er that thonder stynte, comth a reyn!" (727-31)

The sentiment is entirely masculine, the Wife her own victim.

Chaucer brings this long rehearsal of antifeminist data to a close with a crisp proverb from Scripture itself: "A fair womman, but she be chaast also, / Is lyk a gold ryng in a sowes nose" (784), and then allows the Wife a brief cry, "Who wold wene, or who wolde suppose, / The wo that in myn herte was, and pyne?" This, together with her earlier attack against clerks (688-96, 706-09),

225

constitutes the feminine opposition — a total of twelve lines — to the 130-line (642-787 approx.) case leveled against them.

The ending of the Prologue is as sharply articulated as a coda. It contains the first, last, and decisive action in this long, argumentative, expository disquisition. It is an appropriate climax to section three in that its fisticuffs effectively resolve the contention between Alison and Jankyn. For the Wife and for all her partisans the victory is a delicious one. But for readers of the Wife of Bath's Prologue, whose viewpoint has been consistently differentiated from the Wife's, the effect is not the exoneration of woman but the exoneration of man's view of her. Although the marital denouement would seem to be, as the Wife describes it, a mutual accord —

> But atte laste, with muchel care and wo,
> We fille accorded by us selven two. — (811-12)

The next lines clarify for us the Wife's sense of mutuality:

> He yaf to me al the brydel in myn hond,
> To han the governance of hous and lond,
> And of his tonge, and of his hond also. (813-15)

One more condition satisfied, and the good man's humiliation is complete: "And made hym brenne his book anon right tho." Deceived, outlasted, and finally subjugated by a tireless and unscrupulous foe, man surrenders his last defense. But this conclusion is as ironic as the Wife's victories in the other parts of the Prologue — as an interpreter of St. Paul, a berater of old husbands, and scorner of Jankyn's book — for the fall of man signals not only the rise of woman but the renewal of the war on women. Though Alison of Bath may have won a skirmish, the Wife of Bath's Prologue is a dazzling victory for antifeminism. Chaucer has fashioned the victory in an inorganic combination of three distinct approaches to antifeminism. In all three the Wife of Bath is the essential vehicle, but the inconsistencies of attitude in the three sections testify less to the organic unity of her personality than to the inorganic unity of Chaucer's literary structure.

ELEVEN THE PARSON'S TALE: PARADIGM AND APOTHEOSIS

The longest of the Canterbury tales is not a tale, is not literature, is not art. It is a treatise which Chaucer pieced together from various sources.[1] Yet within the total strategy of the *Canterbury Tales* the Parson's Tale plays a supremely important role, both aesthetically and didactically. Not only does it "knytte up al this feeste" and "make an ende"; it also assures the translation of this particular pilgrimage into the collective journey of mankind toward salvation. As the Parson asserts, he means in his tale to show the way "of thilke parfit glorious pilgrymage / That highte Jerusalem celestial."

[1] Though Chaucer's direct sources are unknown, scholarship has revealed close resemblances to parts of two scholastic documents of the thirteenth century, the *Summa* of St. Raymund of Pennaforte and the *Summa vitiorum* of Guilielmus Peraldus. See the summary of scholarship in *Sources and Analogues of Chaucer's Canterbury Tales,* ed. W. F. Bryan and Germaine Dempster, pp. 723-729.

CHAUCER AND THE SHAPE OF CREATION

Both symbolically, that is (in the medieval sense), truly, and architectonically the Parson's Tale is the pinnacle, reaching heavenward, upon which the diverse earthly tales converge.

As a treatise on penitence the Parson's Tale offers little that will please or instruct the modern reader. Just how little it offers is apparent in the fact that two excellent recent editions of Chaucer's works, Donaldson's and Baugh's, have found it expedient to omit the Parson's Tale. Economy is, of course, an important consideration in our cost-conscious age, but obviously there are more definitive reasons, aesthetic and moral, for omitting this tale rather than others. The fundamental reason seems simple enough and conclusive: the Parson's Tale is a prose tract, not a verse narrative, and therefore it is a sport among the Canterbury tales. Even the Melibeus, though in prose and very tractlike, follows a narrative line. But the simple observation that the Parson's Tale is not a literary work and is therefore more or less expendable conveys an important implication, namely, that there is a discrepancy in judgment between Chaucer and ourselves regarding the scope of art and the proper role of the artist in matters of belief and doctrine. Since it is plain that Chaucer took the Parson's Tale very seriously, both as doctrine and as the culmination of his work of literary art, we are faced with some large questions. Assuming, as we tend to do, that a poem must not mean but be, are we able to invest with literary value a work which so manifestly *means*? And there is not only the question of reconciling modern and medieval concepts of the limits of art; we must also ask to what extent Chaucer felt his doctrine to be an encroachment upon his art.

The outlines of answers begin to emerge, I think, from what we know of Gothic art in general and its antecedents, theoretical and spiritual as well as concrete, and from our knowledge of Chaucer's particular practice, both within the *Canterbury Tales* and elsewhere. That Chaucer valued the Parson's Tale more than we do requires no demonstration. Its strategic placement, its length,

228

THE PARSON'S TALE

the Parson's explicit introductory comments, the Parson's personal goodness and unique immunity — among all the ecclesiasts in the General Prologue — from satiric exposure: all these indications attest to the importance, in Chaucer's eyes, of this tale. If we cannot see the art in the Parson's Tale it is because we do not understand art as Chaucer did. The shift of faculties which we must undergo in turning our attention from verse narrative to a prose tract on penitence signals to us the end of art and the end of our interest in the *Canterbury Tales*. For Chaucer, however, the shift from narrative to sermon was an elevation and, in a special sense, a relief. For him the ultimate role of art — irrespective of its mediate roles — was to serve and subserve Truth. In the course of the *Canterbury Tales* the framework of a realistic pilgrimage formed the outer limit of credibility, that is, the criterion of truth against which the limits of the fictions stood clearly defined. But that this truth, the truth of the road to Canterbury, was itself limited had to be recognized if the *Canterbury Tales* was to achieve the completeness of vision which to the Gothic mind was the hallmark of serious human enterprise. The Parson's Tale then is not simply an ending but also a transition, from *a* pilgrimage to *the* pilgrimage. By showing the way to "the fruyt of penaunce," which is "the endelees blisse of hevene" (1076), it displaces the illusion that fiction is truth.

That art can contain both illusion and disillusion is a concept foreign to the organicist imagination but integral to the Gothic. In both *Troilus* and the *Canterbury Tales* the breakdown of illusions signifies the poet's awareness of his mortality and also his deeply felt need to secure his place in the eternal order of things. If we are inclined to dismiss the Parson's Tale from our critical consideration of the *Canterbury Tales* on the ground that it is not art, we should recall that for Chaucer art was separate from and less important than truth, that its nature was to represent contingent truths and move through them ultimately to Truth. Therefore, if he views Chaucer's work in its Gothic context, the modern critic will see more than what his own presuppositions define as art.

Taking into account historical change and variation in man's perspectives, we may justifiably maintain that for ourselves the *presence* of the Parson's Tale at the end of the *Canterbury Tales* is more important than the tale itself. The knowledge of what it is is more meaningful and more illuminating than the experience of reading and rereading it. In this respect the Parson's Tale is for us indubitably different from the other Canterbury tales. Even if we are not to return to it for repeated readings, we need to know what it is.

In addition to being a spiritual apotheosis the Parson's Tale is a structural paradigm. In the prosaic nakedness of its rhetorical structure it displays with the utmost explicitness the principles of inorganic structure that we have found fundamental to Chaucer's narrative art. Revealing its generic roots in the scholastic *Summa*, the Parson's Tale also exemplifies Panofsky's criteria of the Gothic: "(1) totality (sufficient enumeration), (2) arrangement according to a system of homologous parts and parts of parts (sufficient articulation), and (3) distinctness and deductive cogency (sufficient interrelation)."[2] Though the Parson's Tale diverges widely from the relentless regularity and balance of the Thomistic *Summa*, it does adhere to the principle of explicit definition of topics and numerical subordination of divisions and subdivisions. Quantitative structure is an obvious characteristic of the work, though the adjustment of substance to structure is notably irregular; that is, subordinate parts of the subject are not always of appropriately reduced size. The most striking irregularity of this kind is the excursus on the seven deadly sins. This subdivision of Confession assumes such proportions that it overshadows the entire treatise. The importance of this phenomenon, as we shall see, is that it occurs within a

---

[2] Erwin Panofsky, *Gothic Architecture and Scholasticism*, p. 31. See above, pp. 56-60.

rigorously formalistic framework and for this reason raises important questions about the limits of form.

The opening paragraph of the Parson's Tale establishes the
scope of the exposition, the totality which is to be analyzed and
whose parts are to be displayed. Taking its text from Jeremiah,
the sermon states as its subject the noblest of the many "weyes
espirituels that leden folk to oure Lord Jhesu Crist, and to the
regne of glorie." It is the way called Penitence. Within this stated
subject the treatment is to be exhaustive, so that men might know
"what is Penitence, and whennes it is cleped Penitence, and in how
manye maneres been the acciouns or werkynges of Penitence, / and
how manye speces ther been of Penitence, and whiche thynges
apertenen and bihoven to Penitence, and whiche thynges destourben
Penitence." Though the degree of schematism here adumbrated
exceeds by far Chaucer's practice in narrative, the mode of treatment is essentially the same as that employed elsewhere. In *Troilus,*
for example, the introductory stanzas similarly define the scope of
the subject — love, as depicted in the hero's "aventures" — and
specify the stages or elements of that subject, regardless of the
resulting damage to narrative suspense.

Following a long paragraph defining penitence, the Parson's
Tale proceeds to fulfill its stated aims, that is, to fill in the outline
presented in the introductory paragraph.

In the first stage of development, whose purpose is to enumerate and define the actions of penitence (lines 95-100), system clearly
overrides substance. Though the "acciouns" of penitence are explicitly stated to be three, it is difficult to discern in fact what these
three acts are. The first clearly enough concerns baptism, but the
subordinating syntax clouds the meaning: "The firste is that if a
man be baptized after that he hath synned . . ." The main clause of
this sentence digresses further from the stated intention by quoting
an authority: "Seint Augustyn seith, 'But he be penitent for his olde
synful lyf, he may nat bigynne the newe clene lif.' " The second

231

and third acts are similarly articulated but even more unclear in substance, though the intention to formalize and the assumed value of formal enumeration remain very clear. The problem is that "accioun" has been displaced by "defaute," growing out of the digressive quotation from St. Augustine. But even though the meaning and scope of the paragraph undergo this change, the enumerative form is firmly adhered to, and instead of the second and third "acciouns" we find the second and third "defautes": "Another defaute is this, that men doon deedly synne after that they han receyved baptesme. / The thridde defaute is that men fallen in venial synnes after hir baptesme, fro day to day. / Therof seith Seint Augustyn that penitence of goode and humble folk is the penitence of every day" (98-100).

The next major division (lines 101-05) is more consistently developed, substance following closely the enumerated categories. Its abrupt opening — "The speces of Penitence been three" — serves to articulate the unit of exposition and affirm its autonomy within the total scheme of coordinated parts. The three species are "solempne," "commune," and "privee," and brief illustrative examples are provided for each.

The next section, intricately divided, subdivided, and interpolated, constitutes the remaining bulk — some 1,000 lines — of the Parson's Tale. It is a thoroughgoing display of the Gothic zeal for homological structure, that is, for the division of a whole into parts and parts of parts, all formed after the macrocosmic model of the total exposition. The subject (or subsubject) here is the process of perfect penance — its genesis in feeling, its enactment in confession, and its continuing affirmation in satisfaction, or exaction of alms and bodily deprivation. It is characteristic of the Gothic impulse that the process of penitence, though sequential, is represented as a rationally structured configuration. Thus the resulting rhetorical structure displays three equivalent divisions of a stated whole: "Now shaltow understande what is bihovely and necessarie

THE PARSON'S TALE

to verray perfit Penitence. And this stant on three thynges: / Contricioun of herte, Confessioun of Mouth, and Satisfaccioun" (106-107). The terminology of the Parson's exposition is somewhat confusing, despite the explicit clarity of the organization, and it may be helpful to make clear that the rhetorical structure we are presently considering, the exposition of "what is bihovely and necessarie to verray perfit Penitence," is the third major division of the total subject "Penitence"; it is equivalent to the "acciouns of Penitence" and the "speces of Penitence," though much longer than both and more elaborately subdivided.

Contrition, confession, and satisfaction, the three subdivisions of "what is bihovely and necessarie to verray perfit Penitence," are expounded independently in self-contained rhetorical units. The treatment of contrition, beginning at line 112 and running to line 315, insists, in typical fashion, upon clear, quantitative delineation of parts. The following series of quotations illustrates the manner of explicit division. First, a metaphorical definition of the subject: "The roote of this tree [of Penitence] is Contricioun, that hideth hym in the herte of hym that is verray repentaunt, ryght as the roote of a tree hydeth hym in the erthe. / Of the roote of Contricioun spryngeth a stalke that bereth braunches and leves of Confessioun, and fruyt of Satisfaccioun . . . Penaunce is the tree of lyf to hem that it receyven . . ." (112-13, 126).

There follows a four-part analytical definition: "In this Penitence or Contricioun man shal understonde foure thynges; that is to seyn, what is Contricioun, and whiche been the causes that moeven a man to Contricioun, and how he sholde be contrit, and what Contricioun availeth to the soule" (127). Each of these elements of definition is expounded in turn. The second one is chosen, arbitrarily, or at least without explanation, for extensive subdivision:

> The causes that oghte moeve a man to Contricioun been sixe.
> First a man shal remembre hym of his synnes . . . (132)
> The seconde cause that oghte make a man to have desdeyn of

233

synne is this: that, as seith Seint Peter, "whoso that dooth synne is thral of synne"; and synne put a man in great thraldom . . . (141)

    The thridde cause that oghte moeve a man to Contricioun is drede of the day of doom and of the horrible peynes of helle . . . (157)

In this manner the six causes of contrition are systematically expounded, the sixth being itself further subdivided: "The sixte thyng that oghte moeve a man to contricioun is the hope of three thynges; that is to seyn, foryifnesse of synne, and the yifte of grace wel for to do, and the glorie of hevene, with which God shal gerdone man for his goode dedes . . ." (282). At this point we have reached the lowest stage in the descending levels of subdivision. The relentless process, comparable perhaps in more ways than one to Dante's descent through the stages of the Inferno, has reached a vortex. After the third division of the sixth cause of contrition we emerge to the surface to advance to the next section, whence we shall begin another descent into subdivisions. The new topic, parallel to "causes" of contrition, is "manner" of contrition: "Now shal a man understonde in which manere shal been his contricioun . . ." (291). Following the treatment of the causes of contrition and the manner of contrition comes the third and last subdivision: "The laste thyng men shal understonde in contricioun is this: wherof avayleth contricioun . . ." (307), this section running to line 315.

    Having thus completed the exposition of contrition, the treatise moves abruptly to the next major unit, confession, the second of the three major divisions under "what is bihovely and necessarie to verray perfit Penitence." Confession is expounded in the prevailing fashion, except for the extraordinary deviation represented by the excursus on the seven deadly sins. The structural significance of this excursus, as distinct from its doctrinal significance, can be appraised only in relation to its peculiar setting within the context of the total treatise.

THE PARSON'S TALE

Up to the point at which the excursus is introduced — part way into the exposition of confession — the progress of the treatise has been almost painfully systematic, to the extent, as we have seen, that system and enumeration often seem to war with substance. And up to this point the treatise has observed consistently a sense of subordination, the subject being penitence, which is divided into contrition, confession, and satisfaction, the first of which has been scrupulously reduced to its elements and the second of which is begun in the same fashion, with a definition of parts. Thus we are in no way prepared, in this firmly controlled formal exposition, for the annihilation of form. And yet that is precisely what the excursus on sin achieves, for it completely overwhelms not only the section on confession in which it occurs but the entire treatise on penitence. It is almost twice as long as all the other sections of the treatise combined. Thus the most massive of the Canterbury tales splits in two: in part it is a consistently ordered exposition of penitence, and in larger part it is an autonomous, systematic presentation of the seven deadly sins and their respective remedies.[3]

This division in the Parson's Tale and the structural imbalance that accompanies it crystallize, in unambiguous expository form, Chaucer's fundamental aesthetic problems and his characteristic method of dealing with them. Though it may appear perverse to maintain that this treatise on penitence exemplifies aesthetic problems, I think the reader who has followed me thus far will recognize the connections with basic assumptions of inorganic art as we have deduced them from Chaucer's practice as well as from that of the Gothic builders and theorists. The relationship between the excursus on sin and the framing treatise on penitence is a problem

---

[3] Morton Bloomfield suggests that the disjointed nature of the section on the sins arises from a hurried appropriation of the material from a source other than that which provided Chaucer with the material on penitence; had Chaucer lived he might have smoothed the links. *The Seven Deadly Sins, An Introduction to the History of a Religious Concept, with Special Reference to Medieval English Literature* (East Lansing, Mich., 1952), p. 192.

in the adjustment of substance to structure. Adjustment consists in fitting a given element into a preconceived, prearranged framework. Chaucer solves the problem here in a way which appears to make little sense, for the supplied element overpowers the fixed framework. But this willingness to tolerate such an imbalance is of special interest to us because it is rooted in the quantitative bases of Chaucer's art.

I hope I have made clear by now the extent to which Chaucer's artistic practice consists of the fitting of fixed, often autonomous parts into preconceived and prestated totalities. A situation readily comparable to that of the sins in the Parson's Tale is that of the discourse on predestination in Book Four of *Troilus*. We know that this self-contained Boethian debate was added to the completed poem and that in Chaucer's mind its insertion did not seriously affect the continuity of the narrative. Its presence in the narrative is an aesthetic fact, despite the puzzlement and disappointment of many modern readers who lament its "prosaic" quality and its unseemly length. We must conclude that Chaucer was not concerned about stylistic consistency or dramatic propriety or structural balance. What for him defined artistic propriety was thematic relevance, and relevance was assured by purely nominal means: in the philosophical matrix of the poem, despair at ill fortune relates by direct association to a discussion of free will and necessity. The lineaments of such a discussion were ready to Chaucer's hand in the traditional scholastic arguments on the subject. Only minimal adjustment was required to fit this body of argument into the narrative situation.

Similarly, we recognize at once that the excursus on the sins in the Parson's Tale is not a digression. Since the context in which it occurs is pure exposition rather than narrative, the means for indicating relevance can be even more explicit than in *Troilus*. The context is confession (the second major division of the treatise), and the relevance of sin is plainly stated at the beginning of the treatment of confession: "First shaltow understonde that Confessioun is verray shewynge of synnes to the preest" (317). Henceforth the verbal definition of confession, which entails three parts, deals exclusively with sin. The three parts are "whennes that synnes spryngen, and how they encressen and whiche they been" (320). The third of these provides the rubric for what proves to be only in name a subdivision. The insistence upon nominal connection is important, however, for it is emphasized again when the actual presentation of "whiche they been" occurs: "Now is it bihovely thyng to telle whiche been the sevene deedly synnes, this is to seyn, chieftaynes of synnes" (386). Expositions of the sins, like disquisitions on predestination, lay ready to hand. Chaucer could have turned to any of hundreds of sources as well as to the *Summa vitiorum* of Guilielmus Peraldus.

If the Parson's Tale is unlike the rest of the *Canterbury Tales* in purpose and subject, I think we can recognize a deep kinship in structural predispositions. From essentially the same quantitative concept of structure Chaucer's poetic narratives, in their subtler fashion, develop and take shape according to the expository imperatives that govern his prose treatise. In Chaucer's inorganic aesthetic, exhaustiveness of treatment and clarity of display are primary standards. The creative impulse develops in an analytical and endlessly inventive process of dividing a preconceived totality into its constituent parts. As in the Parson's Tale the subject so displayed is penitence, in *Troilus* it is love, in the Clerk's Tale it is "vertuous suffraunce," in the Knight's Tale nobility of life, in the Merchant's Tale wedlock. The ground upon which this inorganic aesthetic rests is the firm assumption, certified by antique science and philosophy, that existence is finite and comprehensible, that circumscribable totality is a condition of nature, an attribute of divine creation discernible on all levels of being. The "exposed beam" constructions of Chaucer's art reflect the medieval presupposition that wholeness exists and is apprehensible, whether the object of contemplation is the cosmos itself or any element or concept within it. The idea of finitude is essential to Chaucer's aesthetic practice. It manifests itself most strongly in his technical practice of "distancing," that is, of managing his art externally, from a point of view which is not simply "omniscient" in the modern critical sense of the term but much more fully embodied in a suprafictional existence than is the case in such "omniscient" writers as Thackeray or de Maupassant. This technique preserves the objective integrity of the fiction and prevents the illusion from merging with the observer and thus changing its shape with changing observers. In Chaucer's inorganic aesthetic, firmness of outline assures the possibility of structure.

Pursuing further the paradigmatic value of the Parson's Tale we find that structural analogies obtain not only between it and individual tales but also between it and the *Canterbury Tales* as a total aesthetic structure. Characteristically the "unity" of an inorganic work achieves a collocation of autonomous parts by holding such parts within a governing conceptual framework. The result, as we have seen, can be a gathering of parts widely disparate in size and character and dissonant in tone. The *Canterbury Tales* readily suggests such an inorganic unity. As the Parson's Tale contains within the framing concept of penitence a place for virtually every contingency of human conduct in this life, so does the *Canterbury Tales,* within its framework as presented in the General Prologue, make provision for a similarly comprehensive presentation of human society. Mankind is anatomized in the pilgrim-types and synthesized in the idea of pilgrimage.

The basic structural procedure, both in the treatise and in the *Tales,* is the inorganic one of additive collocation. Depending upon the ingenuity of the maker, a limitless number of new divisions can be adduced or new parts added, since the work does not grow *ab ovo* but is built up of parts whose relevance to the controlling idea can be defined nominally, by rationalistic deduction. Thus, though the presentation of the deadly sins seems to bulge out of all proportion to its setting in the Parson's Tale, its relevance to confession justifies its presence. Once such an exterior connection is secured, considerations of size become immaterial, since the connected part retains its autonomy and is free to fulfill the requirements of its own nature.

In the *Tales* a similar detachability of parts is everywhere apparent. The appearance of the Canon and his Yeoman, for example, though not "prepared" in the General Prologue, is easily accommodated. All that is necessary to gather them into the *Tales,* and thus make possible the Yeoman's Tale of alchemy, is a means of connecting them to the social framework; hence they ride up and join the wayfaring group. In the same way the whole question of the suitability of tale to teller is answerable only in terms of superficial and nominal connections. A churl will tell a churl's tale, but which shall be for which churl, or which noble tale or romance for which aristocrat, or which of many relevant possibilities for any type becomes a matter of exterior correspondences, which can be adjusted by detachable links and prologues. It is not a matter of integral development and inner inevitability. The relations between tellers and tales are determined by external criteria of genre, type, and subject, all of which are fixed, objective determinants. Although at times the tale may seem to grow organically out of the teller and dramatically "express" him, analysis seems to indicate, as in the case of the Merchant's Tale, that the illusion of organic expressivism is "applied" to the tale in the prologue and fades away as the autonomy of the tale asserts itself.

In one important respect the Parson's Tale differs from the others in relation to the total structure of the *Tales.* A tale such as the Merchant's or the Wife of Bath's, having established its "appropriateness" to the teller and thereby its relevance to the framing idea of the social order, can go on to persevere in its own nature as an independent story. The Parson's Tale, on the other hand, bears a deep thematic relevance to the framework of the *Tales.* The explicit introductory remarks of the Parson concerning the way of "thilke parfit glorious pilgrymage," coupled with the tale's emphatic position as the culmination of a long enterprise, impart to the tale unusually heavy significations of serious portent. Through its nature as a treatise on penitence, the tale indeed fulfills these aesthetic implications and verbal prophecies. It shows the true way as none of the other tales, even religious tales such as the Second Nun's and the Prioress', could, for it moves beyond the symbolic game of illusion to the reality of revealed truth. Being a sermon on a Scriptural text, the Parson's Tale explicates the word of God, as conveyed by the prophet Jeremiah:

> Stondeth upon the wyes, and seeth and axeth of olde pathes . . . which is the goode wey, / and walketh in that wey, and ye shal fynde refresshynge for youre soules, etc. / Manye been the weyes espirituels that leden folk to oure Lord Jhesu Crist, and to the regne of glorie. / Of whiche weyes ther is a ful noble wey and a ful covenable, which may nat fayle to man ne to womman that thurgh synne hath mysgoon fro the righte wey of Jerusalem celestial; / and this wey is cleped Penitence . . . (76-80)

The tale follows the way of the prophet to God, and for this reason it moves beyond the limits of man's makings at the same time that it moves beyond the limits of modern man's literary interest.

Because the Parson's Tale is Truth it lacks the idiosyncrasies of fiction. It offers Chaucer none of the prerogatives of his normally wide range of poetic and rhetorical techniques. The platform of the public entertainer is gone, and with it the possibilities of distancing and perspective that Chaucer exploited so fully in his play with the narrator-role. Differentiation of style and varieties of tone and of figurative language are also absent, not to mention the possibilities of meter and rhyme. In short, the Parson's Tale is not the work of a poet, a maker of beautiful lies; it is the work of a servant of God. That Chaucer could be both such a Christian *and* the maker of such beautiful fictions is perhaps the most conclusive demonstration we

240

can offer of the nonorganicist sensibility. In Chaucer we find art and belief coming together without merging. The result, to use Wölfflin's terms once more, is not a "unified unity" but a "multiple unity," which allows each element its full play and autonomy yet holds them together within a controlling outline. The sensibility is "dissociated" but not disunified. Thus the Parson's Tale sacrifices none of its Truth for being a part of a fiction, nor does the fiction of the *Canterbury Tales* lose any of its literary persuasiveness for standing in its place within the edifice of Truth. In the ultimate perspective of God's vision, contingent reality does not dissolve, for it is the palpable sign of Truth. Such was the structure of Creation, that the penitential journey of man's life was both very real — as the Parson's sermon makes abundantly plain — and at the same time a mere imperfect image of "the endelees blisse of hevene."

BIBLIOGRAPHY OF WORKS CITED

Abrams, M. H. *The Mirror and the Lamp*. New York: 1953.

Ackerman, James S. " 'Ars sine scientia nihil est'; Gothic Theory of Architecture at the Cathedral of Milan." *The Art Bulletin,* 31:84-109 (1949).

Aiken, Conrad. "William Faulkner: The Novel as Form," in *William Faulkner: Two Decades of Criticism,* ed. F. J. Hoffman and Olga W. Vickery. East Lansing, Mich.: 1951.

Alan of Lille. *De planctu naturae. PL,* vol. 210.

Aquinas, St. Thomas. *Summa theologica,* trans. English Dominican Fathers. 2nd ed. London: 1922.

Aristotle. *Metaphysics,* trans. W. D. Ross. 2nd ed. Oxford: 1928.

Atkins, J. W. H. *English Literary Criticism: The Medieval Phase.* London: 1952.

Augustine, Saint. *On Christian Doctrine,* trans. D. W. Robertson, Jr. Indianapolis and New York: 1958.

———— *Soliloquies,* trans. Thomas F. Gilligan. New York: 1948.

———— *The City of God,* trans. G. G. Walsh and Grace Monahan. New York: 1952.

———— *The Trinity,* trans. Stephen McKenna. Washington, D.C.: 1963.

Baldwin, Ralph. "The Unity of the Canterbury Tales," *Anglistica,* V. Copenhagen: 1955.

Baugh, Albert C. "The Original Teller of the Merchant's Tale," *MP,* 35:16-26 (1937).

———— ed. *Chaucer's Major Poetry.* New York: 1963.

Baum, Paull F. *Chaucer: A Critical Appreciation.* Durham, N. C.: 1958.

Bell, Eric Temple. *The Magic of Numbers.* New York: 1946.

Bethurum, Dorothy, ed. *Critical Approaches to Medieval Literature.* New York: 1960.

Blackmur, R. P. *Language as Gesture.* New York: 1952.

Bloomfield, Morton W. "Authenticating Realism and the Realism of Chaucer," *Thought,* 39:335-358 (1964).

———— "Distance and Predestination in *Troilus and Criseyde,*" *PMLA,* 72:14-26 (1957).

———— *Piers Plowman as a Fourteenth-Century Apocalypse.* New Brunswick, N. J.: 1961.

———— *The Seven Deadly Sins, An Introduction to the History of a Religious Concept, with Special Reference to Medieval English Literature.* East Lansing, Mich.: 1952.

———— "Symbolism in Medieval Literature," *MP,* 56:73-81 (1958).

Boethius. *De consolatione philosophiae. PL,* vol. 63, trans. Richard Green. Indianapolis and New York: 1962.

———— *De musica. PL,* vol. 63.

———— *De arithmetica. PL,* vol. 63.

Bowden, Muriel. *Commentary on the General Prologue to the Canterbury Tales.* New York: 1948.

Brenner, Gerry. "Narrative Structure in Chaucer's *Troilus and Criseyde,*" *Annuale Medievale,* 6:5-18 (1965).

Bronson, Bertrand H. "Afterthoughts on the Merchant's Tale," *SP,* 58:583-596 (1961).

———— "Chaucer's Art in Relation to His Audience," in *Five Studies in Literature.* Berkeley, Calif.: 1940.

———— *In Search of Chaucer.* Toronto: 1960.

Bruyne, Edgar de. *Etudes d'esthétique médiévale.* 3 vols. Bruges: 1946.

Bryan, W. F., and Germaine Dempster, ed. *Sources and Analogues of Chaucer's Canterbury Tales.* New York: 1953.

Chaucer, Geoffrey. *Complete Works,* ed. F. N. Robinson. 2nd ed. Boston: 1957.

Claghorn, George S. *Aristotle's Criticism of Plato's "Timaeus."* The Hague: 1954.

Collingwood, R. G. *The Idea of Nature.* Oxford: 1945.

BIBLIOGRAPHY OF WORKS CITED

Cornford, F. M., "Mysticism and Science in the Pythagorean Tradition," *Classical Quarterly,* 16:137-150 (1922); 17:1-12 (1923).

———— trans. *Plato's Cosmology.* London: 1952.

Crombie, A. C. *Medieval and Early Modern Science.* 2 vols., rev. ed. Garden City, N.Y.: 1959.

Crosby, Ruth. "Chaucer and the Custom of Oral Delivery," *Speculum,* 13:413-432 (1938).

Curry, W. C. "Destiny in Chaucer's *Troilus,*" *PMLA,* 45:129-168 (1930).

Curtius, Ernst Robert. *European Literature and the Latin Middle Ages,* trans. Willard R. Trask. New York: 1953.

Dante Alighieri. *The Convivio,* trans. P. H. Wicksteed. London: 1903.

———— *Dantis Alagherii Epistolae,* ed. and trans. Paget Toynbee. Oxford: 1920.

———— *La Vita nuova,* trans. Mark Musa. New Brunswick, N. J.: 1957.

David, Alfred. "The Hero of the *Troilus,*" *Speculum,* 37:566-581 (1962).

Dempster, Germaine. *Dramatic Irony in Chaucer.* New York: 1959.

———— "The Original Teller of the *Merchant's Tale,*" *MP,* 36:1-8 (1938).

Dobrée, Bonamy. *English Literature in the Early Eighteenth Century.* Oxford: 1959.

Donaldson, E. Talbot, ed. *Chaucer's Poetry.* New York: 1958.

———— "Chaucer the Pilgrim," *PMLA,* 69:928-936 (1954).

———— "The Ending of Chaucer's *Troilus,*" in *Early English and Norse Studies,* ed. Arthur Brown and Peter Foote. London: 1963.

———— "Patristic Exegesis in the Criticism of Medieval Literature: The Opposition," in *Critical Approaches to Medieval Literature,* ed. Dorothy Bethurum. New York: 1960.

Everett, Dorothy. *"Troilus and Criseyde,"* in *Essays on Middle English Literature,* ed. Patricia Kean. Oxford: 1955.

Faral, Edmond, ed. *Les Arts poétiques du XIIe et du XIIIe Siècles* Paris: 1924.

Fletcher, Angus J. S. *Allegory; the Theory of a Symbolic Mode.* Ithaca, N. Y.: 1964.

Ford, Ford Madox. *Joseph Conrad: A Personal Remembrance.* New York: 1965.

Frank, Robert W., Jr. "The Art of Reading Medieval Personification Allegory," *ELH,* 20:237-250 (1953).

Frankl, Paul. *The Gothic.* Princeton, N. J.: 1960.

———— *Gothic Architecture.* Baltimore, Md.: 1962.

Frost, William. "An Interpretation of Chaucer's Knight's Tale," *RES,* 25:289-304 (1949).

Geoffrey of Vinsauf. *Poetria nova,* in Edmond Faral, ed. *Les Arts poétiques du XIIe et du XIIIe Siècles.*

Gilson, Etienne. *La Philosophie de saint Bonaventure.* Paris: 1924.

Green, Richard H. "Dante's 'Allegory of Poets' and the Medieval Theory of Poetic Fiction," *CL,* 9:118-128 (1957).

———— trans. Boethius, *The Consolation of Philosophy.* Indianapolis and New York: 1962.

Halverson, John. "Aspects of Order in the Knight's Tale," *SP,* 57:606-621 (1960).

Heath, Thomas L. *A History of Greek Mathematics.* 2 vols. Oxford: 1921.

Holman, C. Hugh. "Courtly Love in the Merchant's and the Franklin's Tales," *ELH,* 18:241-252 (1951).

Honig, Edwin. *Dark Conceit: The Making of Allegory.* Evanston, Ill.: 1959.

Howard, Donald R. "Chaucer the Man," *PMLA,* 80:337-343 (1965).

Hugh of St. Victor. *Eruditionis didascalicae. PL,* vol. 176.

BIBLIOGRAPHY OF WORKS CITED

Hughes, Dom Anselm. *Early Medieval Music.* New Oxford History of Music, vol. 2. London: 1954.

Huizinga, Johan. *The Waning of the Middle Ages.* London: 1924.

James, Henry. "The Art of Fiction," in *The Major Critics,* ed. C. S. Holmes, Edwin Fussell, and Ray Frazer. New York: 1957.

Jantzen, Hans. *High Gothic,* trans. James Palmes. London: 1962.

Jones, Richard F. "A Conjecture on the Wife of Bath's Prologue," *JEGP,* 24:512-547 (1925).

Jordan, Robert M. "Chaucer's Sense of Illusion: Roadside Drama Reconsidered," *ELH,* 29:19-33 (1962).

———— "The Narrator in Chaucer's *Troilus,*" *ELH,* 25:237-257 (1958).

Kaske, Robert E. "Chaucer and Medieval Allegory," *ELH,* 30:175-192 (1963).

Kellogg, Robert. See Scholes, Robert.

Kimpel, Ben. "The Narrator of the *Canterbury Tales,*" *ELH,* 20:77-86 (1953).

Kittredge, G. L. *Chaucer and His Poetry.* Cambridge, Mass.: 1915.

———— "Chaucer's Discussion of Marriage," *MP,* 9:435-467 (1912).

Klibansky, Raymond. *The Continuity of the Platonic Tradition during the Middle Ages.* London: 1939.

Kubler, George. *The Shape of Time: Remarks on the History of Things.* New Haven and London: 1962.

Lewis, C. S. *The Allegory of Love.* London: 1936.

Lowes, J. L. *Geoffrey Chaucer.* Oxford: 1934.

Lubac, Henri de. *Exégèse médiévale: Les quatre sens de l'Écriture.* 2 vols. Paris: 1959-61.

Lüdeke, Henry. "Die Funktionen des Erzählers in Chaucers epischer Dichtung," *Studien zur englischen Philologie,* vol. 72. Halle: 1928.

Lumiansky, R. M. *Of Sundry Folk: The Dramatic Principle in the Canterbury Tales.* Austin, Tex.: 1955.

Macrobius. *Commentary on the Dream of Scipio,* trans. William H. Stahl. New York: 1952.

Mâle, Emile. *The Gothic Image: Religious Art in France of the Thirteenth Century,* trans. Dora Nussey (from 3rd French ed., 1918). New York: 1958.

Malone, Kemp. *Chapters on Chaucer.* Baltimore, Md.: 1951.

Manly, John M. *Some New Light on Chaucer.* New York: 1926.

———— ed. *Chaucer's Canterbury Tales.* New York: 1928.

———— and Edith Rickert, ed. *The Text of the Canterbury Tales.* 8 vols. Chicago: 1940.

Mazzeo, Joseph A. *Medieval Cultural Tradition in Dante's "Comedy."* Ithaca, N. Y.: 1960.

McGalliard, John C. "Chaucerian Comedy: The Merchant's Tale, Jonson, and Molière," *PQ,* 25:343-370 (1946).

Meech, Sanford. *Design in Chaucer's "Troilus."* Syracuse, N. Y.: 1959.

Migne, J. P., ed. *Patrologiae cursus completus; series latina.* Paris: 1844-1903.

Mizener, Arthur. "Character and Action in the Case of Criseyde," *PMLA,* 54:65-81 (1939).

Muscatine, Charles. *Chaucer and the French Tradition: A Study in Style and Meaning.* Berkeley and Los Angeles, Calif.: 1957.

———— "Form, Texture, and Meaning in Chaucer's *Knight's Tale,*" *PMLA,* 65:911-929 (1950).

Neuse, Richard. "The Knight: The First Mover in Chaucer's Human Comedy," *UTQ,* 31:299-315 (1962).

Newman, J. R., ed. *The World of Mathematics.* 4 vols. New York: 1956.

Nicomachus Gerasenus. *Introduction to Arithmetic,* trans. M. L. D'Ooge. New York: 1926.

Owen, C. A., Jr. "The Crucial Passages in Five of *The Canterbury Tales:* A Study in Irony and Symbol," *JEGP,* 52:294-311 (1953).

BIBLIOGRAPHY OF WORKS CITED

—— ed. *Discussions of the Canterbury Tales.* Boston: 1961.

Panofsky, Erwin. *Gothic Architecture and Scholasticism.* Latrobe, Pa.: 1951.

—— ed. and trans. *Abbot Suger on the Abbey Church of St.- Denis and Its Art Treasures.* Princeton, N. J.: 1946.

Patch, Howard R. *On Rereading Chaucer.* Cambridge, Mass.: 1939.

Payne, Robert O. *The Key of Remembrance: A Study of Chaucer's Poetics.* New Haven, Conn. and London: 1963.

Pevsner, Nikolaus. *An Outline of European Architecture.* London: 1948.

Plato. *Timaeus.* Trans. with commentary by F. M. Cornford, in *Plato's Cosmology.* London: 1952.

Pratt, Robert A. "Chaucer's Use of the Teseida," *PMLA,* 62:598-621 (1947).

—— "The Development of the Wife of Bath," in *Studies in Medieval Literature in Honor of A. C. Baugh,* ed. MacEdward Leach. Philadelphia: 1961.

—— "The Order of the Canterbury Tales," *PMLA,* 66:1141-1167 (1951).

Preston, Raymond. *Chaucer.* London and New York: 1952.

Rickert, Edith. See Manly, John M.

Robbins, F. E. "The Development of Greek Arithmetic before Nicomachus," in Nicomachus of Gerasa, *Introduction to Arithmetic,* trans. M. L. D'Ooge. New York: 1926.

Robertson, D. W., Jr. *A Preface to Chaucer: Studies in Medieval Perspectives.* Princeton, N. J.: 1963.

Ruggiers, Paul G. *The Art of the Canterbury Tales.* Madison and Milwaukee, Wis.: 1965.

Scholes, Robert, and Robert Kellogg. *The Nature of Narrative.* New York: 1966.

Schorer, Mark. "Technique as Discovery," *Hudson Review,* 1:67-87 (1948).

BIBLIOGRAPHY OF WORKS CITED

Sedgewick, G. G. "The Structure of the *Merchant's Tale*," *UTQ*, 17:337-345 (1948).

Shanley, J. L. "The *Troilus* and Christian Love," *ELH*, 6:271-281 (1939).

Shelly, P. V. D. *The Living Chaucer.* Philadelphia: 1940.

Shumaker, Wayne. "Alisoun in Wander-Land: A Study in Chaucer's Mind and Literary Method," *ELH*, 18:77-89 (1951).

Simson, Otto von. *The Gothic Cathedral.* 2nd ed. New York: 1962.

Singleton, Charles S. *Dante Studies I.* Cambridge, Mass.: 1954.

Sledd, James. "*The Clerk's Tale:* The Monsters and the Critics," *MP*, 51:73-82 (1953).

Smalley, Beryl. *The Study of the Bible in the Middle Ages.* 2nd ed. Oxford: 1952.

Spicq, Ceslaus. *Esquisse d'une histoire de l'exégèse latine au moyen âge.* Paris: 1944.

Spingarn, J. E. *A History of Literary Criticism in the Renaissance.* New York: 1925.

Stahl, William H., ed. and trans. Macrobius, *Commentary on the Dream of Scipio.* New York: 1952.

Suger, Abbot, See Panofsky, Erwin.

Sypher, Wylie. *Four Stages of Renaissance Style.* Garden City, N. Y.: 1955.

Tatlock, J. S. P. "Chaucer's *Merchant's Tale*," *MP*, 33:367-381 (1936).

——— "The Epilog of Chaucer's *Troilus*," *MP*, 18:625-659 (1920-21).

Turnbull, H. W. "The Great Mathematicians," in vol. 1, *The World of Mathematics,* ed. J. R. Newman. 4 vols. New York: 1956.

Tuve, Rosemond. *Allegorical Imagery.* Princeton, N. J.: 1966.

Underwood, Dale. "The First of *The Canterbury Tales*," *ELH*, 26:455-469 (1959).

BIBLIOGRAPHY OF WORKS CITED

Utley, Francis Lee. "Robertsonianism Redivivus," *Romance Philology,* 19:250-260 (1965).

Wagenknecht, Edward, ed. *Chaucer: Modern Essays in Criticism.* New York: 1959.

Wellek, René. "Concepts of Form and Structure in Twentieth Century Criticism," *Neophilologus,* 42:1-11 (1958).

—— and Austin Warren. *Theory of Literature.* 3rd ed. New York: 1962.

Wenzel, Siegfried. "Chaucer's Troilus of Book IV," *PMLA,* 79:542-547 (1964).

Williams, George. *A New View of Chaucer.* Durham, N. C.: 1965.

Wölfflin, Heinrich. *Kunstgeschichtliche Grundbegriffe.* Munich: 1915.

INDEX

INDEX

INDEX